FOLLOWING THE DETECTIVES

REAL LOCATIONS IN CRIME FICTION

MAXIM JAKUBOWSKI EDITOR

FOLLOWING THE DETECTIVES
REAL LOCATIONS IN CRIME FICTION

NH

NEW
HOLLAND

This edition published in 2011

First published in 2010 by New Holland Publishers (UK) Ltd
London • Cape Town • Sydney • Auckland
www.newhollandpublishers.com
Garfield House, 86–88 Edgware Road, London W2 2EA, United Kingdom
80 McKenzie Street, Cape Town 8001, South Africa
Unit 1, 66 Gibbes Street, Chatswood, NSW 2067, Australia
218 Lake Road, Northcote, Auckland, New Zealand

10 9 8 7 6 5 4 3 2 1

A catalogue record for this book is available from the British Library

ISBN 978 1 84773 936 0

Publisher: Aruna Vasudevan
Editor: Henry Russell
Inside Design: Colin Hall
Cover Design: HelloPaul Ltd
Picture Editor: Susannah Jayes
Cartography: Encompass Graphics Ltd
Production: Melanie Downland

Reproduction by PDQ in the UK
Printed and bound in Malaysia by Times Offset (M) Sdn Bhd

For Dolores,

Who always travels with me,
and agrees to read all the
crime books I approve of!

CONTENTS

LIST OF MAPS IN THE BOOK

CRIME LOCATIONS FEATURED IN THE MAIN ENTRIES

CHICAGO

BOSTON

NEW YORK

WASHINGTON

SAN FRANCISCO

LOS ANGELES

NEW ORLEANS

SOUTHERN
CALIFORNIA

FLORIDA

PACIFIC
OCEAN

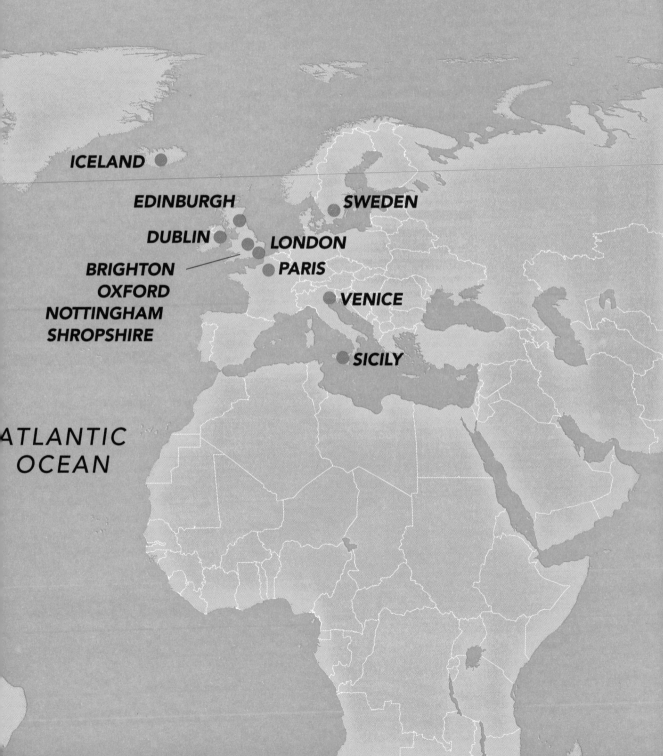

ARCTIC OCEAN

ICELAND

EDINBURGH

DUBLIN

SWEDEN

LONDON

BRIGHTON
OXFORD
NOTTINGHAM
SHROPSHIRE

PARIS

VENICE

SICILY

ATLANTIC
OCEAN

Maxim Jakubowski

INTRODUCTION: A SENSE OF PLACE

For many people who haven't actually lived there, London continues to evoke images of gas-lit streets and fog and, perhaps to a lesser extent, horse-drawn carriages. It is an image that is etched in the collective mind in many parts thanks to the writings of Sir Arthur Conan Doyle and his immortal adventures of Sherlock Holmes.

I once lived for a few years in Northern Italy, and when local acquaintances would meet me and learn that I was from London, their automatic reaction was all too often 'Ah... the fog... the fog...', accompanied by a sorry nod of the head, conveniently forgetting the fact that the Po Valley suffers every winter from day-long blackouts with airports and motorways closed due to fog, and that London's last serious pea-souper actually goes all the way back to the very early 1960s!

Thus are images of places perpetuated by fiction and books, and even more so by crime and mystery fiction, and they lodge forever in the mind of the reader, creating a new parallel reality of sorts. And, under the spell of the evocative prose, fans of the books will be attracted to the real city or country, curious to see how it might differ from the settings he or she has read about. They wish to follow in the footsteps of their favourite detectives and tread the same streets. Tourists now go to Venice and follow Commissario Brunetti tours or to Edinburgh to explore Inspector Rebus's haunts, so fascinated are they by the cities they have been introduced to in detective books.

It has always been one of literature's virtues and attractions that it can powerfully evoke places and times and bring them to life alongside plot and characters. Hardy's Wessex springs to mind, as do Thomas Mann's Venice or the St Petersburg of Dostoyevsky or, again, the teeming London of Charles Dickens.

However, I would argue that crime and mystery fiction offers the perfect blend of storytelling and sense of place, insofar as so many of us identify to a strong extent with the narrators and heroes, and these memorable characters are often intimately at one with the environment they function in. Sherlock Holmes, even when he moves farther afield, is essentially the Baker Street, London, sleuth. Philip Marlowe meanders his way through Los Angeles, Maigret inhabits Paris, as does Rebus Edinburgh and so on, to the extent that the city or place and region becomes an extra character in the stories.

Indeed, it almost appears as if every city or area these days has been colonized by one detective or crime writer or more.

Over the past decade, we have finally had the opportunity to read much crime fiction written in other languages and this has introduced us to further foreign and often exotic, or at any rate different locales. Scandinavian crime fiction from the likes of Henning Mankell, Asa Larsson, Stieg Larsson, Camilla Lackberg, Gunnar Staalesen, Karin Fossum, Liza Marklund, Arnaldur Indridason, Jo Nesbø and many others; French authors such as Thierry Jonquet, Jean-Claude Izzo (whose evocative books turn the Mediterranean city of Marseille into an ideal breeding ground for crime and atmosphere), Jean-Pierre Manchette, Daniel Pennac, Jacques Chessex; Italian practitioners like Giancarlo de Cataldo, Gianrico Carofiglio, Massimo Carlotto, Barbara Baraldi, Carlo Lucarelli; in addition, courageous publishers are introducing us to plentiful crime and mystery fiction from as afar afield as Spain, Argentina, Cuba, Poland, Germany, Russia, Switzerland even. To this we must add a rediscovery of Australian (Peter Temple, Tara Moss, Peter Corris), Canadian (Howard Engel, John McFetridge) and South African writers (Deon Meyer, Margie Orford, Michael Stanley). All bring a new, reinforced sense of place to contemporary crime fiction.

In addition, there is barely a place on our planet where fictional sleuths now don't operate; certainly the fascinating but indispensable investigators we have been unable to cover fully sin this volume can be found in places as diverse as Barcelona, Berlin, Botswana, China, Cuba, Hong Kong, India, Japan, Laos, Malaysia, Mexico, Mongolia, Poland, Russia and South Africa.

It's a list that could go on for endless pages, in addition to the fact that every major British and American city and region must surely by now have a resident sleuth!

With the able assistance of some of the best worldwide commentators on crime and mystery fiction, in this book we've tried to survey the cities, streets and regions made so popular by mysteries and thrillers, and over the course of this book have followed the detectives across the world. It is a project that could have had no end, as every day new territories came to mind and we sadly had to restrict ourselves to a given number. So, no Harry Hole's Oslo (Jo Nesbø), Scarpetta's Virginia (Patricia Cornwell), Elmore Leonard's and Loren D. Estleman's Detroit, Jean-Claude Izzo's Marseille or Temperance Brennan's Montreal (Kathy Reichs).

This is not a travel book, although you could well use it as a handy companion on your journeys, and neither is it a pure reference volume seeking deep insights into classic crime books and the authors who wrote them. Rather, it's something of both, and our hope is that it will encourage you to read mystery writers you might previously have overlooked or even provoke you to go out of your way and explore the real world behind the stories during the course of your travels.

Good writers have the power to evoke a sense of location and to capture the spirit and soul of a place in a most unique manner and when it comes to mystery fiction, you add a few bodies, incomparable thrills, memorable characters and psychological insights and the ensuing results become unforgettable.

So, read crime fiction and travel the world!

HOW TO USE

Following the Detectives features 15 cities and 6 regions around the world that appear prominently in crime fiction.

Each entry includes an essay by a leading expert focusing on particular cafés, restaurants, streets and other places that the character frequents or which may have featured as a crime scene location. There is a film/theatre/TV box and also a useful websites feature, which directs readers to interesting places linked to the entry in question. A double-page colour map picks up on places important to the author and character (*please see key below*).

In addition there are boxes and double-page spreads scattered throughout the book dedicated to authors or literature also located in the cities or areas under discussion.

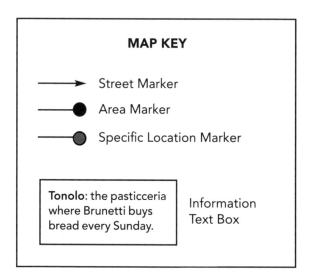

Barry Forshaw

IAN RANKIN & INSPECTOR REBUS'S EDINBURGH

As well as being the most successful male crime writer in the United Kingdom, Ian Rankin (who was born in Scotland in 1960) has another duty: his writings are the most important celebration of the city of Edinburgh in modern crime fiction and, some would argue, in the whole of literature.

The author has even been celebrated by the naming of an Ian Rankin Court in Cardenden, Fife, where Rebus, his detective, grew up.

Rankin carries his responsibilities lightly, and continues to produce a body of work that will ensure his pre-eminence in the field for some time to come. If Charles Dickens (1812–70) is the ultimate chronicler of London, Ian Rankin has performed a similar function for his beloved Edinburgh.

Rankin's novels featuring the wry, damaged Detective Inspector John Rebus have produced a cumulative picture of the city – in all its splendour and squalor – that is quite as rich and evocative as anything in more explicitly literary novels. While Rebus may be cut from a familiar crime-fiction cloth – a messy private life, conflicts with his superiors, alcoholism – Rankin's skill as a novelist nevertheless makes Rebus a weighty and well-rounded character.

The author has said that he started writing the Rebus books to make sense of Scotland – and, for many readers (Scottish or otherwise), he has gone some way to accomplishing that task.

Rankin's and Rebus's youth

John Rebus grew up in Cardenden (in fact, in the same cul-de-sac as the author himself). This miners' row was one of many, built speedily and to a uniform design. The idea was to provide housing for the men working in the coal mines – when coal was a much sought-after commodity. The area itself had grown up around coal, and the brighter sons of the miners got their start in the Auchterderran Secondary School (as did both Rankin and Rebus). Rebus evokes the depressed and rundown nature of the area in *Dead Souls* (1999):

Cardenden had grown up around coal, hurried streets constructed in the

twenties and thirties to house the incoming miners. These streets hadn't even been given names, just numbers.

The blue-collar Scotland of the author's youth may have respectable historical interest, but Rankin was equally familiar (as a first-year student) with a strip bar called Tony's, a soft-core porn cinema on Edinburgh's Nicolson Street, and flyblown motels on the outskirts of the city. As a student he tried but failed (together with three school friends) to rent a flat on the second floor of a tenement on Morrison Street, an area far more upmarket in the 21st century than it was in Rankin's student days. Rankin had already realized that there was more to Edinburgh than the glamorous historical associations that brought in so many tourists, and was keenly interested in the underbelly of the city, as is clear from the books that he was subsequently to write.

Nevertheless, Ian Rankin's love of Scotland is, of course, one of his most characteristic features. And, in choosing Edinburgh as his locus classicus, and by virtue of being such an excellent and successful

crime-fiction writer, he has brought a new brand of tourist to Edinburgh. As he himself said: 'Even Edinburgh City Council now regards me – finally – as an asset. I may have populated the city (in my books) with criminals, prostitutes and bent politicians, but I don't think that people these days consider that such things give the city a bad name' (*Rebus's Scotland*, 2005).

Tackling all issues

The first Rebus book, *Knots and Crosses* (1987), showed that Rankin's literary skills were already burnished to

IAN RANKIN

Ian Rankin is not only the UK's best-selling male crime writer, his celebrity is such that he has been asked to cut a ribbon to open Ian Rankin Court, an upscale housing development in Cardenden, Fife.

His first literary prize (while still at school) was for a national poetry competition; he won second prize for a poem entitled 'Euthanasia'.

Rankin was the world's least successful swineherd (his pigs had very short lives).

Ian and his wife and family lived on a farm in France before he achieved success as a writer.

Rankin has also written books under the pseudonym Jack Harvey.

Rankin has honorary degrees from Abertay Dundee, St Andrews and Edinburgh universities.

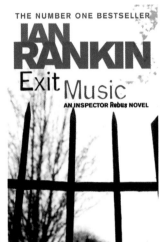

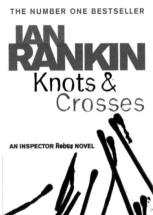

perfection, as was assured in such subsequent books as *Dead Souls*, which treated difficult topics such as paedophilia in a harrowing yet responsible fashion. His most complex novel is possibly *The Hanging Garden* (1998), with its issues of war crimes and sexual slavery skilfully and persuasively handled.

Mortal Causes (1994) is one of the most Edinburgh-centric of Rankin's novels. It begins with a corpse found hanging in the hidden streets below Edinburgh's Royal Mile. The theme here is the sectarian conflict between Catholics and Protestants that bubbles beneath Edinburgh's civilized surface. In *Mortal Causes*, the sharp evocation of Pilmuir (a fictitious conflation of two Edinburgh districts, Pilton and Muirhouse) is as vivid as the characters and the plot. Ian Rankin is a political animal, and he ensures that his rebellious copper follows a similar path. In *Mortal Causes*, Rankin details a march in Cowdenbeath; there had, in fact, been an Orange march by ardent Protestants in the area. The potential for violence and confrontation in the area was never lost on the author. Subsequently, in the same book, he tells readers that, as a young man, Rebus had gone on an Orange Lodge march through Edinburgh city centre, but Rebus realizes that Scotland has more than enough problems of its own

'SOMETIMES READERS GET A BIT CHEESED OFF WHEN REBUS IS QUITE BALANCED IN SOME OF THE BOOKS, BUT HE COULDN'T GO THROUGH THE EXPERIENCES OF BLACK AND BLUE EVERY WEEK – HE'D BE OUT OF THE POLICE, THEY JUST WOULDN'T WANT HIM' – IAN RANKIN

without getting involved in those of Ireland – 'They were like Siamese twins who refuse the operation to separate them'.

In *Black and Blue* (1997), the celebrated Barrowland Ballroom in Glasgow is a venue visited by the sinister Bible John (more recently, the ballroom has become a rock venue). The book itself demonstrates Rankin's growing assurance, with a particularly memorable (and unpleasant) villain. Bible John was a real-life figure: this is one of the first occasions in which the author utilizes a non-fiction character in this way.

Scottish Politics

Set in Darkness (2000) is set at a momentous time for Edinburgh: the city is about to become home to the first Scottish Parliament, but Detective Inspector Rebus finds his assignment as liaison troublesome. Queensberry House, part of the new parliament, is soon echoing to the sound of falling bodies, and one victim is prospective Member of the Scottish Parliament Roddy Grieve. To make matters worse, Rebus finds that a dangerous criminal he thought was rid of is back on the scene. As often before, Rankin is adroit at combining the feel of a raw and compelling narrative with an intelligent political subtext. The Scottish Parliament is, of course, a source of much debate, both for its architecture and the often heated discussions within its walls. The building itself (noted for its striking modern design) was famously – and disastrously – over budget.

Rankin has long argued for his country to have more confidence in itself, and (justified or not) the Scottish Parliament

The Oxford Bar in Young Street – a favourite haunt of both Rebus and his creator.

'AS TIME'S GONE ON, I'VE PROBABLY BECOME A LOT MORE LIKE HIM [JOHN REBUS]: I DRINK AT HIS BAR AND I LIKE TO BE ONE-ON-ONE WITH MY MUSIC LATE AT NIGHT' – IAN RANKIN

has become a receptacle for such aspirations. However, its location, opposite the Palace of Holyroodhouse, could not be more appropriate, with a marked contrast between the new and the old. When Rankin takes Rebus to the parliament building in *Set in Darkness*, he allows himself a provocative discussion of Scottish history (with a certain macabre piquancy added by the fact that a notorious act of cannibalism involving a member of the family of the Duke of Queensbury took place on the very site).

Ian Rankin used the name of this alleyway off Cockburn Street as the title of the 15th Rebus novel.

Rebus's haunts

Needless to say, in a series in which the central character has battled with alcoholism, the drinking dens of Edinburgh are recurrent locations. *Knots and Crosses* features the following wonderful evocation of such places:

Old men sat with their half-pint glasses, staring emptily towards the front door. Were they wondering what was

outside? Or were they just scared that whatever was out there would one day force its way in?

As the author has lamented, many of these much-loved bars have been swept away or gentrified into 'style bars' – transformations that may have attracted a new, trendier clientele but which have precipitately seen off the older regulars. Apart from The Sutherland – a fictitious bar based partly on The Guildford Arms – the author had need of another watering hole and decided to make use of The Oxford Bar near Princes Street. (Rankin was pleased that the bar staff could, by his third visit, pour his beer of choice unprompted.) The Oxford is first identified by name in *Mortal Causes*, in which Rebus is pleased by the generous measures of spirits – and even when the detective is off the booze, notably in *The Hanging Garden*, he remains a regular.

Rankin is, inevitably, ambiguous about his detective's relationship with alcohol (something of a metaphor for the Scottish nation itself, which, as Rankin says, likes to 'take a drink'), but it is absolutely part of the warp and woof of the Rebus books.

There is, of course, a certain transmutation from the real to the fictional in Ian Rankin's Edinburgh. For example, the lap-dancing bar The Nook in *Fleshmarket Close* (2004) does give a nod to the nearby famous Burke and Hare

REBUS ON SCREEN

Scottish Television (STV) produced 14 episodes of the Rebus novels between 2000 and 2007. The first two series starred John Hannah in the title role; in the remaining episodes, the part was played by Ken Stott.

📺 ON TELEVISION

Series 1
'Black and Blue' (2000)
'The Hanging Garden' (2001)

Series 2
'Dead Souls' (2001)
'Mortal Causes' (2004)

Series 3
'The Falls' (2006)
'Fleshmarket Close' (2006)

Series 4
'The Black Book' (2006)
'A Question of Blood' (2006)
'Strip Jack' (2006)
'Let it Bleed' (2006)

Series 5
'Resurrection Men' (2007)
'The First Stone' (2007)
'The Naming of the Dead' (2007)
'Knots and Crosses' (2007)

Club, named after the most famous of Edinburgh grave robbers.

Doubters and dissenters

Among the significant places visited by Rebus during the course of the books might be included the Church of Scotland headquarters at the top of The Mound, near an imposing statue of John Knox (whose illiberal views on women and Catholics are noted by Rankin), but Rebus and his creator are well aware that these monuments are remnants of a hidebound past that the country is only now starting to shake off. In the city's Greyfriars Kirkyard there is a monument to the Seceders and reformers who suffered condemnation for their beliefs – and whose legacy of dissent is alive and well today.

As a total picture of Scotland (and the city of Edinburgh itself), Rankin offers a

The Guildford Arms in West Register Street was part of the inspiration for Rebus's bar The Sutherland.

nigh-unparalleled vision of the industrial and post-industrial landscape, addressing such issues as new technologies in *Let It Bleed* (1996) and oil development in *Black and Blue* (1997). Writing a series about a character who ages in real time has allowed Rankin to take the occasional sideways glance at society or politics – never, though, at the expense of telling the tale. Ian Rankin the social commentator is almost as well known as his crime-writing persona. From the mouth of his dyspeptic copper, we've had a perceptive (and scabrous) analysis of Scottish society and politics spread out across 20 books.

In *The Naming of the Dead* (2006), Rankin made an intriguing background out of media scare stories about the G8 meeting of world leaders in Scotland (2005). Rebus starts on the sidelines of the

massive security arrangements, barely noticed by his superiors, who are happy to keep this difficult copper out of the public eye. He becomes involved when the death of an MP (with the outward appearance of suicide) appears to tie in with hints that a serial killer may be plying his bloody trade.

Retirement and new blood

Exit Music (2007) signals the end for DI John Rebus. However, Rankin decided that he wouldn't make the same mistake that Sir Arthur Conan Doyle (1859–1930) made when he tried to kill off his detective Sherlock Holmes (*see pages 216–225*) by throwing him and his nemesis Moriarty over the Reichenbach Falls. Although *Exit Music* put a full stop to the acclaimed series of crime novels featuring this tough Scottish detective, and ended with a face-off between Rebus and his own Moriarty, this confrontation was less final than Doyle's: Rebus was retired but still may reappear in the future.

All the Rebus novels vividly evoke Auld Reekie (as Edinburgh is lovingly known), and, in 2009, Rankin inaugurated another series set in the city with *The Complaints*, featuring a rather different copper, Malcolm Fox – but one whose beat remained that of the now-retired Rebus.

As for modern Scotland and its leaders, Rankin has said:

> *'I want politicians – English and Scottish – to know that we are watching them – and not letting them get away with anything.'*

And we can be grateful that watching Scotland itself – and its capital – is clearly Ian Rankin's most abiding concern.

USEFUL WEBSITES

'Experience the dark and hidden world of Ian Rankin's best-selling Rebus novels and discover the history and mystery of the real locations, with stunning views of some of Edinburgh's unexplored areas.'
www.rebustours.com

Guided evening walks around the parts of Edinburgh made notorious by the activities of 1820s' bodysnatchers Burke and Hare.
www.westporttours.com/page2.htm

Guided tours of Scotland's new seat of government.
www.scottish.parliament.uk/vli/visitingholyrood/guidedTours.htm

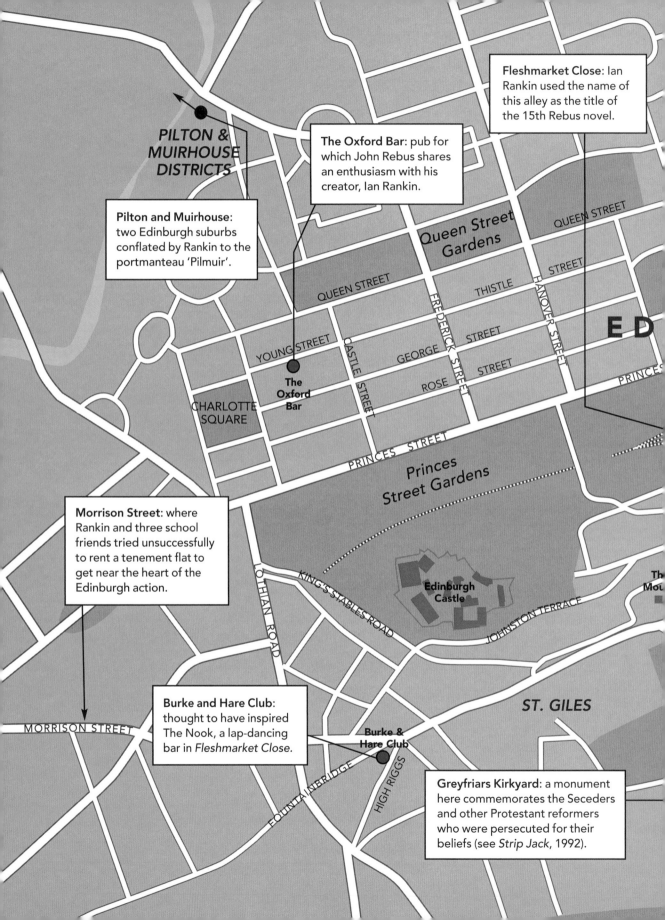

Fleshmarket Close: Ian Rankin used the name of this alley as the title of the 15th Rebus novel.

The Oxford Bar: pub for which John Rebus shares an enthusiasm with his creator, Ian Rankin.

PILTON & MUIRHOUSE DISTRICTS

Pilton and Muirhouse: two Edinburgh suburbs conflated by Rankin to the portmanteau 'Pilmuir'.

Queen Street Gardens

QUEEN STREET

QUEEN STREET

THISTLE STREET

HANOVER STREET

YOUNG STREET

The Oxford Bar

CASTLE STREET

GEORGE STREET

FREDERICK STREET

ROSE STREET

E D

PRINCES

CHARLOTTE SQUARE

PRINCES STREET

Princes Street Gardens

Morrison Street: where Rankin and three school friends tried unsuccessfully to rent a tenement flat to get near the heart of the Edinburgh action.

KING'S STABLES ROAD

LOTHIAN ROAD

Edinburgh Castle

JOHNSTON TERRACE

Th Mou

MORRISON STREET

Burke and Hare Club: thought to have inspired The Nook, a lap-dancing bar in *Fleshmarket Close*.

FOUNTAINBRIDGE

Burke & Hare Club

HIGH RIGGS

ST. GILES

Greyfriars Kirkyard: a monument here commemorates the Seceders and other Protestant reformers who were persecuted for their beliefs (see *Strip Jack*, 1992).

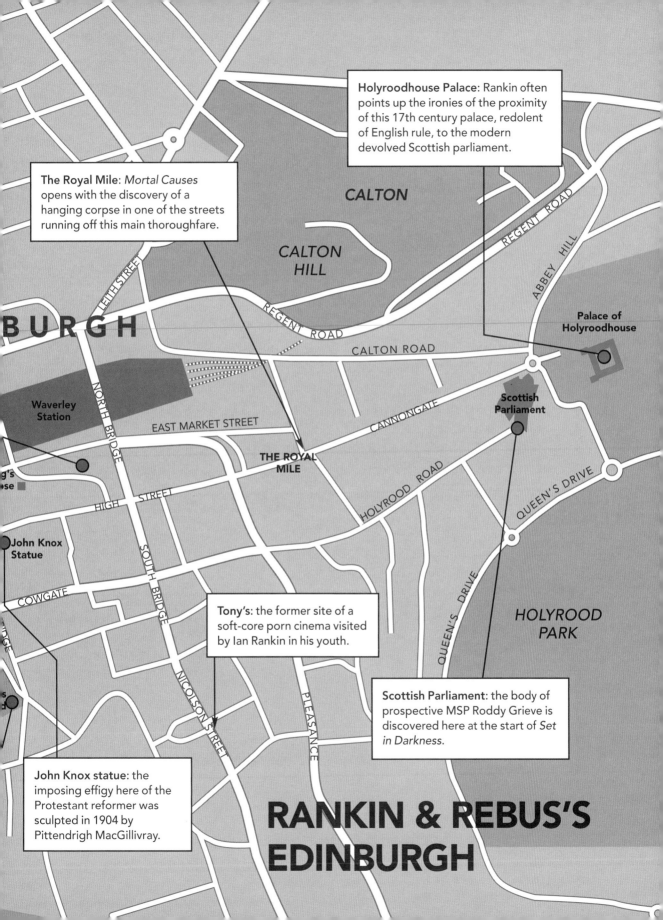

Holyroodhouse Palace: Rankin often points up the ironies of the proximity of this 17th century palace, redolent of English rule, to the modern devolved Scottish parliament.

CALTON

The Royal Mile: *Mortal Causes* opens with the discovery of a hanging corpse in one of the streets running off this main thoroughfare.

CALTON HILL

REGENT ROAD

ABBEY HILL

Palace of Holyroodhouse

BURGH

REGENT ROAD

CALTON ROAD

LEITH STREET

NORTH BRIDGE

Waverley Station

EAST MARKET STREET

CANNONGATE

Scottish Parliament

THE ROYAL MILE

g's se

HIGH STREET

HOLYROOD ROAD

QUEEN'S DRIVE

John Knox Statue

SOUTH BRIDGE

COWGATE

Tony's: the former site of a soft-core porn cinema visited by Ian Rankin in his youth.

QUEEN'S DRIVE

QUEEN'S DRIVE

HOLYROOD PARK

NICOLSON STREET

PLEASANCE

Scottish Parliament: the body of prospective MSP Roddy Grieve is discovered here at the start of *Set in Darkness*.

John Knox statue: the imposing effigy here of the Protestant reformer was sculpted in 1904 by Pittendrigh MacGillivray.

RANKIN & REBUS'S EDINBURGH

Maxim Jakubowski

RAYMOND CHANDLER & PHILIP MARLOWE'S LOS ANGELES

In Raymond Chandler's early short stories featuring a private investigator, the character was called Mallory, Ted Carmady or John Dalmas, until he became Philip Marlowe in *The Big Sleep* (1939).

Ever since, Marlowe has been synonymous with the soft-hearted, caustic-tongued, action-prone American private eye in fiction. With few exceptions, every mystery writer who has followed in the footsteps of Chandler has openly acknowledged the author's iconic influence, and Philip Marlowe is the detective each new detective character is invariably compared to. Marlowe defines what the fictional private eye is all about: 'The loneliness, the quick, sarcastic cynical jibes masking a battered romantic, the love/hate relationship with the cops, the corruption that exists in all levels of society. It's all here' (www.thrillingdetective.com).

Who was Raymond Chandler?

Raymond Chandler was an American who was educated mostly in England, an experience that gave him an interesting perspective on the United States in general and particularly Los Angeles. He came to

writing late in life – he was 45 by the time his first stories began appearing in the detective-story pulp magazines of the day, and 51 when his first novel was published. Critical and commercial acclaim came even later, partly spurred by film adaptations, and by the time Chandler died in 1959 he had written just seven novels and four chapters of the next Marlowe tale, together with just over 20 short stories. The unfinished *Poodle Springs* was completed by Robert B. Parker of the Boston-based PI Spenser series in 1989 (*see pages 98–107*).

As Chandler biographer Tom Hiney points out, Chandler shares many of Marlowe's characteristics:

> *Marlowe is a decent, wisecracking semi-alcoholic. He is also a man whose innate nobility transcends the milieu in which it is his fate to operate: a loner, living in 1940s Los Angeles, watching society around him and wondering what makes people tick, disgusted at the way they were*

being fooled by tycoons and politicians, allowing themselves to be fooled, horrified at the tattiness of the mass production stage of civilization he had found himself in. Marlowe is a private eye; so was his childless, shiftless creator.

Who is Philip Marlowe?

In a letter to an English fan, D.J. Ibberson, in 1951, Chandler noted among other things that Marlowe is 38 years old and was born in Santa Rosa, California. He had a couple of years at college and some experience as an investigator for an insurance company and the district attorney's office of Los Angeles County; he was fired for insubordination (or, as Marlowe put it, 'talking back'). The DA's chief investigator, Bernie Ohls, is a friend and former colleague, and an inside source of information.

Slightly over six feet tall, Marlowe weighs about 190 pounds. He lives at the Hobart Arms, on Franklin Avenue near North Kenmore Avenue and

his office, which is modest, is two miles away at #615 on the 6th floor of the Cahuenga Building, located on Hollywood Boulevard near North Ivar Avenue (between North Cahuenga Boulevard to the west and Vine Street to the east). The office telephone number is Glenview 7537 and he doesn't have a secretary. He generally refuses to take on divorce cases.

Marlowe has particular tastes and interests. An adept chess player, he plays almost exclusively against himself. He smokes and Camels are his cigarette of choice, but at home, he sometimes smokes a pipe. He drinks

Powers Boothe as Philip Marlowe in a TV version of the Chandler books.

MARLOWE, PHILIP

Height: 'slightly over six feet'
Weight: about 190 pounds
Occupation: Private investigator

Favourite drink: Four Roses whiskey

Favourite tobacco: Camel cigarettes

Note to counsel: Chandler warns Marlowe-watchers against 'confusing momentary preference with fixed taste'. The PI is also known to like Old Forester Kentucky bourbon; he sometimes smokes a pipe at home.

whiskey or brandy frequently and in relatively large quantities. For example, in *The High Window* (1942) he gets out a bottle of Four Roses, and pours glasses of the blended American whiskey for himself, for Detective Lieutenant Breeze and for Spangler. At other times he drinks Old Forester, a Kentucky bourbon: 'I hung up and fed myself a slug of Old Forester to brace my nerves for the interview. As I was inhaling it I heard her steps tripping along the corridor.' (*The Little Sister*, 1949).

English education, Californian insight

Billy Wilder (1906–2002), the Austrian-born film director who made a home in California, once remarked: 'Chandler's great strength was a descriptive one. There are very few people who can get the flavour of California. It's very peculiar, you know, that the only person who caught the Californian atmosphere in prose was an Englishman – Chandler'. Wilder and Chandler had huge success writing the screenplay for the 1944 movie adaptation of James M. Cain's 1943 *Double Indemnity*.

Critic Bill Scheller compares Chandler's use of setting to that of Sir Arthur Conan Doyle (*see pages 216–227*):

I've always found it interesting that two of the greatest practitioners of the most plot-dependent of all literary genres excelled just as much at setting as at plot. Sir Arthur Conan Doyle... limmed late Victorian London so exquisitely that you feel as if you could go there and hail a hansom cab. And Raymond Chandler is the other genius of setting, portraying the Los Angeles of the Thirties and Forties every bit as convincingly as he portrayed his knight-errant Marlowe ... Chandler pulled an even neater trick than Conan Doyle ... While the London of Sherlock Holmes, with its damps and fogs and perpetually crepuscular atmosphere, looked like a place where half the population was up to no good, it was harder to summon up that much malevolence out of sunny LA. But summon it Chandler did. It might seem as if noir fiction ought to all happen at night, but that's because directors seldom shot noir movies in broad daylight. In Chandler's novels, plenty of creeps crawl out from under their rocks when the sun is shining.

'I'M A ROMANTIC, BERNIE. I HEAR VOICES CRYING IN THE NIGHT AND I GO TO SEE WHAT'S THE MATTER. YOU DON'T MAKE A DIME THAT WAY... NO PERCENTAGE IN IT AT ALL.' – THE BIG SLEEP, 1939

HUMPHREY
BOGART
AND
LAUREN
BACALL
"THE BIG SLEEP"
MARTHA VICKERS · DOROTHY MALONE
HOWARD HAWK
PRODUCTION
MUSIC BY MAX STEINER · SCREEN PLAY BY WILLIAM FAULKNER, LEIGH BRACKETT & JULES FURTHMAN · FROM THE NOVEL BY RAYMOND CHANDLER
46/95

With the exception of *The Lady in The Lake* (1943), where Marlowe has to make repeated visits outside of Los Angeles to Lake Arrowhead and its mountainous surroundings, all of Chandler's stories and novels take place in Los Angeles and its immediate suburbs of Pasadena and Santa Monica. Chandler changed the latter's name to Bay City, and it is there that the climax of *Farewell My Lovely* (1940) occurs on the pier.

Chandler's own opinion of Los Angeles was far from laudatory; Marlowe rails against it for being, among other things 'lost and beaten and full of emptiness', 'a neon-lighted slum' and a place 'with no more personality than a paper cup'. Even so, whenever Marlowe finds himself half-dreaming of a contented small-town life, he decides to 'take the big, sordid, dirty, crooked city' every time. Ironically, once Chandler had made his fortune in Hollywood, he moved away from LA with haste, settling for his final years with his older wife Cissy in the La Jolla suburb of San Diego in Southern California, near the Mexican border.

Marlowe's LA today

Although Los Angeles has changed enormously since the Philip Marlowe years, with its out-of-control urban sprawl, and many of the landmarks visited by Marlowe (or bars patronized by Chandler himself) no longer exist, it is still difficult to think of the city without 1940s' hardboiled fiction of the Chandler variety and film noir springing to mind – a city of corrupt cops, tuxedoed big-time criminals, desperate small-time grifters and femmes fatales by the bucket.

Indeed, for a vision of Marlowe's Los Angeles, there is no better point of reference than *Chinatown*, the 1974 Roman Polanski movie which is conceivably the best Chandler-type adaptation not actually based on a Chandler story. As a result, Los Angeles and Raymond Chandler (and Philip Marlowe) are still closely associated in the mind.

In fact, Esotouric, a local tour company, operates two separate Raymond Chandler bus tours of the city ('Raymond Chandler's Los Angeles: In A Lonely Place' and 'Chandler's Bay City'), with stopovers at locations that appear at important junctures in the Marlowe investigations, as well as at buildings and places and bars known to have been frequented by Chandler. Visitors can have a Chandler-themed gelato at cult favourite Scoops. A Raymond Chandler crime scene map of LA has been published, along with countless photographic books retracing

PHILIP MARLOWE ON SCREEN

Although in many people's minds the definitive Philip Marlowe is Humphrey Bogart, thanks to his iconic performance in the 1946 film of *The Big Sleep*, Marlowe has also been played by a variety of other actors on film and television, with varying degrees of success. Here is a selection:

 IN FILM

George Sanders, albeit called The Falcon, in *The Falcon Takes Over* (1942), an adaptation of *Farewell My Lovely*

Lloyd Nolan as Michael Shayne (the Marlowe character), in *Time to Kill* (1942), an adaptation of *The High Window*

Dick Powell in *Murder, My Sweet* (1944) an adaptation of *Farewell My Lovely*, under which title it was released in the UK

Humphrey Bogart in *The Big Sleep* (1946)

Robert Montgomery in *The Lady in the Lake* (1947)

George Montgomery in *The Brasher Doubloon* (1947), an adaptation of *The High Window*

James Garner in *Marlowe* (1969), an adaptation of *The Little Sister*

Elliott Gould in *The Long Goodbye* (1973)

Robert Mitchum in *Farewell My Lovely* (1975) and *The Big Sleep* (1978)

Tomas Hanak in the Czech film *Mazany Filip* (2003), inspired by various Chandler stories

 ON TELEVISION

Philip Carey in *Philip Marlowe* (1959–60), an ABC TV series

Powers Boothe in *Philip Marlowe, Private Eye* (1983, 1986), a London Weekend Television series

Danny Glover in *Red Wind* (1995), part of the Fallen Angels series

James Caan in *Poodle Springs* (1998), an HBO film for television

Jason O'Mara in *Marlowe* (2007)

'I HAVEN'T BEEN HERE, YOU HAVEN'T SEEN ME, AND SHE HASN'T BEEN OUT OF THE HOUSE ALL EVENING' – THE BIG SLEEP, 1939

the footsteps of the iconic character through pictures of the city then and now.

It is still possible to retrace Marlowe's footsteps (and drives) from novel to novel, from the lush Sternwood residence on Franklin Avenue and the Geiger bookstore and residences on, respectively, Hollywood Boulevard and Laurel Canyon (in *The Big Sleep*) to Florian's Bar, where Marlowe met up with Moose Malloy in *The Little Sister*, and which is now the address of an appliances store; or visit the Barclay Hotel, formerly the Van Nuys, site of the ice-pick murder in *The Little Sister*.

The Bradbury Building on the corner of 3rd Street and Broadway.

Alternatively you can make a detour to Santa Monica and retrace Marlowe's often-perilous progress through the streets of Bay City, from Ann Riordan's apartment on 25th Street or the shady clinic of Dr Sonderberg at 23rd Street and Colorado.

Another iconic location, although some critics have argued about it, is the Bradbury Building at 3rd and Broadway, which Chandler renamed the Belfont Building, with its stunning atrium, wrought-iron stairwells and open-cage elevators. Marlowe visits the building – later immortalized on screen in *Blade Runner* (1982) – on various occasions.

Armed with a good map and a copy of Chandler's novels, it is still possible to follow in Marlowe's footsteps even today. A further invaluable resource,

Made famous by Chandler, the Bradbury Building has had its status enhanced by its use as a location in Ridley Scott's cult film Blade Runner *(1982).*

in addition to a useful half dozen or so biographies of Chandler by an assortment of American and British writers, is the fan website 'Raymond Chandler's Los Angeles: Shamus Town', which provides a wealth of information and iconography about all things Chandleresque.

Beyond the specific locations, real or imagined by Chandler, one of the reasons that the world of Philip Marlowe is still so alive for readers today, well over 70 years after the private eye first made his appearance in print, is not just the intrinsically human and therefore fallible and contradictory nature of Marlowe's personality – hard-bitten and vulnerable, knowing and naïve. Rather, what stays in mind is the exquisitely sketched sense of place, where just a few lines can drag you into a story and transport you in the wink of an eye into the California of the past:

There was a desert wind blowing that night. It was one of those hot dry Santa Ana's that come down through the mountain passes and curl your hair and make your nerves jump and your skin itch. On nights like that every booze party ends in a fight. Meek little wives feel the edge of a carving knife and study their husband's necks. Anything can happen. You can even get a full glass of beer at a cocktail lounge – 'Red Wind', 1938, now in *Raymond Chandler: Collected Stories* (2002).

USEFUL WEBSITES:

Raymond Chandler's Los Angeles: Shamus Town
www.homepage.mac.com/llatker

Esotouric bus tours: Chandler
www.esotouric.com/chandlerpage

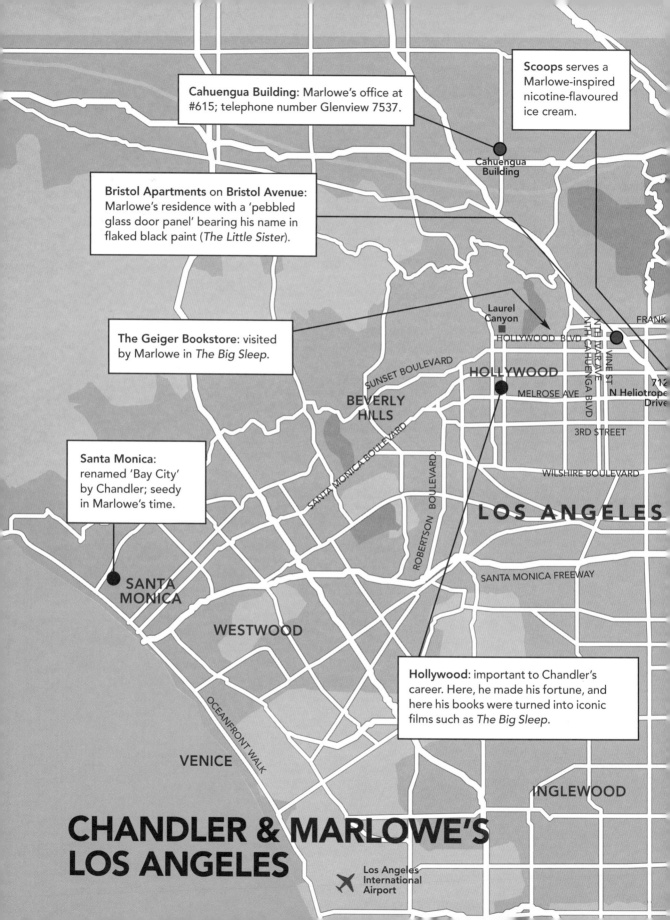

Scoops serves a Marlowe-inspired nicotine-flavoured ice cream.

Cahuengua Building: Marlowe's office at #615; telephone number Glenview 7537.

Bristol Apartments on Bristol Avenue: Marlowe's residence with a 'pebbled glass door panel' bearing his name in flaked black paint (*The Little Sister*).

The Geiger Bookstore: visited by Marlowe in *The Big Sleep*.

Santa Monica: renamed 'Bay City' by Chandler; seedy in Marlowe's time.

Hollywood: important to Chandler's career. Here, he made his fortune, and here his books were turned into iconic films such as *The Big Sleep*.

Cahuengua Building

Laurel Canyon

FRANK

HOLLYWOOD BLVD

N'TH MAR AVE

N'TH CAHUENGA BLVD

VINE ST

71

N Heliotrope Drive

SUNSET BOULEVARD

BEVERLY HILLS

HOLLYWOOD

MELROSE AVE

3RD STREET

WILSHIRE BOULEVARD

SANTA MONICA BOULEVARD

ROBERTSON BOULEVARD

LOS ANGELES

SANTA MONICA

SANTA MONICA FREEWAY

WESTWOOD

OCEANFRONT WALK

VENICE

INGLEWOOD

CHANDLER & MARLOWE'S LOS ANGELES

Los Angeles International Airport

GLENDALE

COLORADO STREET

EAGLE ROCK

Griffith Park

AVENUE

GOLDEN STATE FREEWAY

N. KENMORE AVE

HOLLYWOOD FREEWAY

Elysian Park

CHINATOWN

Bradbury Building

Barclay Hotel

BROADWAY

DOWNTOWN

BOYLE HEIGHTS

HUNTINGTON PARK

HARBOR FREEWAY

WATTS

Pasadena: a favourite Chandler setting. In the 1930s, two-thirds of LA's population lived here. By 2000, the number of residents had doubled but comprised less than 2% of LA's residents.

PASADENA

Sternwood Residence at 3765 Alta Brea Crescent, with entrance doors 'which would have let in a troop of Indian elephants' (*The Big Sleep*).

The Bradbury Building features in Chandler's books as the Belfont Building.

The Barclay Hotel, which features in *The Little Sister* under its old name, the Van Nuys.

Barry Forshaw

DONNA LEON & COMMISSARIO BRUNETTI'S VENICE

It is not necessary for an author to live in a particular locale to render his or her settings authentic, but Donna Leon's vivid recreation of Venice for her Commissario Guido Brunetti novels would seem to owe something to her intimate knowledge of the city.

As much as the beleaguered Brunetti himself, Venice is a powerful protagonist in Leon's elegantly constructed tales. An American expatriate, she has lived in the city since the 1980s, and this has given her a superb knowledge of *La Serenissima* – one of the names by which Venice is known, literally meaning 'the most serene'. Leon is unbeatable at conjuring up the atmosphere of this unique city, which has been evoked with assurance by other chroniclers from artists Canaletto (1697–1768) and J. M. W. Turner (1775–1851) to film director Nicolas Roeg (b. 1928).

Reading a Donna Leon novel is almost as good as a trip to her adopted city, although her view of the dark sides of Italy (multiple levels of corruption and double-dealing) strays quite some way from the tourist trail, and may be one of the reasons she has not sanctioned Italian translations of her work.

From La Fenice to San Polo

Opera is a theme close to Donna Leon's heart: she is a friend of the great Italian soprano Cecilia Bartoli (b. 1966), and is involved in many important classical concerts. The opera house of La Fenice is immensely celebrated in Venice, not just for the musical glories that have taken place within its walls. Famously, the opera house burned down and was later restored to its exquisite former appearance – and it is here that we first encounter Guido Brunetti in a Donna Leon novel. In *Death at La Fenice* (1992), Brunetti is reminded of many aspects of Venice's glorious past. The area surrounding the opera house, the Campo San Fantin, is the location of one of the city's most illustrious restaurants, Antico Martini, a famous venue for classical studies, the Ateneo Veneto, and the site of a Renaissance church, Chiesa di San Fantin. In this book, Brunetti considers the marked contrast between the glory of bygone days and its more shopworn present.

In *Death at La Fenice* we learn also that the Commissario's apartment is in the San Polo region, near the less-visited Santa Croce district. The eastern area

of San Polo was once the historical centre of Venice, and the area still has a liveliness granted to it by the Rialto stalls, which are not too far away. The bells of the church of San Polo are a familiar noise to Guido Brunetti, and the area is repeatedly described as having a great appeal for him. He and his family have an exquisite view from their apartment, which is a constant source of joy to him; he is able to see the Dolomite mountain range from the kitchen. The slower pace of life at home – not to mention his wife Paola's cooking – offers a respite from the rigours of his job. Another striking vista is presented to the detective when he walks down Calle Traghetto della Madonnetta to gaze at the Grand Canal.

Brunetti muses about the flexibility of the bylaws that affect this patch – his own home is surrounded by areas full of rundown buildings as well as the splendidly maintained historical sites. In *Death at La Fenice* he worries that he doesn't legally own his flat. He is right to worry, as some years later (in *Friends in High Places*, 2000) he finds himself the target of a government initiative to control and bring into line all of Venice's illegal buildings – including the one he is identified as living in.

Exploring the city

Excellent novels such as *Death in a Strange Country* (1993) and *The Anonymous Venetian* (1994) followed Leon's debut Brunetti novel.

The rail and road causeway of the Ponte della Libertà is the area in which Brunetti is nearly killed in the latter work (a young policewoman, in

Donna Leon

Donna Leon will not sanction translation of her books into Italian.

Leon has a passionate interest in serious music (notably the operas of Handel). She organizes numerous classical concerts in her adoptive country and sings and tours in a baroque choir herself.

Leon's books sell best in Germany.

Leon has lived and taught English literature in Switzerland, Iran, China, Italy and Saudi Arabia.

fact, pays with her life) and it is also where a body is found on a train in *A Venetian Reckoning* (1995).

A Noble Radiance (1997) is a distinctive entry in the series. Notable sources of pleasure for Brunetti are the boat trips that he is able to take from his apartment, during which he muses on the problems and pleasures of living in Venice – along with the challenges of whatever case he is working on. Arriving home from the Questura (the police headquarters), a walk down a secluded alley to his home from the canal often prompts him to think about the history of Venice, as in *Death in a Strange Country*, where he reminds himself not to grow oblivious to the beauty of his city with its great Gothic and Neoclassical edifices the Doge's Palace in Piazza San Marco and the Palazzo Grassi in Campo San Samuele, among others.

Having featured in *Death at La Fenice*, the famous cemetery of San Michele reappears in *Death in a Strange Country*. This is where the detective's father is buried (as we learn in the first book) and it is also the site of some of the autopsies of the series. Brunetti's colleague, the pathologist Ettore Rizzardi, appears frequently in the series, usually in collusion with the detective against the intransigence of the authorities. In *Death in a Strange Country*, Brunetti takes a boat to San Michele in order to view a body. The island itself is the site of the grave of the composer Igor Stravinsky (1882–1971), along with the tombs of generations of Venetians, and Leon's descriptions of the cemetery have a peculiar poignancy. In this book, Brunetti also pays a visit to the Ospedale Civile in Campo Santi Giovanni e Paolo, famous for both the hospital and its pathology and autopsy facility.

Knowing the right people

A particularly strong volume in Leon's series of novels is *Friends in High Places*, her ninth book, which has Brunetti making enemies as he looks into serious drug peddling and the abuses of loan sharks. As the title suggests, much is possible in Italy in terms of establishment corruption and abuse of the system as long as you have the requisite well-placed contacts. Brunetti faces a continuing struggle against such compromised officials in the books. San Polo is featured again here as the site of Brunetti's 'illegal' house.

A Sea of Troubles (2001) is evidence of a deepening and a refinement of Leon's art. Two fishermen have been killed on the island of Pellestrina, south of the Lido on the Venetian lagoon. Brunetti finds it difficult to penetrate the close-knit community, locked behind a code of loyalty

Cooking the books

Food is a vital part of Brunetti's world and the markets and food of Venice feature largely in the books. In response to popular demand – and her own awareness of the importance of gastronomy in Italian culture – Donna Leon has authorized and contributed background culinary stories to a cook book by Roberta Pianaro based on the recipes used by the Commissario's wife, Paola (*A Taste of Venice*, 2010). One of the highlights is a unique and mouth-watering recipe for risotto.

and an insularity that the Mafia would be proud of. However, solving the murders is not his only problem: when Signorina Elettra, secretary to the Questore (the chief of the Questura), volunteers to come to the island, Brunetti finds himself obliged to protect her – and, furthermore, to deal with the confused feelings he has for her.

Apart from his family home, the place in which Brunetti spends most of his time is the Questura. It is his base of operations, and its location in the quiet Sestiere di Castello (the actual Questura has moved to Piazzale Roma) is used by Leon as an ironic contrast to the grim dealings with death and corruption that take place within the police station. The nearby Church of San Lorenzo, once allowed to fall into disrepair, has been lovingly restored to its former glory, and Brunetti watches work on it progress through the windows of the Questura.

Wilful Behaviour (2002), Donna Leon's 11th Brunetti novel, has none of the repetition that often besets so many long-running series. A prestigious art collection owned by an elderly Austrian woman is kept, rather unwisely, in her flat. When she is found dead, Brunetti soon uncovers secrets involving collaboration and the exploitation of Italian Jews during the war.

The brick wall he encounters seems impregnable – very few people are willing to talk, but this time his wife, Paola, becomes involved.

A living city

These are detective novels that do not merely utilize Venice as an exotic backdrop for mysteries and bloodletting: we are also given brilliantly observed vignettes of workaday Venice in *Wilful Behaviour*. The Church of the Pietà is principally used these days for concerts – appropriately, since it is known as the church of Antonio Vivaldi (1678–1741). This is where the great baroque composer (known in his day as the Red Priest) wrote his concerti for the orphan girls who were placed in the care of the church. There is an echo of just such a neglected young girl in this book – the death of a young woman takes Brunetti to another ecclesiastical setting in which a murder has taken place.

Doctored Evidence (2004) has Brunetti encountering a seemingly open-and-shut case: a wealthy Venetian is found savagely murdered in her apartment and her missing maid, a Romanian immigrant, is the prime suspect. The maid is tracked down, but meets a grisly end on a railway track, while attempting to escape. Needless to say, Brunetti does not takes things at face value, and when it transpires that the money found on the maid is not stolen money, Brunetti engages in a little unofficial sleuthing and uncovers a very tangled web of motives indeed – with revelations quite different from the attempts to cover up municipal shenanigans that have often been the worm in the bud of previous Brunetti cases.

The Campo San Stefano is a much-frequented locale in Donna Leon's novels, and it is inevitable that the Commissario is intimately familiar with the square and its denizens. This is the second largest square on the eastern side of the Grand Canal (after its more celebrated counterpart, the Piazza San Marco). It has been a popular venue for bullfights, festivals and political rallies, and the detective is often to be found here, sipping an espresso or listening to the public loudspeakers booming out political sloganeering.

Through a Glass Darkly (2006), like all Leon's work, has the exuberance of a Puccini opera, and the title turns out to be a play on the word 'glass'. On a bright spring day in Venice, Brunetti and his associate, Vianello, help the latter's friend Marco, who is under arrest after an environmental protest. After his release, Marco is attacked by his splenetically angry father-in-law, owner of a glass factory (hence the pun of the title). Marco's wife believes that the old man may actually kill him for his eco-friendly views. Although the themes Leon juggles here are not new (the customary establishment chicanery, for instance),

there is a freshly energized passion in both Leon's (and Brunetti's) reaction to the ecological threat, evidence of the author's passion for Venice and its environs, which suffer badly from dumped toxic waste.

In *Through a Glass Darkly*, the iconic Pasticceria Tonolo is identified as the site of the small bakery that Brunetti regularly visits on Sundays to pick up brioche for his family (the bakery is also, of course, a favourite with his gourmet wife, Paola). Much visited by locals and tourists alike, Tonolo is one of Venice's finest pastry shops.

Revealing the darker side of the city

In these novels, we can cruise down the Grand Canal or stroll over the Rialto Bridge in Donna Leon's agreeable (if severe) company, but she's not in the business of just presenting a roseate tourist's eye view of Venice. Italy, in Brunetti's dark world, is a country where corruption reaches to the highest levels of government (and recent political turmoil will no doubt provide more grist for the author's mill). However picturesque the settings, there is little that is comfortable about the struggle to bring justice to a chaotic universe. And if something is rotten in the state of Italy, Commissario Guido Brunetti is the man to drag it kicking and screaming into the light – as in *Suffer the Little Children* (2007), one of the most complex and socially engaged of the Brunetti novels. Here the Commissario

'THE MERE USE OF ONE'S EYES IN VENICE IS HAPPINESS ENOUGH, AND GENEROUS OBSERVERS FIND IT HARD TO KEEP AN ACCOUNT OF THEIR PROFITS IN THIS LINE' – HENRY JAMES 'VENICE: AN EARLY IMPRESSION' (1872)

GUIDE TO BRUNETTI ON SCREEN

The Brunetti novels have been slow to transfer to cinema. This is perhaps surprising, given their dramatic themes and exquisitely picturesque settings, but part of the reason may be the refusal of American-born Donna Leon to authorize Italian-language editions of her work. This has naturally restricted her appeal in her adopted country and hence the likelihood of finding local financial backing for a movie or TV series. Asked to justify her decision, Leon explains: 'I do not want to live where I am famous … I don't like being approached by people in a deferential way'.

 **IN FILM**

German series starring Joachim Król as
    Commissario Brunetti:
Venezianische Scharade (2000)

Vendetta (2000)
Nobiltà (2002)
In Sachen Signora Brunetti (2002)

finds a can of worms prised open after a respected hospital paediatrician is the victim of a vicious attack: one of Brunetti's fellow policemen had broken into the doctor's house and abducted his baby son.

In the Piazza San Marco some of Venice's loveliest buildings can be found, including the Doge's Palace and St Mark's Cathedral, although it is also an area that gives some visitors pause for the sheer excess of the offerings on display. As Brunetti walks through this imposing square in several of Leon's books, including *Quietly in Their Sleep* (1997) and *A Venetian Reckoning*, his feelings are ambiguous – especially towards the hordes of tourists who are always thronging there during the summer months, since they contrast starkly with the great artists who visited the area in the past. In *Suffer the Little Children*, Brunetti recalls some of the most famous: the poet Lord Byron (1788–1824), the composer Richard Wagner (1813–83), who complained about the Venetians' refusal to applaud his music, and the novelist Henry James (1843–1916). Brunetti is a secular individual in a Catholic society: the Basilica di San Marco is a place that fills him with a certain reverence, but also prompts thoughts of the city's bloody past.

Navigating the waterways

Leon has long gone native – in no uncertain terms. Her familiarity with Brunetti's waterlogged beat is transmuted into vivid and evocative narratives: the Grand Canal

and the Rialto Bridge are often the dark passageways to another, darker Italy, where hidden (and not-so-hidden) sleaze in politics and daily life is very much an everyday thing (as newspaper headlines remind us).

The Girl of His Dreams (2008), the 17th Brunetti novel, demonstrates how much life is left in the Leon/Brunetti criminal world. The body of a young girl is found floating near some steps on the Grand Canal – but there have been no reports of missing children. The search for the identity of the youthful victim and her family takes Brunetti to many varied destinations, including a gypsy encampment on the mainland. Eventually, he turns up some very grisly secrets. As ever, it is not only the villains who thwart Brunetti at every turn – it is the venality and clandestine nature of the establishment that hamper him, almost as a matter of course.

In *The Girl of His Dreams*, Brunetti's investigations take him to the Dorsoduro and the Palazzo Guardi that overlooks the Grand Canal. As so often in the books, the beauty of the city is contrasted with its underlying violence. And, as ever, Donna Leon is the most provocative and stimulating of guides.

The English writer Michael Dibdin evoked Italian cities with notable skill, but no other writer, including native Italian crime fiction practitioners, has matched Leon's authority and imagination in conjuring up the country she has chosen to live in and, in Guido Brunetti, she has created one of the great European policemen.

Useful websites & addresses

Donna Leon Online
www.randomhouse.co.uk/minisites/donnaleon

Brunetti Walking Tour of Venice
There are several tours available. This two-hour walk takes in Brunetti's haunts and many of the great works of architecture featured in the novels of Donna Leon.

www.private-guides.com/guide-in-italy/fiona-giusto-venice-1-498/brunetti-venice-3474/index.php

Pasticceria Tonolo, Dorsoduro 3764
This pastry shop opened in 1953; a favourite of Guido Brunetti and millions of other people, it often features among Venice's Top 10 tourist places to eat.

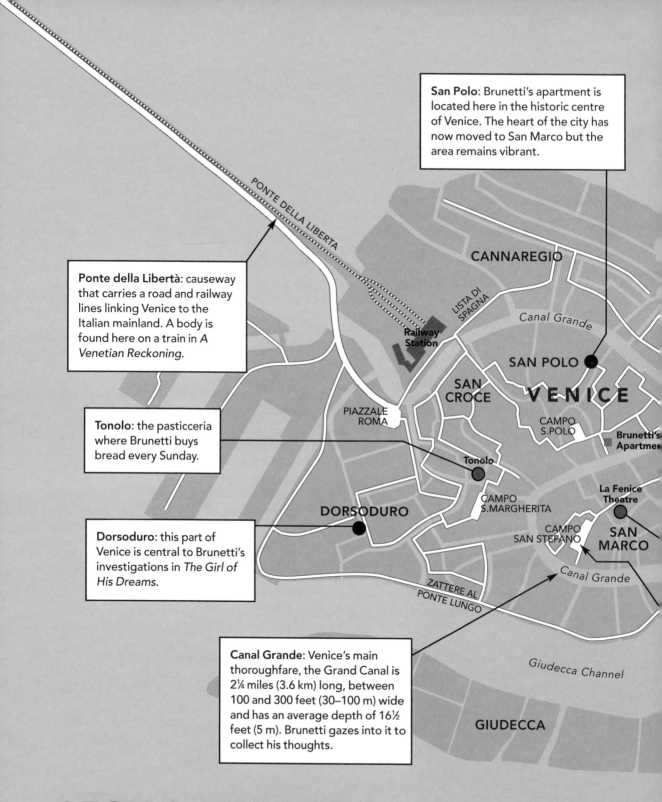

San Polo: Brunetti's apartment is located here in the historic centre of Venice. The heart of the city has now moved to San Marco but the area remains vibrant.

Ponte della Libertà: causeway that carries a road and railway lines linking Venice to the Italian mainland. A body is found here on a train in *A Venetian Reckoning*.

Tonolo: the pasticceria where Brunetti buys bread every Sunday.

Dorsoduro: this part of Venice is central to Brunetti's investigations in *The Girl of His Dreams*.

Canal Grande: Venice's main thoroughfare, the Grand Canal is 2¼ miles (3.6 km) long, between 100 and 300 feet (30–100 m) wide and has an average depth of 16½ feet (5 m). Brunetti gazes into it to collect his thoughts.

PONTE DELLA LIBERTA

CANNAREGIO

LISTA DI SPAGNA

Canal Grande

Railway Station

SAN POLO

V E N I C E

SAN CROCE

PIAZZALE ROMA

CAMPO S.POLO

Brunetti's Apartmen

Tonolo

CAMPO S.MARGHERITA

La Fenice Theatre

DORSODURO

CAMPO SAN STEFANO

SAN MARCO

CAMPO SAN STEFANO

Canal Grande

ZATTERE AL PONTE LUNGO

Giudecca Channel

GIUDECCA

LEON & BRUNETTI'S VENICE

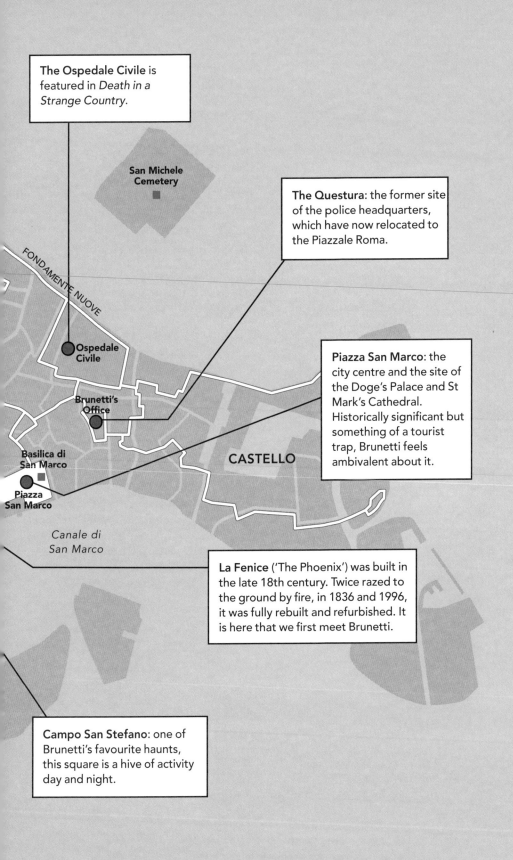

The Ospedale Civile is featured in *Death in a Strange Country*.

San Michele Cemetery

The Questura: the former site of the police headquarters, which have now relocated to the Piazzale Roma.

FONDAMENTE NUOVE

Ospedale Civile

Piazza San Marco: the city centre and the site of the Doge's Palace and St Mark's Cathedral. Historically significant but something of a tourist trap, Brunetti feels ambivalent about it.

Brunetti's Office

Basilica di San Marco

CASTELLO

Piazza San Marco

Canale di San Marco

La Fenice ('The Phoenix') was built in the late 18th century. Twice razed to the ground by fire, in 1836 and 1996, it was fully rebuilt and refurbished. It is here that we first meet Brunetti.

Campo San Stefano: one of Brunetti's favourite haunts, this square is a hive of activity day and night.

Dick Adler and Maxim Jakubowski

SARA PARETSKY & V.I. WARSHAWSKI'S CHICAGO

In V.I. Warshawski, Sara Peretsky has created a distinctive private eye – a Chicagoan to her fingertips who could probably not function or exist anywhere else on earth.

Chicago began with the railroads and its geographic position – between the U.S. eastern seaboard, the Midwest and Canada – quickly turned it into a boom town with all that that entails, including a strong heritage of violence, rackets and corruption. Indeed, it became the city of gangster Al Capone (1899–1947) and is still associated for many with the excesses of the Prohibition years (1920–33), crooked politics and the development of jazz a saving grace. What crime writer could ask for a better stage?

Sara Paretsky has used Chicago to create her popular series featuring the tough but deeply committed private investigator V.I. (first name's Victoria, but people use it at their peril) Warshawski. The first of these novels, *Indemnity Only*, appeared in 1981; the 13th in line, *Hardball*, became an instant best-seller on its publication in 2009. The series has become a landmark, and Paretsky is often mentioned by critics in the same breath as Raymond Chandler (1888–1959), Dashiell Hammett (1894–1961) and Ross MacDonald (1915–1983).

Just as Chandler captured the 'mean streets' of Los Angeles, Hammett brought to life the underbelly of San Francisco, and Macdonald dug beneath the lush gardens of Santa Barbara, so Paretsky has set her novels firmly in the geography of Chicago – from V.I.'s childhood home – where she lived with her policeman father and opera-loving mother – on 92nd Street in South Chicago to her present home on Racine Avenue in Lincoln Park, where she runs daily with two large dogs owned by Mr Contreras, her downstairs neighbour.

V.I. never forgets her South Chicago past. For example, in *Fire Sale* (2005) she goes back to her old high school in Bessemer Park to coach a girls' basketball team and winds up in all kinds of trouble: investigating a factory explosion in which she herself is injured, she uncovers a web of intrigue in the owner's family.

Women in crime

Explaining why she made Warshawski such a unique blend of thought and action, Sara Paretsky commented:

I always loved mysteries but I got tired of reading about women who were vamps. Sexually active women had to be evil or virgins. If they were chaste, they couldn't act at all, but waited around to be rescued, or victims – graphic rape and dismemberment of women continue to titillate readers. With V.I., I created a fourth "V" – a woman who could solve her own problems. The fact that she had a sex life was just part of her humanity, not a sign of her moral character.

The success of the series and the character owes a lot to Warshawski's gender, with Paretsky creating one of the first major positive female characters in the genre, paradoxically within the perception that Chicago was a particularly manly town: American poet Carl Sandburg (1878–1967), for example, called it 'City of the Big Shoulders', 'a tall bold slugger set vivid against the little soft cities'. This contrast between Chicago's masculinity and V.I.'s supposedly weaker sex, together with the heroine's instinctive reaction against this state of affairs, lie at the centre of Paretsky's books, and while the city grows no less mean from book to book, her detective hardens and conquers obstacles with increasing verve and determination.

In *Scene of the Crime* (2008), David Geherin, Professor of English at Eastern Michigan University, describes how Sara Paretsky feminizes Chicago by giving V.I. Warshawski a support network of friends and family that sets her apart from the usual male lone wolf sleuth characterized

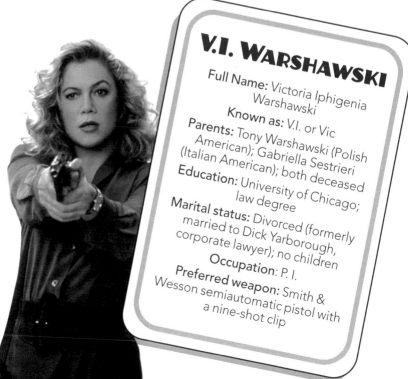

V.I. WARSHAWSKI

Full Name: Victoria Iphigenia Warshawski

Known as: V.I. or Vic

Parents: Tony Warshawski (Polish American); Gabriella Sestrieri (Italian American); both deceased

Education: University of Chicago; law degree

Marital status: Divorced (formerly married to Dick Yarborough, corporate lawyer); no children

Occupation: P. I.

Preferred weapon: Smith & Wesson semiautomatic pistol with a nine-shot clip

by Chandler and Hammett. This extended family helps Paretsky domesticate the dangers that surround her main character and make sense of the violence and contradictions that assail her at every turn of the plots. In addition, V.I. is solidly anchored to the city by an accumulation of reassuring habits. She regularly eats at the Belmont Diner in an old working-class neighbourhood; she drinks at the Golden Glow, a saloon in the South Loop that's been there forever. In addition, V.I. is a Cubs fan and often attends baseball games at Wrigley Field (*see below image*).

Raising the game

Throughout the V.I. Warshawski series, not only does the tough heroine change psychologically as she encounters more and more of the evil in the modern world and Chicago in particular, but Paretsky also maps the gentrification of ethnic areas and the blight that modernization leaves behind, the poverty and the inequalities. Some critics have taken offence at the increasing politicization of Paretsky's crime novels – she has even written a few books in which V.I. does not appear – including *Ghost Country* (1998) and

*The Green Mill
bar on North
Broadway.*

Bleeding Kansas (2008) – and her social
conscience is becoming ever more acute.

In reflecting modern mores Paretsky
has also become a faithful chronicler of
the way Chicago and America are
changing and she goes well beyond the
basic remit of crime and mystery fiction.
In this respect, the roles of Paretsky and
Warshawski have proved pioneering and
been at the root of an explosion of new

crime writing set in Chicago. At the
forefront of this new movement is The
Outfit, a group of authors whose collective
name is taken from that of an old
nickname for the Mob and who look upon
Paretsky as their queen bee.

Influences

Paretsky once acknowledged as her
mentor Stuart M. Kaminsky (1934–2009),
another fine chronicler of the Chicago
crime scene. One of his series, about a

'THE VASTNESS OF THE CITY AT NIGHT
WAS OVERWHELMING. RED FLARES GLOWED
AGAINST A YELLOW SKY, FOLLOWED BY MILE
ON MILE OF UNBENDING LIGHTS: STREET
LIGHTS, NEON SIGNS, TRAFFIC LIGHTS,
FLASHING POLICE BLUES – LIGHTS THAT
DIDN'T ILLUMINATE BUT THREW SHADOWS
AND MADE THE CITY SEEM A MONSTER,
READY TO DEVOUR THE UNWARY'
– V.I. FOR SHORT (1995)

'HERE IS THE DIFFERENCE BETWEEN DANTE, MILTON, AND ME. THEY WROTE ABOUT HELL AND NEVER SAW THE PLACE. I WROTE ABOUT CHICAGO AFTER LOOKING THE TOWN OVER FOR YEARS AND YEARS' – CARL SANDBURG (1961)

close-to-retirement Chicago police detective named Abe Lieberman, shows that Kaminsky had a unique eye for the city's meanest streets. 'Terror Town is roughly bordered on the north by Seventy-fourth Street, on the south by Seventy-ninth Street, and on the east and west by Yates and Exchange', he writes about a South Side neighbourhood where residents are 11 times more likely to be victims of violent crime than those living in the rest of the city. 'The police enter the streets of Terror Town with the same foreboding as Marines in Baghdad.'

The unusually savage murder of a young single mother brings Lieberman and his long-time partner, Bill Hanrahan, to Terror Town. Also on Lieberman's daily docket are an attack on a semi-famous former Cubs player at his favourite hot-dog establishment (Lenny & Al's on Montrose) and the chilling antics of a religious maniac who sidelines in extortion. Through it all, Lieberman tries hard not to gobble down vast quantities of unhealthy food and to keep as close as he can to the tenets of his Judaism. He is also a devout family man. His

North Side will ring true to anyone who knows the Rogers Park or Uptown sections of Chicago, and the many subplots create a narrative pace like a car chase. Multiethnic Chicago could hardly ask for a better ventriloquist than Kaminsky. The city comes warmly alive when hardened gang members wax sentimental over the Cubs and in the erudite speech of Abe, which contrasts markedly with the sudden, savage force he can apply to a kneecap when necessary.

This deep empathy with the common man, allied to Chicago's ever-present undercurrent of violence, is a trait Paretsky inherited from Kaminsky and provides an accurate reflection of the city's essence.

Water mark

Chicago stands on the shores Lake Michigan. This vast expanse of fresh water – the third largest of the North American Great Lakes, 321 miles (517 km) long, 118 miles (190 km) wide and up to 923 feet (281 m) deep – is another element of the city's essence, a significant and sometimes dominant influence on the lives of all Chicagoans. Its importance is reflected in Paretsky's books, where the Lake is ever present. Often during the course of her cases

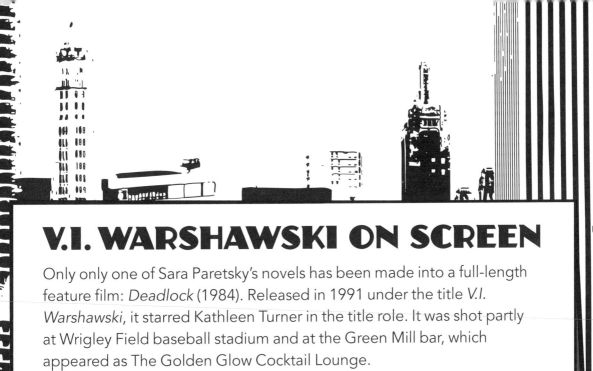

V.I. WARSHAWSKI ON SCREEN

Only only one of Sara Paretsky's novels has been made into a full-length feature film: *Deadlock* (1984). Released in 1991 under the title *V.I. Warshawski*, it starred Kathleen Turner in the title role. It was shot partly at Wrigley Field baseball stadium and at the Green Mill bar, which appeared as The Golden Glow Cocktail Lounge.

Turner later played Warshawski in two six-part radio dramatizations for the BBC: *Deadlock* (also 1991) and *Killing Orders* (1993). In a third Paretsky-based BBC radio serial, *Bitter Medicine* (1996), the leading role was played by Sharon Gless, best known as Sergeant Christine Cagney in the 1980s, U.S. TV series *Cagney and Lacey*.

 **IN FILM**

V.I. Warshawski (1991), directed by Jeff Kanew and starring Kathleen Turner in the title role

 **ON RADIO**

Deadlock (also 1991), BBC Radio
Killing Orders (1993), BBC Radio
Bitter Medicine (1996), BBC Radio

CHICAGO THE ONE AND ONLY

Sam Reaves (b. 1954), a notable Chicago crime writer, explains why the Big Town on the Lake is unlike any other American city:

You don't come to Chicago for the scenery, that's for sure. LA has oceans and mountains and palms, and all that sunshine beating down through the smog. An LA novel involves lots of landscape because they have a lot out there. In Chicago we have no landscape. In Chicago we have weather instead. Big bad chunks of it. We have mean, smack-you-in-the-face, morale-sapping Arctic weather in winter and thick, wet, tantrum-triggering Mississippi Delta weather in the summer. Weather-wise, Chicago sits in the Intemperate Zone. The weather extremes reflect other extremes – the penthouse suites a quarter of a mile up looking down on the wasted blocks that never came back from the Martin Luther King riots, the sprawling rail yards a mile or two south of the world's finest collection of Impressionist paintings, Fermi and Friedman's cloistered halls hunkered down on the heart of the hardscrabble South Side. In Chicago you can't be particular who you rub elbows with.

'HAVE YOU EVER SEEN WHAT I CAN DO WITH A NUTCRACKER?' – V.I. WARSHAWSKI (FILM, 1991)

V.I. finds herself visiting its shores or daydreaming of swimming there in the sun.

Water to the horizon, corruption, ice and snow, and a crusading lady. Chicago could have done much worse.

Chicago's historical connection with crime from violent prohibition years to its contemporary status as a hot bed of corruption and political party machinery (this is the city where Barack Obama established his credentials from an early stage in the hustle and bustle of local politics) has meant that it is a city with a million stories, and Paretsky continues to mine these quite indefatigably in her books, as did pioneering Chicago chronicler Fredric Brown or newer writers like Marcus Sakey. The Windy City remains an ideal blank canvas to chronicle crime in all its forms and this is unlikely to change.

USEFUL WEBSITES

The offical site of V.I.'s beloved baseball team, the Chicago Cubs
http://chicago.cubs.mlb.com/index.jsp?c_id=chc

Official website of the Green Mill cocktail and jazz bar at 4802 North Broadway, Chicago
http://www.greenmilljazz.com

Lake Michigan shoreline itinerary takes in 15 significant locations in Paretsky's V.I. Warshawski novels
http://www.communitywalk.com/vi_warshawskis_chicago

Rogers Park, an uptown district of Chicago; the setting of several incidents in the work of Kaminsky.

Wrigley Field: home of the Chicago Cubs, V.I's favourite baseball team.

North Racine: street on Lincoln Park where V.I. Warshawski now lives.

The Golden Glow, a saloon that's been there forever.

St. Justin Martyr: Sara Paretsky's childhood home.

KENNEDY EXPRESSWAY

W IRVING PARK RD

ELMWOOD PARK

N CICERO AVENUE

CHICAGO

CICERO

OGDEN AVENUE

STEVENSON

S CICERO AVENUE

BURBANK

OAK LAWN

PARETSKY & WARSHAWSKI'S CHICAGO

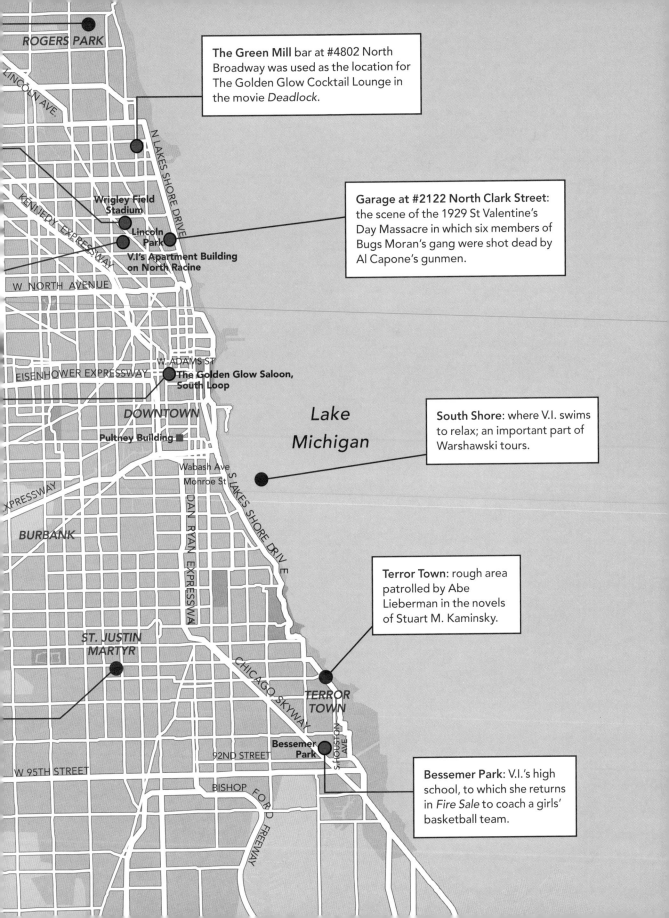

ROGERS PARK

LINCOLN AVE.

N LAKES SHORE DRIVE

KENNEDY EXPRESSWAY

The Green Mill bar at #4802 North Broadway was used as the location for The Golden Glow Cocktail Lounge in the movie *Deadlock*.

Garage at #2122 North Clark Street: the scene of the 1929 St Valentine's Day Massacre in which six members of Bugs Moran's gang were shot dead by Al Capone's gunmen.

Wrigley Field Stadium

Lincoln Park

V.I's Apartment Building on North Racine

W NORTH AVENUE

W ADAMS ST

EISENHOWER EXPRESSWAY

The Golden Glow Saloon, South Loop

DOWNTOWN

Pultney Building

Wabash Ave
Monroe St
S LAKES SHORE DRIVE E

DAN RYAN EXPRESSWAY

EXPRESSWAY

BURBANK

Lake Michigan

South Shore: where V.I. swims to relax; an important part of Warshawski tours.

ST. JUSTIN MARTYR

CHICAGO SKYWAY

Terror Town: rough area patrolled by Abe Lieberman in the novels of Stuart M. Kaminsky.

TERROR TOWN

S HOUSTON AVE

W 95TH STREET

92ND STREET

Bessemer Park

BISHOP FORD FREEWAY

Bessemer Park: V.I.'s high school, to which she returns in *Fire Sale* to coach a girls' basketball team.

Peter Rozovsky

ARNALDUR INDRIDASON & ERLENDUR'S ICELAND

People disappear easily in Arnaldur Indridason's Iceland, but the soil has a way of yielding them up again. An earthquake cracks the land, drains a lake and uncovers a body; a victim turns up in a construction-site excavation; in spring, corpses come to light in a lake, where winter ice had concealed all signs of their disappearance.

Even Arnaldur's indoor murder discoveries are excavations of a kind. Subsiding land leads investigators to a body in a basement in *Tainted Blood* (2004) (*Jar City* in the United States), while in *Voices* (2006) a man dies in the tiny subterranean room where he had lived for years. 'The setting is a character' is a commonplace in modern discussion of crime fiction; in Arnaldur, the setting is a narrative agent as well. The landscape swallows up victims, whether of murder, accident or natural disaster; demographic disruption lays them bare again.

Family secrets

Through each investigation, Reykjavík Police Inspector Erlendur Sveinsson – solitary, taciturn, but somehow never quite unhappy – muses on missing-person cases, including that of his brother, who disappeared years previously in

a blizzard that nearly took the young Erlendur's own life.

The first Erlendur novel translated into English, *Tainted Blood* hinges on long-buried family secrets and, like subsequent books, is much more a whydunnit than a whodunnit. At its root is a tale of violence and revenge as old as any Bible story or Greek tragedy. The means by which that revenge is exacted, however, is possible only in a nation as small, isolated and traditionally homogeneous as Iceland. Suffice it to say that the novel's British title is not entirely metaphorical.

Silence of the Grave (2005), Arnaldur's Dagger Award-winning follow-up novel, takes the action outdoors, deepening and intensifying Erlendur's relationship to his native land. It opens with a weary medical student who has shepherded his much younger brother to a birthday party making a grim discovery:

*He knew at once it was a human bone,
when he took it from the baby who was
sitting on the floor chewing it.*

Humour of a deadpan kind is very much a feature of Arnaldur's Iceland. The bone leads Erlendur to a story of horrific domestic abuse in the past and its echoes in the present, and if that has you rolling your eyes and thinking 'kitchen-sink drama', you haven't read the novel. Not only is Arnaldur unsparing in his description of abuse inflicted slowly and cruelly over time, he also has a character remark the insufficiency of the term 'domestic abuse' for acts of such enormity.

The novel also marks Erlendur's first consistent statement, for English readers at least, of his equivocal feelings about post-World War II Iceland and his own place in it, a preoccupation that will remain strong in subsequent books:

*[Erlendur] had been born
elsewhere and considered
himself an outsider even
though he had lived in the
city most of his life and had*

*seen it spread across the bays and
hills as the rural communities
depopulated.*

An outsider? Erlendur's very name is Icelandic for 'foreign'.

Voices moves back indoors, to a Reykjavík hotel where an employee has been found dead and where Erlendur stays for the course of the investigation because he does not feel like going home. The victim is a former doorman and holiday Santa at the hotel and, it transpires, a former child star

Bernard Scudder

Behind every work of literature that finds success in a foreign language there is a great translator, and in the case of both Arnaldur Indridason and Yrsa Sigurdardottir that translator was Bernard Scudder.

Born in Canterbury in 1954, Scudder read English at the University of York and then Icelandic at Reykjavik University.

He did not live to see the publication of his last completed translation. Copies of the English version of *Silence of the Grave* arrived at his home by post on the day of his funeral in October 2007.

THE INTERNATIONAL BESTSELLER

WINNER
OF THE
CWA GOLD
DAGGER

SILENCE
OF THE
GRAVE

A REYKJAVIK MURDER M...

Arnald
Indridaso

'A fascinating mystery' ... Indridason is a writer worth seeking out'
Daily Telegraph

VINTAGE

who had lost his heavenly voice when he matured.

The indoor setting de-emphasizes the intimate bond with Iceland and its soil that is usual in Arnaldur's books. But this does not preclude his customary wry observations about the country and, given the touristic milieu, about its foreign visitors:

Tourists who were planning to spend Christmas and the New Year in Iceland because it seemed to them like an adventurous and exciting country. Although they had only just landed, many had apparently already bought traditional Icelandic sweaters, and they checked into the exotic land of winter.

Erlendur's pointed retort to a hotel manager who appears more concerned with protecting his business interests than with aiding the quest for justice harks back to an influence Arnaldur has repeatedly acknowledged: the spare prose style, often comic in effect, of the old Icelandic sagas. From Arnaldur:

A panorama of Reykjavik, capital of Iceland.

'I hope you're not disturbing my guests', he said.
Erlendur took him to one side, 'What are the rules about prostitution in this hotel?'

From the 13th-century *Njals Saga*:

Hallgerd was outside. 'There is blood on your axe', she said. 'What have you done?'
'I have now arranged that you can be married a second time', replied Thjostolf.

Crime in a quiet country

Arnaldur has sometimes lamented that Iceland's lack of crime makes life difficult for its crime writers (according to national police statistics, three homicides and one manslaughter in 2005, the year *Arctic Chill* appeared in its original language). Moreover, the crimes tend not to be the sort to capture the imagination. In *The Draining Lake* (2007), Arnaldur has his narrator muse that Erlendur and his colleagues:

'... were more accustomed to dealing with simple, Icelandic crimes without mysterious devices or trade attachés who weren't trade attachés, without foreign embassies of the Cold War, just Icelandic reality: local, uneventful, mundane and infinitely removed from the battle zones of the world'.

'INDRIDASON HAS A REMARKABLE UNDERSTANDING OF GRIEF AND ITS PERSISTENCE… [HE] COMBINES PSYCHOLOGICAL ACUTENESS WITH GREAT STYLISTIC ECONOMY AND A PLEASING PACE' – JANE JAKEMAN, *INDEPENDENT* (2009)

The draining lake of the title nicely symbolizes Iceland's physical vulnerability. It also exposes a personal tragedy and an aspect of Iceland's history that does not accord with its pacific, insular reputation: that of Cold War outpost. The body in the lake, weighted down by Cold War-era radio equipment bearing Russian inscriptions, takes the investigation back to a time when bright young Icelanders were sent to study in communist East Germany. Once again, the land has laid bare the truth. Or perhaps the scarcity of crime in the present spurs Arnaldur to write about crimes with roots in the past. (The lake in question, Kleifarvatn, is real, and it began draining after an earthquake in 2000. *Kleifarvatn* is the novel's title in its original Icelandic.)

If the active agency of geology is unique to the work of Arnaldur, the book's novelistic excavation of a hidden wartime past may remind crime-fiction readers of *The Redbreast* (2007) by the Norwegian Jo Nesbø (b. 1960) and, more distantly, of the exposés of the post-war Swedish welfare state in the popular and influential Martin Beck novels co-written between 1965 and 1975 by Maj Sjöwall (b. 1935) and Per Wahlöö (1926–75).

Iceland's vulnerability is not just physical. The country's small size makes self-concealment difficult. This naturally gives Erlendur and his colleagues something to think about as they seek a motive in yet another missing-person case:

'Can you get away with bigamy in Iceland?' Sigurdur Óli asked.
'No', Elinborg said firmly. *'There are too few of us.'*

In moments of impatience and frustration, characters may find Iceland small-minded. The dead former child star's teacher in *Voices* tells police: 'They make such an awful fuss about small things in Iceland, even more now than they used to; it's a national trait in a country of under-achievers'. Erlendur's colleague Elinborg observes (or complains) that 'No one is ever allowed to excel in this dwarf state'.

Incomers

In *Arctic Chill* Arnaldur's examination of Iceland turns to demography and immigration. As always, Erlendur is sympathetic yet unsentimental. A brief exchange early in the book expresses this and also reveals with telegraphic concision the temperamental differences between Erlendur and his two main colleagues:

'Where do you think he's from?' Sigurdur Óli wondered.
'He looks Asian to me', Elinborg said.
'Could be Thai, Filipino, Vietnamese, Korean, Japanese, Chinese', Sigurdur Óli reeled off.
'Shouldn't we say he's an Icelander until we find out otherwise?' Erlendur said.

Later, Arnaldur puts the following words in the mouth of a character who is not quite the xenophobe he at first seems:

'I've got nothing against immigrants…. But I'm against changing everything that's traditional and Icelandic just to pander to something called multiculturalism, when I don't even know what it means'.

This character expresses revulsion at crimes against immigrants and gives full support for government programmes to help integrate newcomers into Icelandic society. Another character says: 'This is all so new to us. Immigrants, racial issues'. Another muses on the problem of immigrant children who refuse to integrate: 'Same problem with the Icelanders living in Denmark. Their children refused to learn Danish.'

Finally, any number of crime writers might have delivered lengthy exposition on the dreary conditions under which immigrants live. Here's how Arnaldur does it: 'Erlendur was astonished there was no lift in such a tall building.' No diatribe against immigration, no easy, ringing indictment of prejudice in any of the foregoing. Instead, Erlendur and his creator, in their customary spare prose, making a heartfelt, humane effort to understand their country and its changes.

How humane? Icelandic names tend to have meanings, so recognition that immigrants may attach similar significance to their own names is a beautifully subtle, heartfelt message of brotherhood:

'Niran', Erlendur said to himself, as if to hear how the name sounded. 'Does that mean anything in particular?'

'It means eternal', the interpreter said.

'Eternal?'

'Thai names have literal meanings, just like Icelandic ones'.

Traditional names, too, are part of Arnaldur's fictional landscape. Icelandic law and custom govern names and favour tradition, thus Skarphedins, Bergthóras and Gunnars populate these books, just as they do the Icelandic sagas.

Mother–son, father–daughter

Hypothermia (2009) feels lighter in tone than the previous novels. Erlendur reminisces about his affinity with his late mother, and he and his troubled daughter come closer than ever to mutual understanding. But even intimate family relations are bound up with Iceland's soil, its climate and its demographic shifts. Erlendur's mother:

… had still been only middle-aged when his [Erlendur's] father had died but there was never anyone else in her life. She said she enjoyed being alone. She kept in touch with friends and relatives out east, and former neighbours who had also moved to Reykjavík. Iceland was changing; people were drifting away from the countryside.

'IS THERE SUCH A THING AS A PERFECT CRIME-FICTION NOVEL? PROBABLY NOT, BUT IF THERE WERE, THIS [ARCTIC CHILL] WOULD SURELY BE A STRONG CONTENDER' – MAXINE CLARKE, *EUROCRIME* (2008)

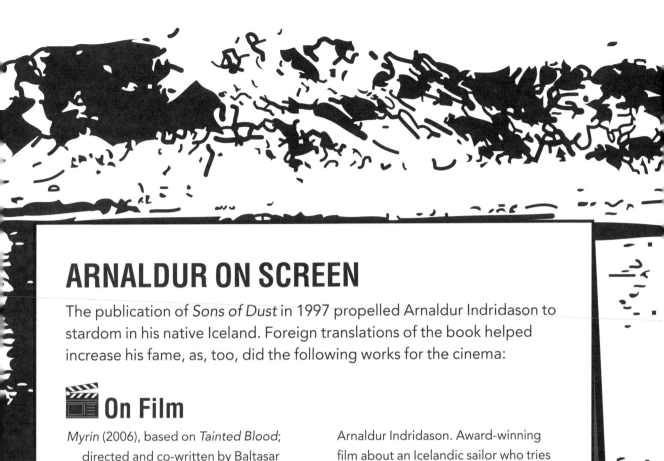

ARNALDUR ON SCREEN

The publication of *Sons of Dust* in 1997 propelled Arnaldur Indridason to stardom in his native Iceland. Foreign translations of the book helped increase his fame, as, too, did the following works for the cinema:

On Film

Myrin (2006), based on *Tainted Blood*; directed and co-written by Baltasar Kormákur and Arnaldur Indridason. The role of Erlundur is played by Ingvar Eggert Sigurdsson.

Reykjavik–Rotterdam (2008), directed and co-written by Óskar Jónasson and Arnaldur Indridason. Award-winning film about an Icelandic sailor who tries to solve his financial problems on a trip to the Netherlands. A planned Hollywood remake will be directed by Baltasar Kormákur, who played the lead in the original, and star Mark Wahlberg.

Medieval Witchcraft and Modern Murder Cases

In 2007, the publication in English of *Last Rituals* brought the mercurial talent of Yrsa Sigurdardóttir (b. 1963) to the attention of a global audience. The novel is the first in a crime series featuring Thóra Gudmundsdóttir – a lawyer, single mother of two and part-time private investigator whose cases, like those of Erlendur Sveinsson, are modern mysteries with deep roots in Iceland's past.

Last Rituals opens with the discovery at the university in Reykjavik of the body of a German student. His eyes have been cut out and mysterious symbols carved into his chest. A likely-looking suspect is soon arrested, but the victim's relatives, unconvinced that this is the right man, ask Thóra to take another look at what the police maintain is an open-and-shut case. When Thóra and her assistant, Matthew Reich, start delving they make chilling discoveries about their country's bloody history – torture, witch hunts and executions.

Crime writer Mark Billingham (b. 1961) described *Last Rituals* as 'dark, deep and icy as an Icelandic fjord … a rich and rewarding debut novel'. The international success of the work has so far led to three further Thóra Gudmundsdóttir mysteries: *Ashes to Dust* (2007), *Veins of Ice* (2008) and *My Soul To Take* (2009). Meanwhile, Yrsa Sigurdardóttir, a wife and mother of two, has remained in her daytime job as a civil engineer.

Eva Lind, the disturbed, drug-addicted daughter, has miscarried a child and almost died in previous books. Her meetings with her father have usually ended with her shouting and storming out of his apartment, furious at her father for having left the family when she and her brother were small. The thaw begins in earnest when Erlendur feels ready to share with his daughter his fascination with books about deaths, disasters and missing-person cases, particularly that of his brother. Erlendur reads to his daughter the story of the long-ago blizzard. Eva Lind listens, and, before the novel's end, daughter joins father for a quiet Sunday outing and acts as a useful sounding board for his theories about a current case.

Examining the past

Erlendur's Iceland is filled with ghosts, or at least with people who believe in them or speak of them casually. Though decidedly an unbeliever in the supernatural, Erlendur feels an affinity with those who do believe. He is, after all, much concerned with the past and with vanished persons who haunt those left behind.

The preoccupation with the past has its humorous side, too. Arnaldur must have enjoyed describing a building that:

> … had once been a community centre, in the days when young men wore their hair in Brylcreemed quiffs and their girlfriends sported perms and they used to go crazy on the dance floor to the new American rock 'n' roll, before they eventually vanished into oblivion…. The yellow lino on the floor was full of holes, the shiny white paint on the walls had long ago succumbed to the grime, and the air freshener had not yet been invented that could overcome the stench of mould rising from the floor and wooden walls. It was like stepping back fifty years in time.

For Erlendur, driven by tales of vanished persons, the past is a constant presence. Sigurdur Óli is of no such gloomily poetic temperament. He complains:

> 'All these people are dead and buried long ago. I don't know why we're chasing them'.

Erlendur knows why.

Useful websites & addresses

Literary Walking Tours
Tryggvagata 15, Reykjavik

Reykjavik City Library walking tour with discussions of Icelandic literature, from the Saga period to newly published books.
http://visitreykjavik.is/desktopdefault.aspx/tabid-13/28_read-1131

Scheduled tours to the heart of Iceland and its writings
www.isafoldtravel.is/scheduled-tours/tours/iceland-saga-trail

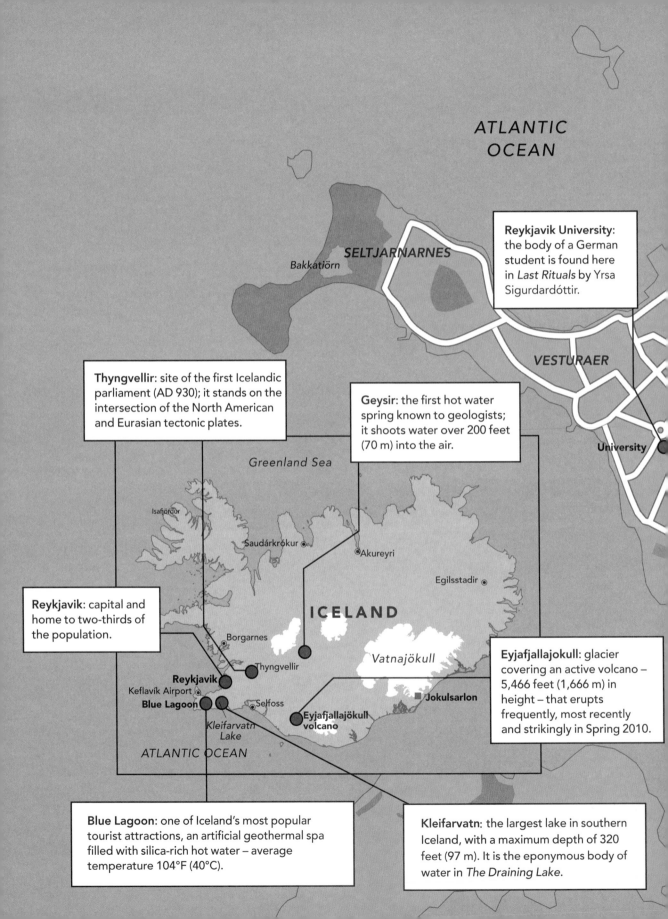

ATLANTIC
OCEAN

SELTJARNARNES

Bakkatiörn

Reykjavik University:
the body of a German
student is found here
in *Last Rituals* by Yrsa
Sigurdardóttir.

VESTURAER

Thyngvellir: site of the first Icelandic
parliament (AD 930); it stands on the
intersection of the North American
and Eurasian tectonic plates.

Geysir: the first hot water
spring known to geologists;
it shoots water over 200 feet
(70 m) into the air.

University

Greenland Sea

Isafjörður

Saudárkrókur

Akureyri

Egilsstadir

ICELAND

Reykjavik: capital and
home to two-thirds of
the population.

Borgarnes

Thyngvellir

Vatnajökull

Eyjafjallajokull: glacier
covering an active volcano –
5,466 feet (1,666 m) in
height – that erupts
frequently, most recently
and strikingly in Spring 2010.

Reykjavik
Keflavík Airport
Blue Lagoon

Selfoss

Jokulsarlon

*Kleifarvatn
Lake*

**Eyjafjallajökull
volcano**

ATLANTIC OCEAN

Blue Lagoon: one of Iceland's most popular
tourist attractions, an artificial geothermal spa
filled with silica-rich hot water – average
temperature 104°F (40°C).

Kleifarvatn: the largest lake in southern
Iceland, with a maximum depth of 320
feet (97 m). It is the eponymous body of
water in *The Draining Lake*.

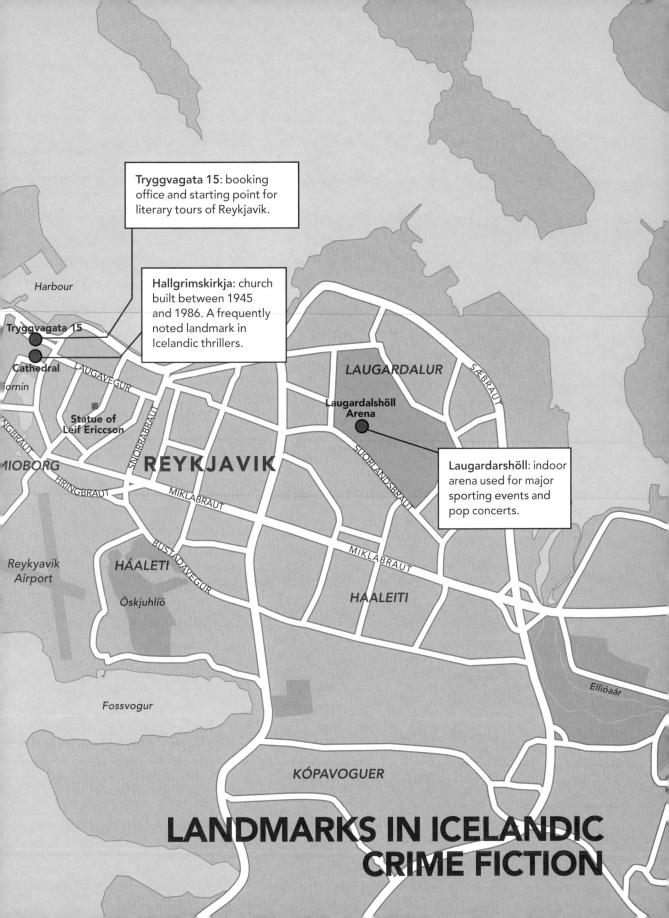

Tryggvagata 15: booking office and starting point for literary tours of Reykjavik.

Hallgrimskirkja: church built between 1945 and 1986. A frequently noted landmark in Icelandic thrillers.

Laugardarshöll: indoor arena used for major sporting events and pop concerts.

Harbour

Tryggvagata 15

Cathedral

Tjornin

Statue of Leif Ericcson

LAUGAVEGUR

MIOBORG

HRINGBRAUT

SNORRABRAUT

REYKJAVIK

MIKLABRAUT

LAUGARDALUR

SÆBRAUT

Laugardalshöll Arena

SUÐRLANDSBRAUT

Reykyavik Airport

HÁALETI

BUSTADAVEGUR

Öskjuhlíð

MIKLABRAUT

HAALEITI

Fossvogur

Elliðaár

KÓPAVOGUER

LANDMARKS IN ICELANDIC CRIME FICTION

Oline Cogdill

JOHN D. MacDONALD & TRAVIS McGEE'S FLORIDA

Florida was tailor-made for mystery writers and crime novelists. It was pioneered by pirates, settled by schemers and dreamers, and humbled by hustlers, fraud and foreclosures. And every now and then a hurricane comes along and blows it all away.

Miami Beach became one of the nation's premier destinations during the 1940s and 1950s – thanks mainly to the efforts of organized crime. Three decades later, when the world again turned its attention to Florida, it wasn't the fine weather and beautiful beaches that made people notice the Sunshine State – it was the cocaine cowboys on the television show *Miami Vice* (1984–90).

Sunshine and subterfuge

In part, what makes Florida crime fiction compelling is what also draws the tourists – breathtaking views, beautiful beaches and balmy weather. Novelists here know what residents admit: that beneath this picture-postcard setting is the dramatic contrast of dark deeds, especially those of politicians and criminals.

To understand that duality is to understand Florida's appeal to writers drawn to themes of greed, overdevelopment, the environment

and bizarre behaviour found nowhere else. For most readers, two authors are synonymous with that unique niche in mystery fiction: John D. MacDonald and Carl Hiaasen – men working two decades apart but who shared the anarchic yet compassionate sensibility that is quintessential Florida.

John D. MacDonald's tales about self-proclaimed beach bum, 'salvage consultant' and private detective Travis McGee began Florida crime fiction as we know it today. McGee was the epitome of the knight-errant who was constantly fighting the good fight, rescuing the damsel in distress. While McGee rescued more than his fair share of damsels – and bedded many of them along the way – his good fight often centred on his fears about the changing Florida environment.

When the Harvard-educated MacDonald introduced McGee in *The Deep Blue Goodbye* (1964), he used the character to explore the collision of environmental concerns, human

corruption and a diverse population. Those themes would echo through 21 mysteries about McGee, who lived on his boat *The Busted Flush*, anchored at Slip F18 at Bahia Mar marina in Fort Lauderdale. A plaque at the resort hotel's real-life marina now honours the fictional McGee.

MacDonald had the foresight to set the McGee novels in the then-sleepy town of Fort Lauderdale rather than the international city of Miami, which is about 30 miles (48 km) south and light years away in cultural sophistication. In 1960, the population of Broward County, where Fort Lauderdale remains the flagship city, was about 334,000; today is nearly 1.8 million. In 1964, Fort Lauderdale had many dirt roads, a small-town feel and was known primarily as a destination for college students on Spring Break, as illustrated in the 1960 movie *Where the Boys Are*.

MacDonald's novels foretold an out-of-control urban sprawl, pristine beauty spoiled by greedy developers as

in *Pale Gray for Guilt* (1968). Nearly every Florida mystery author who has come after MacDonald has touched on the challenges to the ecology.

No one thought much about the Everglades then. But MacDonald did, as he showed in *Bright Orange for the Shroud* (1965) in which he wrote:

Now, of course, having failed in every attempt to subdue the Glades by frontal attack, we are slowly killing it off by tapping the River of Grass. In the questionable

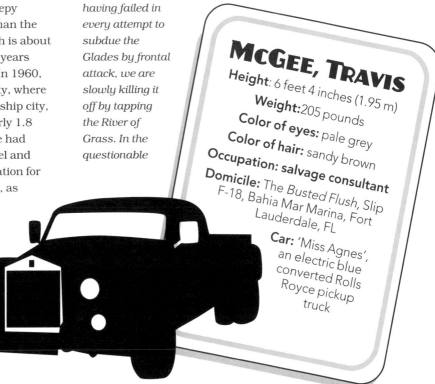

McGee, Travis

Height: 6 feet 4 inches (1.95 m)
Weight: 205 pounds
Color of eyes: pale grey
Color of hair: sandy brown
Occupation: salvage consultant
Domicile: The Busted Flush, Slip F-18, Bahia Mar Marina, Fort Lauderdale, FL
Car: 'Miss Agnes', an electric blue converted Rolls Royce pickup truck

'THIS IS A COMPLEX CULTURE.... THE MORE INTRICATE OUR SOCIETY GETS, THE MORE SEMI-LEGAL WAYS TO STEAL' – THE DEEP BLUE GOODBYE

name of progress, the state in its vast wisdom lets every two-bit developer divert the flow into drag-lined canals that give him 'waterfront' lots to sell.

Today, Western Broward is one of the most densely populated areas of the county, where expensive housing developments have been created on land that used to be a part of the Everglades. Still, MacDonald might be amused that during heavy rains many of these expensive homes flood as the Everglades tries to reclaim its own.

But MacDonald's novels did more than just rail against what he called 'the plastic aromas of the new Florida' (*The Empty Copper Sea*, 1978).

The McGee novels also portrayed an alternative community foreign to most readers at the time. McGee's sidekick Meyer, a respected economist, lived on the cabin cruiser *John Maynard Keynes* near *The Busted Flush*. The tight-knit boating community where McGee and Meyer lived was a romanticized but effective broadside against the wealthy boaters out for a Sunday afternoon getaway and the 'unsympathetic' Florida houses that McGee denigrated in *The Deep Blue Goodbye*. The Bahia Mar community was a forerunner of Dinkin's Bay,

MacDONALD ON SCREEN

John D. MacDonald's work has provided film-makers with a rich vein of material, although title changes to the screen versions have frequently obscured their literary antecedents.

 In Film

MacDonald's novel *The Executioners* (1957) inspired two films entitled *Cape Fear* about a rapist who stalks the family of a lawyer who helped put him in jail. The first version, released in 1962, was directed by British-born J. Lee Thompson; the 1991 remake was by Martin Scorsese. Both starred Gregory Peck and Robert Mitchum, but each time in different roles.

Soft Touch (1953) was the basis for *Man-Trap* (1961), directed by Edmond O'Brien and starring Jeffrey Hunter and David Janssen.

In 2010, pre-production discussions were taking place about a new movie, also entitled *Travis McGee*, with Oliver Stone provisionally slated to direct and Leonardo DiCaprio to take the lead.

On Television

On television, *Travis McGee* (1983) was directed by Andrew V. McLagen and starred Sam Elliot. The script was by MacDonald himself and Stirling Silliphant, Oscar winner for In the *Heat of the Night* (1967).

The novel *Cry Hard, Cry Fast* (1955) formed the basis in 1967 of a two-part episode of *Run for Your Life*, a series in which Ben Gazzara, having been told that he has only a short time to live, decides to do all the things he had previously missed out on.

The numerous other adaptations of his work include two 1980 TV movies: one a version of *The Girl, the Gold Watch and Everything* (1962), the other of *Condominium* (1977).

FLORIDA'S GREAT APPEAL

Even when most mystery fiction was set in California, New York, London and a few English villages, Florida was a viable location for imaginary crime and detection. In the view of many, the earliest example was *Don Blasco of Key West* (1896) by Archibald Clavering Gunter (1847–1907). But if John D. MacDonald was the first Florida writer to make a mainstream mark beyond potboilers, the genesis of the Florida crime novel as a serious literary genre arguably began with Charles Willeford (1919–88). Hoke Moseley, who features in four novels, including *Miami Blues* (1984) was a detective with badly fitted dentures who lived in a rundown Art Deco hotel on the verge of being condemned to make way for the development that would become South Beach. Moseley wasn't comfortable with the changes in Miami or with his savvy new partner, a Cuban American woman. But mostly Moseley wasn't comfortable with himself. Depressed and asocial, Moseley was on a constant collision course with Miami's criminals who were more normal – and interesting – than he.

Today the true heir to John D. MacDonald is widely regarded as the influential James W. Hall (b. 1947). With *Under Cover of Daylight* (1987), Hall created a series about Thorn, a taciturn loner with many of Travis McGee's sensibilities who barely ekes out a living handcrafting expensive fishing flies. Yet Thorn, who lives in Key Largo but makes frequent visits to Miami, is often drawn into violent situations by a relentless sense of justice in 11 of Hall's 16 novels. Hall, who retired in 2009 after 36 years as a professor of literature and writing at Florida International University, not only picked up MacDonald's mantle but also proved himself to be Florida's most consistently superior mystery writer with his involving plots and characters.

'THE HARD THING TO DO IS THE RIGHT THING TO DO' – LONELY SILVER RAIN (1985)

the locale for Randy Wayne White's Gulf Coast novels about Marion 'Doc' Ford.

In 1964, the world was drastically changing and South Florida along with it. In that presidential year, Martin Luther King became the youngest recipient of the Nobel Peace Prize and Nikita Khrushchev was deposed as leader of the Soviet Union. A brash young boxer named Cassius Clay took the world heavyweight championship in a historic fight staged in Miami. The second US performance of a rising British pop group called The Beatles was broadcast live on *The Ed Sullivan Show* from Miami's posh Deauville hotel. Politicians and celebrities began to see South Florida as a destination – not a detour.

Consider 1964 as the year that the Florida mystery as we know it today was born.

MacDonald's legacy

In 1986, the year MacDonald died, Carl Hiaasen launched a second wave of crime fiction, even more irreverent but even more relevant. Although a newspaper reporter who still writes a regular opinion column for *The Miami Herald*, Hiaasen proved himself through 12 mysteries to be a social critic equal to Jonathan Swift (1667–1745) in his keen observations. In Hiaasen's first satire, *Tourist Season* (1986), his villain stuck a rubber alligator down the throat of a member of the Miami chamber of commerce. Today, Hiaasen still mixes the comic absurdity indigenous to South Florida with serious looks at the now-classic themes of irresponsible development, tourism, corrupt politicians and a multiethnic population that inform most of the region's mysteries.

MacDonald and Hiaasen created an infrastructure on which Florida mysteries have been built ever since – as exemplified by James W. Hall, Jonathon King, Edna Buchanan, Les Standiford, Carolina García-Aguilera, Barbara Parker and many authors in between. It's a tradition of novels and screenplays stemming in part from a world in which reality rivals fiction.

USEFUL WEBSITES

Frommer's Tour itineraries include key locations in the work of John D. MacDonald.

http://www.frommers.com/destinations/florida/0222010007.html

A comprehensive listing of Florida authors and their work

http://floridaauthors.wetpaint.com/page/Mystery

LANDMARKS IN FLORIDA CRIME FICTION

Gulf of Mexico

St. Petersburg: main setting for James Swain's seven-novel series about Tony Valentine, a retired 60-something cop turned casino consultant.

Sarasota: home city of Lew Fonesca, a depressed process server in the novels of Stuart M. Kaminsky.

Sanibel Island: thanks to Randy Wayne White's hero, Doc Ford's Sanibel Rum Bar & Grill has become a major attraction for visitors to Sanibel.

The Clevelander Hotel: in South Beach; a recurrent setting in the police procedurals of James O. Born.

Orange Bowl: outdoor athletics stadium; a recurrent setting in the police procedurals of James O. Born.

Versailles: renowned Cuban restaurant featured in the novels of Carolina García-Aguilera.

Calle Ocho: the main street of Miami's Little Havana and the model for Douglas Fairbairn's *Street Eight*.

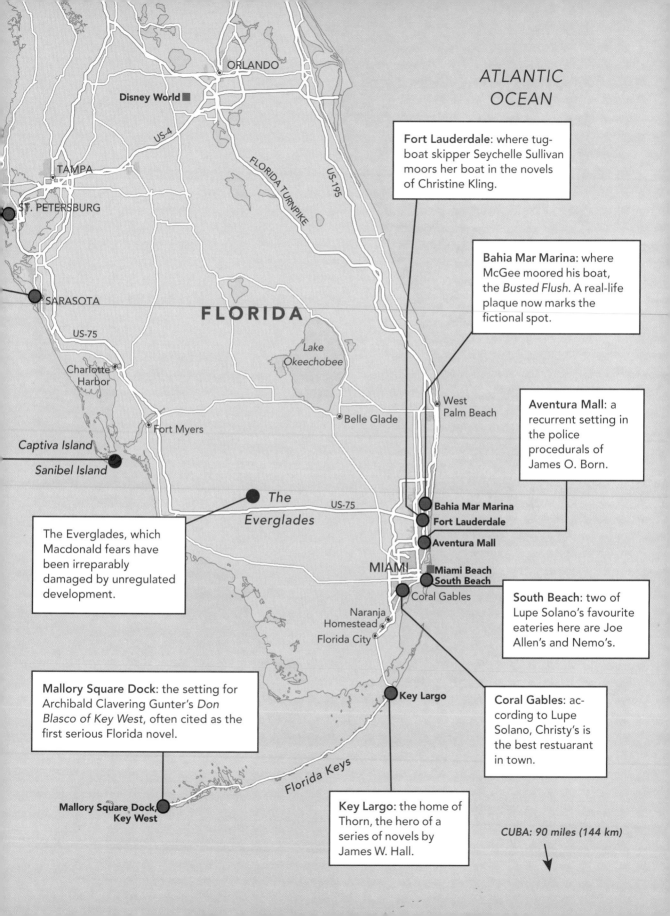

ATLANTIC OCEAN

Fort Lauderdale: where tug-boat skipper Seychelle Sullivan moors her boat in the novels of Christine Kling.

Bahia Mar Marina: where McGee moored his boat, the *Busted Flush*. A real-life plaque now marks the fictional spot.

Aventura Mall: a recurrent setting in the police procedurals of James O. Born.

ORLANDO

Disney World ■

TAMPA

ST. PETERSBURG

US-4

FLORIDA TURNPIKE

US-I95

SARASOTA

FLORIDA

US-75

Lake Okeechobee

Charlotte Harbor

• Belle Glade

• Fort Myers

Captiva Island

Sanibel Island

West Palm Beach

The Everglades

US-75

Bahia Mar Marina
Fort Lauderdale
Aventura Mall

The Everglades, which Macdonald fears have been irreparably damaged by unregulated development.

MIAMI

Miami Beach ■
South Beach
Coral Gables

Naranja
Homestead
Florida City

South Beach: two of Lupe Solano's favourite eateries here are Joe Allen's and Nemo's.

Mallory Square Dock: the setting for Archibald Clavering Gunter's *Don Blasco of Key West*, often cited as the first serious Florida novel.

Key Largo

Coral Gables: according to Lupe Solano, Christy's is the best restuarant in town.

Florida Keys

Mallory Square Dock, Key West

Key Largo: the home of Thorn, the hero of a series of novels by James W. Hall.

CUBA: 90 miles (144 km)

MODERN THEMES IN FLORIDA'S CRIME FICTION

Modern Florida fiction reflects the many changes that have occurred in the state's cultural, social and ethnic diversity. Many Florida mysteries focus on the growing influence of Hispanics arriving from the Caribbean and South America, an ethnic and cultural shift that has culminated today in a region with a population that is 38% Hispanic. Douglas Fairbairn (b. 1926) was one of the first – if not the first – to write about Cuban exiles and the potent mix of politics that their presence has created. In his gritty *Street Eight* (1977) he depicted an Anglo car dealer in Miami who hires a Cuban salesman to keep up with the changing demographics. The thoroughfare of the title is now called Calle Ocho, the main street of Miami's Little Havana.

In the 1990s, this ethnic diversity became integral to plots, themes and characters. Barbara Parker (1947–2009) highlighted diversity with her Gail Connor/Anthony Quintana series about partners in a law firm, beginning with the Edgar-nominated *Suspicion of Innocence* (1994). Connor's Anglo family had roots that ran deep in Miami while the Cuban-born Quintana exemplified the exile community. Parker was known for her precise research. Each of her 12 novels, eight in the Connor/Quintana series, used that research as the basis of stories that explored facets of Florida, specifically Miami, from the arts to politics to its emphasis on family ties.

Taking it another step, Carolina García-Aguilera (b. 1949) used her own Latin American background to create Lupe Solano, the first Cuban American female private investigator who debuted in *Bloody Waters* (1996). Born in Havana, Cuba, García-Aguilera emigrated to the United States in 1960, a year after the Cuban Revolution. To prepare to become a mystery writer, García-Aguilera became a licensed private investigator.

García-Aguilera's writing contains the nuances of exiled Cuban politics, the history of the Communist island, and a strong sense of life in Miami. The life of Lupe Solano

reflects that of a young single Cuban American woman who despite her independence still lives at home. Lupe also was a faithful patron of area restaurants – in each novel she visits Versailles, the renowned Cuban restaurant on Calle Ocho; Lupe also made readers salivate on her visits to Joe Allen's and Nemo's, both on South Beach, and Christy's on Coral Gables. Although García-Aguilera put Lupe on hold after *Bitter Sugar* (2001), she later revived her most famous character.

Similarly, the mysteries of Edna Buchanan (b. 1939) are centred on Britt Montero, a Miami police reporter whose father was executed by a Castro firing squad when she was three years old.

Legal matters

In the 1990s, Florida's court system – in many ways as off-centre as its crimes – gave rise to some quirky legal thrillers. Paul Levine (b. 1948) worked as a newspaper reporter, a law professor and a trial lawyer in Miami before becoming a full-time writer. Beginning with *To Speak for the Dead* (1990), Levine published seven humour-laden, hard-edged Jake Lassiter novels during that decade. A Miami Dolphins' linebacker turned hard-nosed lawyer, Lassiter had a smart mouth and a self-deprecating personality that did him few favours. Levine steeped his series in details that seem unusual outside Florida, such as the courthouse steps being cleaned daily to remove chicken parts and goats' heads used in Santeria religious rituals. Jake would sometimes lose his way in Little Havana because numbered streets were renamed to honour heroes favoured by the Miami City Commission such as General Maximo Gomez Boulevard and Jose Canseco Street. Such observations helped Levine win the John D. MacDonald Florida Fiction Award, and *To Speak for the Dead* was named one of the 10 best mysteries of the year by the *Los Angeles Times*.

The genre is also well represented by James Grippando (b. 1958), to date the author of 13 thrillers, eight of which focus on Miami criminal defence lawyer Jack Swyteck and his outrageous sidekick, Theo Knight. Swyteck is the son of a former Florida governor, with whom he has a fractious relationship, and a Cuban American mother who died in childbirth. While the law is central to his novels, Grippando also delves into loyalty and familial bonds. The Swyteck series began with *The Pardon* (1994); the most recent was *Born To Run* (2008).

FLORIDA: OUT OF THE MAINSTREAM

Florida's penchant for the bizarre has given birth to self-contained genres found nowhere else. When it comes to offbeat, perhaps the oddest Miami mysteries are Jeff Lindsay's novels about serial killer Dexter Morgan, a sociopathic vigilante who channels his murderous nature to dispatching killers far worse than he, especially paedophiles. Dexter is an innocent compared to his vile victims. The series began with *Darkly Dreaming Dexter* (2004).

Inspired by Carl Hiaasen, Tim Dorsey produced a string of comic novels – including *Florida Roadkill* (1999), *Triggerfish Twist* (2002) and *Torpedo Juice* (2005) – in which a loveable serial killer named Serge A. Storms roams Florida.

Although most Florida fiction has been set in Miami, other parts of the state have not been entirely neglected. The Everglades provide a rich setting for former newspaper reporter Jonathon King, whose *The Blue Edge of Midnight* won the 2002 Edgar Allan Poe Award for best first novel. The success of this book spawned a series featuring Max Freeman, a former Philadelphia cop who has retreated to a remote cabin in the National Park to contemplate his life.

The region's waterways provide the background for the mysteries by Christine Kling featuring tugboat captain Seychelle Sullivan. Sullivan has been called the female Travis McGee because, like John D. MacDonald's hero, she lives on boats in Fort Lauderdale. Kling's books reflect a social conscience as she depicts the plight of Haitian children used as slaves and teenage girls becoming strippers.

To the west, Randy Wayne White owns the Gulf Coast with his ever-changing novels about Marion 'Doc' Ford, a mild-mannered marine biologist with a murky past as a government operative. White has consistently showcased the unspoilt beauty of Sanibel Island and, in a fiction-meets-reality twist, his favourite restaurant, Doc Ford's Sanibel Rum Bar & Grill, has become a major attraction for visitors.

P.J. Parrish has moved her series hero Louis Kincaid, a young mixed race detective, to Captiva Island with many scenes that capture the area's beauty and the small-town atmosphere of nearby Fort Meyers. Kincaid's cases have taken him throughout Captiva

and into the mangroves across long bridges that span causeways and to nearby Charlotte Harbor, a natural estuary spanning the west coast of Florida from Venice to Bonita Springs.

In 1999, Stuart M. Kaminsky began a six-novel series about Lew Fonesca, a depressed process server in Sarasota. Further up the road in St. Petersburg, James Swain set a seven-novel series about Tony Valentine, a retired 60-something cop turned casino consultant.

Orlando – world-famous for Disney World – has been neglected by most writers, though many have set individual scenes here. The exception is building contractor Bob Truluck, who wrote two novels set in his hometown. The first, *Street Level*, won the 1999 St. Martin's Press/Private Eye Writers of America prize for Best First Private Eye Novel.

At the southern tip of Florida, Key West thrives on its eccentricities and so do the stories set there. The Alex Rutledge novels of Tom Corcoran show Key West's idiosyncrasies as well as the reality of living there. Rutledge is a photographer who freelances for the local police department, giving him a unique view of the city. Among the other authors who showcase Key West is Michael Haskins, whose *Chasin' the Wind* appeared in 2008.

During the 1990s, Laurence Shames' seven comic novels about Mafia members settling in Key West perfectly captured the island's quirkiness. Broadly laced with humour, Shames still injected a vein of seriousness into these entertaining novels. Also during the 1990s, four novels by John Leslie featuring private investigator and piano player Gideon Lowry seemed perpetually set during the night.

Humour is a facet of many Florida mysteries but comic timing is paramount in the novels of Elaine Viets and Deborah Sharp. Viets' *Dead End Job* series revolves around Helen Hawthorne, a once highly paid executive who now lives off the grid in Fort Lauderdale and takes menial jobs that pay in cash. Set in the Central Florida prairie, Sharp's 'Mama' novels take the reader on a merry ride through the state's back roads, ranches and citrus groves. Mama herself is an oft-married, larger-than-life Florida native with a penchant for loud clothes whose sensible daughter Mace is the series' real heroine.

Few police procedurals were set in Florida until James O. Born – a special agent with the Florida Department of Law Enforcement (FDLE) – based five novels on aspects of his career. His settings include The Clevelander Hotel in South Beach, The Aventura Mall, The Orange Bowl in Miami, and smaller towns such as Belle Glade, Homestead, Naranja and Florida City.

Martin Edwards

COLIN DEXTER & INSPECTOR MORSE'S OXFORD

The poet Matthew Arnold (1822–88) memorably described Oxford as 'that sweet city with her dreaming spires' and, despite the traffic and the bustle of the 21st century, he would no doubt still agree that, to this day, 'she needs not June for beauty's heightening'.

Oxford's historic prestige is reflected in the fact that it received its charter from King Henry II (reigned 1154–89), and that its university is the oldest in the English-speaking world, as well as one of the most renowned. Oxford is rich in places reeking of history, an element that helped to cement the popularity of Colin Dexter's Inspector Morse series of books. The city's most notable landmarks, many of which appear in Dexter's novels, include the Martyrs' Memorial in St Giles', which commemorates the burning at the stake for heresy of Protestant martyrs Hugh Latimer, Nicholas Ridley and Thomas Cranmer in 1555. The architecture is as distinctive as Arnold's phrase suggests, while the rivers Thames and Cherwell flow through the city, meeting just south of it; above Iffley Lock, the Thames is known as the Isis. Christ Church Cathedral uniquely combines a college chapel with a cathedral, the Ashmolean Museum is

the oldest museum in the UK, while the Bodleian Library was opened in 1602 and now holds more than eight million volumes. Yet, for all its charm and for all the tranquillity of the college quadrangles and green spaces, Oxford has seen more than its fair share of murders, at least in fiction. The reason for Oxford's popularity as a setting for murder and mayhem is not so much the inherently criminal tendencies of the local population as the enthusiasm of alumni of the university, and others associated with it, for writing detective stories. For instance, more than 30 former students of Balliol College alone have published crime fiction.

The body count in the books of Colin Dexter featuring Inspector Morse and in the British television series named after his character reached 80 before Dexter killed off his hero. Dexter was quoted as saying in 1999 that the city had become the country's murder capital, and it was time to put an end to that – although he reckoned without the subsequent spin-off

television series *Lewis*, starring Morse's sidekick. It is often forgotten, however, that Oxford was the setting for a considerable number of successful murder stories long before Dexter created Endeavour Morse (*see box on page xx*).

When Colin Dexter, a classicist and crossword puzzle fanatic who at the time worked for the University Examinations Board, introduced Inspector Morse in *Last Bus to Woodstock*, he was participating in a well-established tradition. The book was published in 1974 and, in the years that followed, the cases of Morse and his sidekick Sergeant Lewis earned considerable acclaim. However, it was only after the books were adapted for British television, starting in 1987 with *The Dead of Jericho*, with John Thaw in the lead role, that Morse became a household name. Intelligent, irascible, tight-fisted, beer-drinking and Wagner-loving, Morse is a memorable character, while Kevin Whately's portrayal of Lewis (in the early books, an older man from Wales; on the small screen a youngish Geordie) from the outset provided a perfect counterpoint.

Drinking and thinking

Both on the page and on television, the Morse stories make superb use of locations both within the university and beyond. The detective's love of liquid refreshment, for instance, sees him patronizing a variety of pubs. In *The Secret of Annexe 3* (1986), Morse and Lewis take their 'lunchtime calories' at The Eagle and Child in St Giles', while The Bear Inn features in *Death is Now My Neighbour* (1996) and the Turf Tavern in *The Daughters of Cain* (1994). Another Morse favourite, The Perch Inn, is

MUSIC AND MORSE

Together with beer, the main love of Morse's life is music, which features heavily in the books and TV adaptations. The opening titles of the very first Morse TV episode, 'The Dead of Jericho', were intercut with shots of the Oxford colleges to a soundtrack of a choir singing, while Morse simultaneously plays baroque music very loudly on his car stereo.

'I'VE NEVER SAID ANYTHING SIGNIFICANT ABOUT MOTIVE.... FOR ME, IT'S THE TWISTS AND TURNS OF THE WHODUNNIT' – COLIN DEXTER, *GUARDIAN* (2000)

located at Binsey, overlooking Port Meadow, while the books have immortalized The Trout Inn at Lower Wolvercote. The Trout, which dates from the 17th century, is beautifully located on the Thames by Godstow Bridge and benefits from a terrace facing the river; it now boasts a 'Morse Bar', and framed covers of Dexter's novels hang on the wall.

Oxford's most famous hotel, The Randolph, on the corner of Magdalen Street and Beaumont Street, features in 'The Wolvercote Tongue', a screenplay based on a storyline by Dexter, which he later turned into a novel, *The Jewel That Was Ours* (1991). A party of American tourists are staying at the 19th-century hotel when an extremely valuable jewel, the 'Wolvercote Tongue', goes missing and its owner is found dead. The Randolph has featured in other original television episodes, such as 'The Infernal Serpent' and 'Second Time Around' and it, too, now has its own 'Morse Bar'. The Mitre in the High Street, formerly a hotel but now a bar and restaurant, appears in two episodes – 'Happy Families' and 'The Last Enemy'.

Jericho, lying to the northwest of the city centre, and Oxford's earliest suburb, historically derived commercial importance from the fact that the Oxford Canal passes through its heart. The Bookbinder's Arms (now The Old Bookbinder's Ale House), on the corner of Victor Street and Canal Street, was transformed into 'The Printer's Devil'

in *The Dead of Jericho* (1981). When this book was adapted for the first episode of *Inspector Morse*, the pub again featured, but this time under its own name – although the interior scenes were shot in another location. The Bookbinder's stands opposite Canal Reach (Combe Road in reality), where Anne Scott (Anne Staveley on screen) and George Jackson, two victims of the killer, both lived.

Oxford and television

Many of the city's most famous locations feature in the television series. The Bodleian Library crops up in several episodes, notably 'The Twilight of the Gods', in which the Welsh opera singer Gwladys Probert is shot from one of its windows. A gun is later found behind some of the books. In the same story, the suave Andrew Baydon is due to receive an honorary doctorate at the nearby Sheldonian Theatre. Gwladys accompanies him, giving rise to speculation that the bullet may have been meant for Baydon. Meanwhile, the stunningly designed Radcliffe Camera, believed to be the first round library in England, is so photogenic that inevitably it also features in the background of many scenes.

The city's attractive Botanic Gardens, which date back to 1621, appear in 'The Settling of the Sun' and 'Deceived by Flight'. The building of the Holywell Music Room, said to be the oldest surviving

'HE MADE MORSE'S FAULTS POIGNANTLY HUMAN, AND PERCEPTIVELY DEPICTED THE MAN'S INSIGHT INTO HIS OWN SHORTCOMINGS' – JOHN THAW'S OBITUARY, *INDEPENDENT* (2002)

concert hall in the world, began in 1742, when a subscription was started, and was completed six years later; it is now administered by the University Faculty of Music. It is the setting for a masterclass given by Gwladys Probert in 'The Twilight of the Gods' and a couple of scenes in 'Who Killed Harry Field?' Equally appealing are Magdalen College and Magdalen Bridge, both regularly featured in the television series. In the final episode, 'The Remorseful Day', Lewis stands on a terrace overlooking the Cherwell, while Colin Dexter makes his customary Hitchcock-like cameo appearance, this time in a wheelchair, as a member of a group of elderly tourists.

The Oxford Union, founded in 1825, is a student society that has its premises in St Michael Street. Harold Macmillan (1894–1986), a former British Prime Minister and Chancellor of the University, described it as 'an unrivalled training ground for debates in the Parliamentary style which no debating society in any democratic country can equal'. Its former presidents include many other politicians, including Pakistan's Benazir Bhutto (1953–2007), who in 1988 became the first woman elected to lead a Muslim state. Morse attends the debating chamber in 'Greeks Bearing Gifts', as he listens to a talk given by Randall Rees. A short distance away is the Covered Market, which first opened in 1774. Such a busy place is an ideal setting for chase scenes, and was used for that purpose in both 'Absolute Conviction' and 'Greeks Bearing Gifts'.

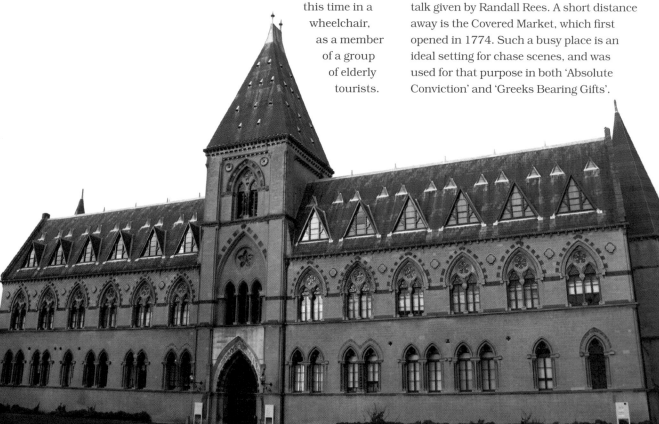

MORSE ON SCREEN

The 13 Inspector Morse novels spawned 33 episodes of the television series first shown on the British network ITV.

 ## ON TELEVISION

Series 1

'The Dead of Jericho' (1987)

'The Silent World of Nicholas Quinn' (1987)

'Service of All the Dead' (1987)

Series 2

'The Wolvercote Tongue' (1987)

'Last Seen Wearing' (1988)

'The Settling of the Sun' (1988)

'Last Bus to Woodstock' (1988)

Series 3

'Ghost in the Machine' (1989)

'The Last Enemy' (1989)

'Deceived by Flight' (1989)

'The Secret of Bay 5B' (1989)

Series 4

'The Infernal Serpent' (1990)

'The Sins of the Fathers' (1990)

'Driven to Distraction' (1990)

'Masonic Mysteries' (1990)

Series 5

'Second Time Around' (1991)

'Fat Chance' (1991)

'Who Killed Harry Field?' (1991)

'Greeks Bearing Gifts' (1991)

'Promised Land' (1991)

Series 6

'Dead on Time' (1992)

'Happy Families' (1992)

'The Death of the Self"' (1992)

'Absolute Conviction' (1992)

'Cherubim and Seraphim' (1992)

Series 7

'Deadly Slumber' (1993)

'The Day of the Devil' (1993)

'Twilight of the Gods' (1993)

Specials

'The Way Through the Woods' (1995)

'The Daughters of Cain' (1996)

'Death is Now My Neighbour' (1997)

'The Wench is Dead' (1998)

'The Remorseful Day' (2000)

OXFORD CRIME

Although Inspector Morse's (principally) television adventures put Oxford on the map as the 'murder capital of England', crime and mystery had haunted the hallowed streets of the city long before Colin Dexter created the character of the irascible policeman.

As early as 1929, Adam Broome's *The Oxford Murders* introduced Chief Inspector Bramley in the first university-based detective novel. This was soon eclipsed by the success of J.C. Masterman's *An Oxford Tragedy* (1933), where the sleuthing was undertaken by Viennese lawyer-criminologist Ernest Brendel. Michael Innes introduced his series policeman John Appleby in *Death at the President's Lodging* (1936); Appleby then appeared in another 36 novels and several collections of short stories. Another eminent Oxford scholar and crime writer was composer Bruce Montgomery who wrote as Edmund Crispin; his *The Moving Toyshop* (1946) sees the titular establishment move all across the city.

Other notable appearances by Oxford in mystery books include Dorothy L. Sayers' *Gaudy Night* (1935), featuring the popular sleuth Lord Peter Wimsey, in which Somerville College is portrayed as Shrewsbury College; an outstanding novel by the famous broadcaster Robert Robinson, *Landscape with Dead Dons* (1956); and Argentine author Guillermo Martinez's *The Oxford Murders* (2005), which won the Crime Writers' Association Gold Dagger.

Life after Morse

The death of John Thaw in 2002, and the fictional demise of the character he portrayed with such gruff humanity, might have been expected to spell the end for the Morse franchise on television, especially as the last of Dexter's 13 novels appeared as long ago as 1999. However, *Lewis*, a series starring Kevin Whately and Laurence Fox, was aired in 2006 and soon established itself as a perhaps unexpectedly successful spin-off. In this series, Lewis has at last been promoted, and Fox plays the cool and cerebral DS James Hathaway, who chose a career in the police rather than one in the priesthood. The high production levels of *Inspector Morse* have been maintained, together with the strong focus on evocative and visually appealing locations in the city. The Bodleian features yet again, for example in the episode 'And the Moonbeams Kiss the Sea', when an engineer is found shot in the head in the library's basement. The attraction of Oxford as a setting for fictional murder, thus shows no obvious sign of abating.

USEFUL WEBSITES

Morse-coded walking tour of the city bookable online
www.visitoxford.org/thedms.asp?dms=72&shop=8&prod=855&p1=shop

Drink where Colin Dexter and his creation drank
www.oxfordpubguide.co.uk/centralpubs.html

The Randolph Hotel has its own themed Morse Bar
www.macdonaldhotels.co.uk/randolph

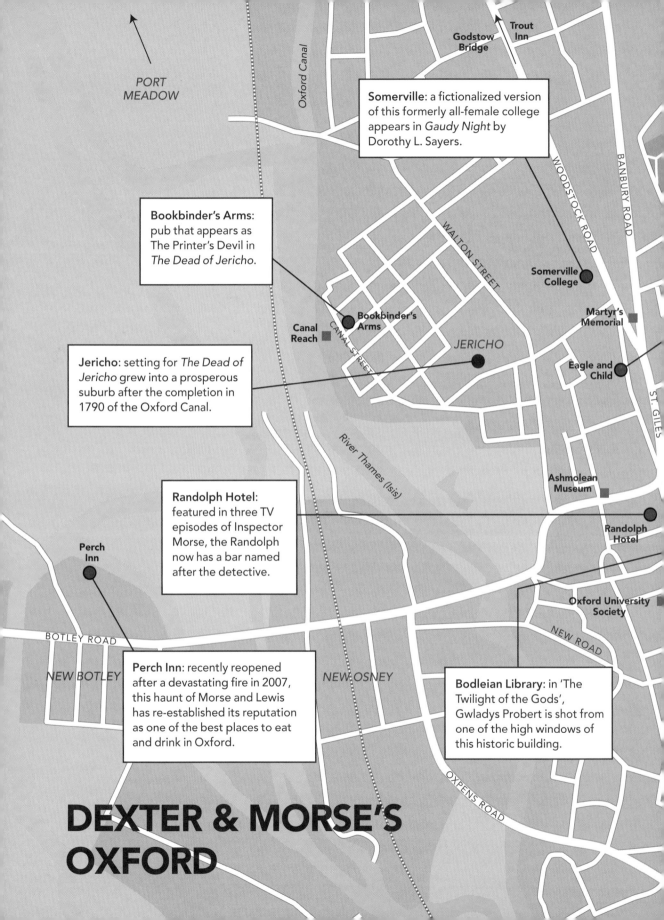

PORT MEADOW

Oxford Canal

Godstow Bridge

Trout Inn

WOODSTOCK ROAD

BANBURY ROAD

Somerville: a fictionalized version of this formerly all-female college appears in *Gaudy Night* by Dorothy L. Sayers.

Bookbinder's Arms: pub that appears as The Printer's Devil in *The Dead of Jericho.*

WALTON STREET

Somerville College

Martyr's Memorial

Canal Reach

CANAL STREET

Bookbinder's Arms

JERICHO

Eagle and Child

ST. GILES

Jericho: setting for *The Dead of Jericho* grew into a prosperous suburb after the completion in 1790 of the Oxford Canal.

River Thames (Isis)

Ashmolean Museum

Randolph Hotel: featured in three TV episodes of Inspector Morse, the Randolph now has a bar named after the detective.

Randolph Hotel

Perch Inn

Oxford University Society

NEW ROAD

BOTLEY ROAD

NEW BOTLEY

Perch Inn: recently reopened after a devastating fire in 2007, this haunt of Morse and Lewis has re-established its reputation as one of the best places to eat and drink in Oxford.

NEW OSNEY

Bodleian Library: in 'The Twilight of the Gods', Gwladys Probert is shot from one of the high windows of this historic building.

OXPENS ROAD

DEXTER & MORSE'S OXFORD

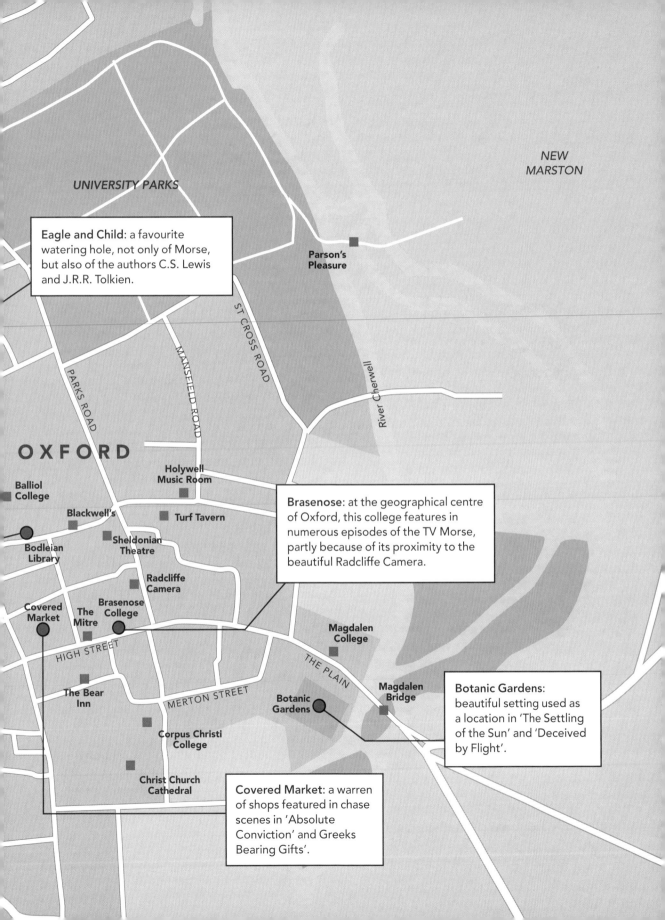

Eagle and Child: a favourite watering hole, not only of Morse, but also of the authors C.S. Lewis and J.R.R. Tolkien.

Brasenose: at the geographical centre of Oxford, this college features in numerous episodes of the TV Morse, partly because of its proximity to the beautiful Radcliffe Camera.

Botanic Gardens: beautiful setting used as a location in 'The Settling of the Sun' and 'Deceived by Flight'.

Covered Market: a warren of shops featured in chase scenes in 'Absolute Conviction' and Greeks Bearing Gifts'.

NEW MARSTON

UNIVERSITY PARKS

Parson's Pleasure

ST CROSS ROAD

MANSFIELD ROAD

PARKS ROAD

River Cherwell

OXFORD

Holywell Music Room

Balliol College

Blackwell's

Turf Tavern

Bodleian Library

Sheldonian Theatre

Radcliffe Camera

Magdalen College

Covered Market

The Mitre

Brasenose College

HIGH STREET

THE PLAIN

Magdalen Bridge

The Bear Inn

MERTON STREET

Botanic Gardens

Corpus Christi College

Christ Church Cathedral

Barry Forshaw

HENNING MANKELL & WALLANDER'S SWEDEN

Before the current (welcome) flood of crime fiction in translation, the occasional non-English-speaking crime writer, such as the prolific French novelist Georges Simenon (1903–89), achieved classic status. However, if there's one modern writer who is the Trojan horse for foreign crime in translation, it is Sweden's Henning Mankell.

His laconic detective Kurt Wallander (something of an alter ego for the similarly laconic Mankell) is one of the great creations of modern crime fiction: overweight, diabetes-ridden, and with all the problems of modern society leaving scars on his soul. Wallander is as rounded a character as any in more literary fiction.

In such books as *Sidetracked* (1995) and *Firewall* (1998), non-Swedish readers were taken into Scandinavian settings that were subtly similar to countries such as the United Kingdom, but also fascinatingly different. Wallander's Sweden is not a good advertisement for the success of the welfare state – the cracks in the consensus of Scandinavian society widening, Swedish family life riven by deep psychological traumas. But like his father-in-law, the film director Ingmar Bergman (1918–2007), Mankell frequently confounds all stereotypical expectations of Nordic gloom and produces books crammed with humanity and optimism (plus the bloodshed and murder that are prerequisites of the crime genre).

A social conscience

The keen social conscience that illuminates Mankell's books chimes with his own commitment to make disadvantaged people's lives better: he has done a great deal of theatre work in Africa, and his reach as a writer extends beyond the crime genre, with such books as the ambitious *Kennedy's Brain* (2007), *Depths* (2004) and *Eye of the Leopard* (1990). The last named, straddling the 1970s and 1980s, is a vigorous examination of the relationship between white farmers and their native workers in Africa, with the protagonist battling a hostile land and descending into his own mental firestorm. However, one of the key pleasures of the books is the entrée given to readers to Henning Mankell's Sweden.

Faceless Killers (1991), the remarkable debut novel for Wallander, established several things: the astonishing narrative grip, a powerfully realized protagonist and – the icing on the cake – the wonderfully realized Swedish locations, here the west of Wallander's home patch of Ystad. In this book, the fallout from two brutal killings kick-starts the first case we see Wallander tackling: an elderly couple is murdered, with no apparent motive. The murders take place in a striking stately home, the impressive country house of Marsvinsholm, which is now a highlight on the Wallander tours that have sprung up in the town.

Walking with Wallander

The Wallander walks in Ystad have one key location: the detective's apartment at 10 Mariagatan. This is Wallander's bolthole, where he feeds his soul with the glories of grand opera – an enthusiasm he shares with a British copper, Colin Dexter's Morse (*see pages 78–87*). The great composers are a way of minimizing the pain Wallander still feels from the fact that his wife left him. Mankell tourists can be seen looking in vain for the first-floor window

mentioned in the books, but which is an authorial invention. Similarly, you could do worse than read a Wallander book while eating at the splendid Hotel Continental – if you are lucky, you might even get to sit at Wallander's preferred table. But with the growing influx of Wallander tourists, the odds are not good.

The White Lioness (1993) has the calm of southern Sweden ruffled by the disappearance of estate agent Louise Akerblom, a pious Methodist. Wallander has little idea that his quest for the truth about the woman's disappearance will take him as far as South Africa. Visitors to Ystad can stroll to the tourist office in the square by the train

Mankell Matters

Henning Mankell is now seen as one of the key cultural exports of his native Sweden, in much the same way that the film director Ingmar Bergman once was. Mankell is, in fact, married to the director's daughter Eva, and has been writing a biographical TV series about the later years of father-in-law.

Mankell divides his time between Sweden and Maputo in Mozambique.

He is the Artistic Director of Maputo's Teatro Avenida.

Mankell also writes children's books, including *The Cat Who Liked Rain* (2007).

station and find the house rented by KGB hard man Rykoff for the African assassin in this book. While in the vicinity of the train station, it might be worth noting that you'd be near the location where a scalped body was discovered in a hole in the road in *Sidetracked*. And, speaking of *Sidetracked*, this perfectly honed novel has as strong a sense of locale as anything Mankell has written – so it might be the ideal book to take if you're planning a Sweden/Mankell trip.

Firewall sets Europe alight

By the time of *Firewall*, the word was out and the days of Mankell being the preserve of a canny few were over. In this novel, Mankell's long-term protagonist moves into a new area of crime: cyberspace. Various deaths have occurred, including the user of a cash machine and a taxi driver killed by two young girls. The country is plunged into a blackout by an electricity failure, and a grim discovery is made at a power station: but what is the connection? Wallander finds himself on the trail of cyber terrorists with shady anarchic aims. But he is hampered along the way by his own seemingly malfunctioning team of policemen and women.

In Ystad, on the north face of a hill with an old water tower, is the police station, Wallander's base of operations in the struggle to reduce a murder rate

that rivals the equally unlikely one in Dexter's Oxford. Any trip to Ystad, of course, should include a stop at the detective's café of choice, Fridolf's Konditori (you are obliged to try the delicious Wallander cake – and you'll just have to come back if it is not on the menu on the day of your visit).

One Step Behind (1997), one of the leanest and most pithy of the Wallander books, sports a particularly memorable locale, the striking Hagestad Wildlife Protection Area. Located near the house of UN Secretary-General Dag Hammarskjöld (1905–61) at Backåkra, the site is vividly utilized by Mankell in this book for the gruesome killing of three teenagers dressed in period costume to celebrate midsummer. Perhaps for all the wrong reasons, this is a notably favoured spot for Mankell tourists. However, leaving aside its grisly associations, Hagestad is well worth visiting in its own right for its outstanding natural beauty – coastal walks across sand dunes, meadows and flower-lined trackways surrounded by tall oaks and pine trees containing the nests of numerous rare species of bird.

A new Wallander

By the early 21st century, Mankell was demonstrating a nagging taste for something new, and *Before the Frost* (2002) brings Linda Wallander, Kurt's daughter, to the forefront as a new

Marsvinsholm, the 17th-century castle 7 miles (12 km) west of Ystad.

central character. In the dark forest near Ystad, a grim find is made: human hands and a severed head, arranged in a grim mockery of prayer. A Bible, seemingly heavily annotated by the killer, is also found. But this is just one of a series of bizarre incidents that have been taxing Inspector Kurt Wallander, including attacks on domestic pets, so it is perhaps not an ideal time for his daughter to make her debut as another detective on the force.

As for the famous forest that runs parallel to the (frequently deserted) beach, visitors often find that renting bikes is the best way to get the feel of this atmospheric locale, using the well laid-out cycle tracks. In the middle of the forest is Soldat's Hus (Soldier's Cottage), a good spot to grab a coffee. Real-life soldiers may be found in the forest on manoeuvres.

The return of Kurt Wallander

Much to the relief of Wallander fans, the man himself is back in *The Man Who Smiled* (1994, but not published in English until after Linda's first outing), but now he is having a very tough time of it. After being forced to kill someone, Wallander has decided to quit the police force. Drink becomes an easy option but does not help relieve his depression and when a solicitor friend whose father has died asks for Wallander's help in looking into his death, he declines – only to become involved when the solicitor himself is murdered. Reluctantly, Wallander returns to work, only to find himself embroiled in a double murder. The investigation points in the direction of a mysterious captain of industry – and Wallander is soon in immediate danger. Plotting here is as impeccable as ever, and those in the English-reading world who feared that regular doses of Wallander had been abruptly curtailed were grateful for this surprise reappearance of the dour Swedish copper.

WALLANDER ON SCREEN

The Swedish TV series starred Krister Henriksson as Kurt Wallander. The first of the 26 episodes was based on the novel that introduced the detective's daughter; the rest were all stories devised by Mankell but previously unpublished.

All six episodes of the BBC's English-language television version of the Wallander series were based on Mankell's novels. They starred the Oscar-winning British actor Kenneth Branagh.

📺 SWEDISH TV

Series 1 (2005)
'Before the Frost'
'The Village Idiot'
'The Brothers'
'The Darkness'
'The African'
'The Tricksters'
'Mastermind'
'The Photographer'
'The Container Lorry'
'The Castle Ruins'

'Blood Ties'
'Jokers'
'The Secret'

Series 2 (2008)
'The Revenge'
'The Guilt'
'The Courier'
'The Thief'
'The Cellist'
'The Priest'
'The Infiltration'

'The Sniper'
'The Angel of Death'
'The Phantom'

'The Heritage'
'The Dun'
'The Witness'

📺 ENGLISH TV

Series 1 (2008)
'Sidetracked'
'Firewall'
'One Step Behind'

Series 2 (2010)
'Faceless Killers'
'The Man Who Smiled'
'The Fifth Woman'

Although Mankell also wrote some non-Wallander books – including *Depths* (2004), a darkly compelling tale set in 1914 Sweden, and *Italian Shoes* (2006), which begins with a naked man standing in the freezing cold of the Swedish archipelago, an axe in his hand – English readers, especially, were more than happy to welcome Wallander back again with the publication of *The Pyramid* in the UK in 2008 (originally published in Swedish in 1998).

The Pyramid fills in some of the gaps in Kurt Wallander's past. Wallander, of course, first appeared in a full-length novel in *Faceless Killers*, when he was a senior police officer just out of his thirties and with his private life in chaos. The stories in the book describe his early years: the events, the people and the crimes that forged the man we first met in that debut novel. We encounter Wallander as a beat cop attempting to crack a murder in his spare time; we follow him in his tentative first steps with Mona, the woman he has decided to marry (and who has already left him by the time of the events in the first novel), and we are shown why his relationship with his father is so difficult. The ingredients that make the full-length Wallander novels so winning are all here in a much more concentrated form: a cool, analytical treatment of crime, the evocative conjuring of the Scandinavian locales, and (best of all) the puzzling, fascinating character of the tenacious policeman at the centre of the narrative.

Location, location

All in all, if you are a fan, you owe yourself a visit to Kurt Wallander's Ystad. Apart from anything else, there are nearly 60 locations from the books (and the much-acclaimed Swedish television series, which many prefer to the BBC one featuring British actor Kenneth Branagh) to track down. There's 18 Harmonigatan, for instance, the home of the deeply unpleasant psychopath in *One Step Behind* (1997) who murders a friend of Wallander's, or another home of a killer in Liregatan, where the ruthless feminist Yvonne Ander (in *The Fifth Woman*, 1996) tabulated the details of her victims. Most of all, though, Wallander's own haunts and hangouts will draw you to this fascinating town – and country.

Useful websites

Wallander walking tours organized by the Ystad Tourist Bureau
www.inspector-wallander.org/guide/sweden

Visit Sweden guide to Wallander world
www.visitsweden.com/sweden/Regions--Cities/Southern-Sweden/Culture/Ystad--Kurt-Wallander

'3-day roundtrip in the footsteps of Wallander with gastronomic delight'
www.travelgatesweden.se/adventure-travel-packages/wallander-tour-gastro

SCANDINAVIAN CRIME

Crime fiction from the Scandinavian countries has become increasingly popular due to the success of Henning Mankell, while the trilogy by the late Stieg Larsson has become an international bestselling phenomenon.

A further selection of crime from the cold includes:

Stieg Larsson: Lisbeth Salander and Mikael Blomkvist trilogy.
   Read *The Girl with the Dragon Tattoo* (2008).

Jens Lapidus: Stockholm Noir trilogy. Read *Easy Money* (2010).

Håkan Nesser: Inspector Van Veeteren series. Read *Borkmann's Point* (2006).

Ake Edwardsson: Erik Winter series. Read *Sun and Shadow* (2005).

Jo Nesbø: Harry Hole series. Read *The Devil's Star* (2005).

Asa Larsson: Rebecka Martinsson series. Read *The Blood Spilt* (2007).

Camilla Lackberg: Patrik Hedstrom series. Read *The Ice Princess* (2008).

Karin Fossum: Inspector Sejer series. Read *He Who Fears the Wolf* (2003).

Liza Marklund: Annika Bengtzon series. Read *The Bomber* (2001).

Johan Theorin: Prize-winning Swedish author of stand-alone mysteries.
   Read *Echoes from the Dead* (2008).

Mari Jungsted: Anders Knutas series. Read *Unseen* (2006).

Maj Sjöwall and Per Wahlöö: Martin Beck series. Read *The Laughing Policeman* (1971).

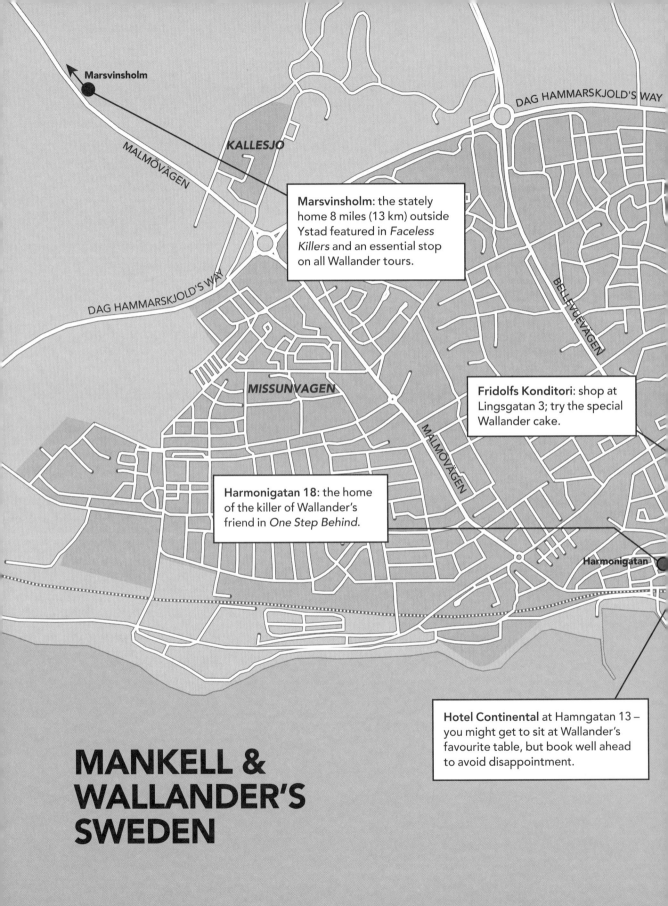

Marsvinsholm: the stately home 8 miles (13 km) outside Ystad featured in *Faceless Killers* and an essential stop on all Wallander tours.

Fridolfs Konditori: shop at Lingsgatan 3; try the special Wallander cake.

Harmonigatan 18: the home of the killer of Wallander's friend in *One Step Behind*.

Hotel Continental at Hamngatan 13 – you might get to sit at Wallander's favourite table, but book well ahead to avoid disappointment.

Marsvinsholm

MALMÖVÄGEN

KALLESJO

DAG HAMMARSKJOLD'S WAY

DAG HAMMARSKJOLD'S WAY

BELLEVUEVAGEN

MISSUNVAGEN

MALMÖVÄGEN

Harmonigatan

MANKELL & WALLANDER'S SWEDEN

Police Station: Wallander's place of work on one of the main roads into town.

Hagestad Wildlife Protection Area: picturesque park where three teenagers are killed in *One Step Behind*.

Cineteken Film Museum: fine collection of props, stills and other Wallander memorabilia from the series.

10 Mariagatan: the exterior of Wallander's flat is an essential stop on any Mankell tour of Ystad.

Sankt Knuts Torg: site of flat rented by KGB agent Rykoff in *The White Lioness*; nearby a corpse was discovered in roadworks in *Sidetracked*.

Railway Station: a scalped corpse was discovered near here in *Sidetracked*.

Police Station

DRAGONGATAN

METALLGATEN

MILITÄRVÄGAN

YSTAD

KRISTIANSTADSVÄGEN

FRIDHEMSGATAN

Wallander's Flat

Cineteken Film Museum

Hagestad Wildlife Protection Area

BLEKEGATAN

REGEMENTSGATAN

STORA ÖSTERGATAN

ÖSTERLEDEN

UREGATAN

LINGSGATAN

Tourist Office

Fridolfs Konditori

Hotel Continental

Railway Station

BORNHOLMSGATAN

HAMNGATAN

SANKT KNUTS TORG

Michael Carlson

GEORGE V. HIGGINS & EDDIE COYLE'S BOSTON

Boston, at least to those who live there and especially to those who write about it, is less a place than a state of mind. Its natives sport an attitude of aggressive superiority that disguises an innate sense of faded glory, of reduced expectations.

Once the city at the heart of America, the birthplace of that country's revolution and the centre of its religious, intellectual and commercial life, Boston has long since been relegated from pre-eminence in any of those areas, as if America left it on a bypass while building its superhighway to the 21st century.

The spiritual centre of the city is its baseball stadium, Fenway Park. Like Boston itself, it is a relic of an earlier era, and its outward charm masks its discomforts and impracticalities. The team that plays in Fenway, the Red Sox, are the city's common ground: even Boston detectives wear Red Sox caps. Although dominant in the early part of the 20th century, the Red Sox' then-owner, Harry Frazee (1881–1929), needed money to finance Broadway shows, so he sold the 1918 champions' best player, George Herman

Ruth, Jr. (1895–1948) – known universally as 'Babe Ruth' – to New York's Yankees in 1919. Boston waited another 86 years for a title, while the Yankees amassed 26. In a typically Bostonian way, the Sox' perennial failure, the city's frustration, became a mark of pride, a symbol of an ability to understand that life was as much about failure as about success, disappointment as much as pleasure, and that all the money in the world could never overcome that, even though New Yorkers might think it could. It is significant that the song played on the stadium's PA is The Standells' 1966 hit, 'Dirty Water', whose chorus goes 'Well I love that dirty water, oh Boston you're my home'.

In some ways, Boston can be compared to San Francisco, a metaphoric island apart from the rest of America: both cities have maintained a sense of aristocratic privilege. Yet Boston never boasted the exotic underworld settings whose fog enveloped San Francisco's most famous detective, Sam Spade. Boston's traditional

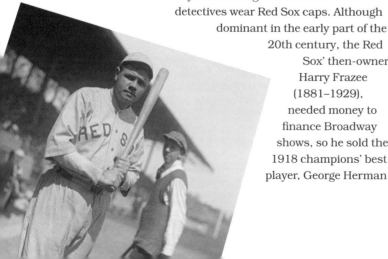

criminal element is down-to-earth, as gritty as the majority of the city. Boston writers delight in turning a spotlight on the hidden criminals, the otherwise respectable people who commit crimes for compelling reasons. In terms of detective stories, for years Boston remained very much a second-class citizen in a genre dominated by New York and California. But all that was to change in the 1970s with the arrival of two writers, Robert B. Parker and George V. Higgins.

Spenser's Boston

Parker's tough yet sensitive former boxer, Spenser, who appeared in 39 novels (and a successful television series) saw nothing exotic in Boston crime, but instead portrayed its world with a sardonic precision that refined the Raymond Chandler-style wisecrack to a fine art. Spenser, like Chandler's character Marlowe, is a former investigator for the District Attorney's office, and, like Marlowe, he left for political reasons, the implication being that he couldn't pursue his investigations to their fullest. But Spenser himself remains in the heart of old Boston, on the smart edge of Back Bay. He's worked out of three offices, all near the Public Gardens, which is also where he lives, in an apartment on Marlborough Street, just a stone's throw from his office on the corner of Boylston and Berkeley streets. This is a high-rent district today, though it was somewhat less so when the series began in 1973. Parker sketches in his settings with economy, but they are always real, something that is important to the writer. As he said in a 1997 interview:

> *It's the way Raymond Chandler made LA real. I need the mood a cityscape can provide, the way light shines through a window...*

CHUCK HOGAN, NEW CONTENDER

If the title *Prince of Thieves* suggests George Higgins, the reality of Chuck Hogan's excellent 2004 Boston-based novel is much closer to the work of Lehane. It's a classic 'one last job' scenario with a twist – bank robber (and disgraced former hockey star) Doug MacRay has fallen in love with a hostage taken in a bank robbery he masterminded and now faces a jealous rival in an FBI agent. The crime drama runs parallel to the family dramas of Charlestown and is portrayed with the same ferocity as Lehane displays in *Mystic River*.

Spenser doesn't slum it, either, except when going to the gym, though Henry Cimoli's Harbor Health Club on Atlantic Avenue near Rowe's Wharf has now suffered gentrification, too. But he's also learned to go with the flow. His preferred drinking spot is not a seedy bar, but the classy Bristol Lounge at the five-star Four Seasons Hotel; similarly, his favourite restaurant, Grill 23, just down Berkeley Street, is one of Boston's poshest. Given Spenser's own cooking skills, as deft with pesto as with pistol, this should be no surprise.

Spenser's psychologist girlfriend, Susan Silverman, lives just across the Charles River on Linnaean Street in Cambridge, the seat of Harvard University and home to hoity-toity and airy-fairy academics, whom Spenser has always enjoyed befuddling with his unexpected erudition. The first Spenser novel, *The Godwulf Manuscript* (1973), had an academic story at its core, and it shouldn't

Mystic River near Boston, Massachusetts.

'I READ PARKER'S SPENSER SERIES IN COLLEGE. WHEN IT COMES TO DETECTIVE NOVELS, 90 PERCENT OF US ADMIT HE'S AN INFLUENCE, AND THE REST OF US LIE ABOUT IT' – HARLAN COBEN, ATLANTIC MONTHLY (2007)

be surprising that Parker, a former professor at Boston's Northeastern University, has taken his detective to any number of colleges and elite prep schools along the way. Spenser is drawn frequently to the smart suburbs, even figuring in one crossover with another Parker series character, Jesse Stone, chief of police in Paradise, on Boston's North Shore and modelled on the former fishing port of Marblehead.

Speaking about the importance of location to a novelist's work, Robert B. Parker once said:

> There's a conceit that place matters more, I think, to a writer than it does.... If Raymond Chandler had lived in Chicago, Marlowe would still be Marlowe, and I think if I lived in Cincinnati Spenser would be working in Cincinnati.

His numerous fans might disagree with him, however.

Higgins's Boston

While Parker was establishing Spenser, George V. Higgins was busy dissecting the inner workings of Boston, as if the city were a malfunctioning timepiece and he were a master watchmaker. His basic theme is understanding, or failing to understand, how things work, with particular reference to the give and take of business, lawful and unlawful.

Higgins's remarkable debut novel, *The Friends of Eddie Coyle* (1972), covered the whole range of Boston locales. A suburban railway

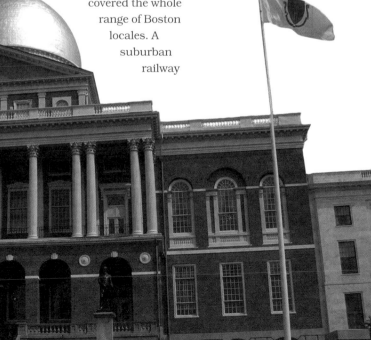

'HIGGINS WAS AN EXCEPTIONAL, PERHAPS THE EXCEPTIONAL, POSTWAR AMERICAN POLITICAL NOVELIST' – GREY GOWRIE, FORMER CHAIRMAN, ARTS COUNCIL OF ENGLAND

station in Sharon and the leafy Memorial Drive along the Charles River in Cambridge become places where gunrunners do business. Sharon is conveniently close to the former Massachusetts Correctional Institute in Walpole (MCI Walpole), which hangs over the novel like the sword of Damocles. Coyle is killed by his 'friend' Dillon, one of the many ironies in Higgins's tale, after being treated to a Boston Bruins ice hockey game at the old Boston Garden (now the TD Banknorth Garden) on Causeway Street. In the brilliant 1973 Peter Yates' film adaptation of the novel, Robert Mitchum, as Coyle, speaks his last words celebrating the skill of the Bruins' star: 'Numbah faw, Bawby Awe' ('Number four, Bobby Orr').

Higgins's only series character, featuring in four novels, was the engaging defence attorney Jerry Kennedy, who bears more than a little resemblance to Higgins himself. Kennedy serves as a worldly-wise narrator of the small corruptions that constitute the reality of day-to-day life in politics, legal practice and business. Kennedy ran two offices, the first

close to Spenser's in the Little Building at Boylston and Tremont streets, which is now a part of Emerson College, and then at 20 Beacon Street, directly opposite the State House, home of the Massachusetts state government, and, in Higgins's terms, a cross between the Roman Senate and the corrupt politicians' lobby in the Willard Hotel.

Interestingly, in Jeremiah Healy's much underrated series featuring lawyer-turned-detective John Francis Cuddy, Cuddy's office is also near the State House, on Tremont Street: if he walks far enough south, past Boston Common and the Public Garden, he might bump into Spenser. Cuddy's defining characteristic is his habit of visiting his wife's grave, to talk with her, share his problems and concerns. The cemetery is fictional, but set overlooking the harbour in South Boston.

The wider world

Two of Higgins's most instructive novels are actually set outside of Boston in the Berkshire Mountains of Western Massachusetts. In *The Mandeville Talent* (1991) a retired investigator, Baldo Ianucci, helps a young couple solve the murder of a woman's grandfather, a prominent banker. Baldo teaches them about the way life works, right down to showing them what to look for when a real estate agent is conning them.

BOSTON ON SCREEN

Boston is a popular film location and features in many movies. Widely acclaimed as an authentic reflection of the Higgins novel on which it is based, *The Friends of Eddie Coyle* (1973) was directed by Peter (*Bullitt*) Yates and starred Robert Mitchum in one of the greatest performances of his career.

Mystic River (2003), based on the novel of the same name by Dennis Lehane (*see page 105*), was directed by Clint Eastwood and shot at his insistence on location. It garnered two Oscars – for Sean Penn as Best Actor and Tim Robbins as Best Supporting Actor. Similarly, *Shutter Island* (2010), directed by Martin Scorsese and starring Leonardo DiCaprio, Mark Ruffalo and Ben Kingsley, received mixed notices on its first release. Film critic Philip French describes it in the *Observer* as 'a film… we will need to revisit before making a proper assessment'.

PARKER ON TELEVISION

The most enduring TV version of Robert B. Parker's work was *Spenser: For Hire* starring Robert Urich, which ran for 65 episodes between 1985 and 1988. The narrator is a voiceover, as in the novels.

Spenser: Ceremony (1993)

Spenser: Pale Kings and Princes (1994)

Spenser: The Judas Goat (1994)

Spenser: A Savage Place (1995)

Poodle Springs (1998)

Spenser: Small Vices (1999)

Thin Air (2000)

Walking Shadow (2001)

Monte Walsh (2003)

Stone Cold (2005)

Jesse Stone: Night Passage (2006)

Jesse Stone: Death in Paradise (2006)

Jesse Stone: Sea Change (2007)

Jesse Stone: Thin Ice (2009)

The plot – which revolves around the Berkshires' status as a posh getaway for Bostonians, including a scene set at Tanglewood, the outdoor concert venue of the Boston Pops. Higgins based it on a real murder in New Hampshire which he had himself investigated while working for the Massachusetts Attorney General. Higgins returned to the Berkshires in *A Change of Gravity* (1997), which was set in Holyoke.

Higgins's novels are composed mainly of dialogue. As the author explained:

The characters are telling you the story. I'm not telling you the story, they're going to do it. If I do it right, you will get the whole story.

USEFUL WEBSITES

A wide selection of walking tours, including one that concentrates on literary Boston and another that takes tourists into the city's seamier side.
www.bostonbyfoot.org

Guide to Spenser's Boston
www.bullets-and-beer.com/Boston.htm

Official site of the longtime Cinderellas of major league baseball.
http://boston.redsox.mlb.com/index.jsp?c_id=bos

Fenway Park baseball stadium, home of the Boston Red Sox.

DENNIS LEHANE

Writer Dennis Lehane called *The Friends of Eddie Coyle* 'the quintessential Boston novel'. Lehane, also known for his Boston-based books, may have been over-generous, because his own *Mystic River* (2001) may surely be considered in the same breath as Higgins's classic. Lehane rightly praises the way Higgins captured the 'tribalism' and 'fatalism' of the city, something he himself captures in *Mystic River*, which also evokes the very essence of Boston even though it is set, nominally at least, in a fictional place called East Buckingham. This is Lehane's amalgam of Charlestown, the actual area just across the Mystic River from Boston, with Boston's South End, or 'Southie', across the Fort Point Channel, and Dorchester, south of Southie.

Lehane grew up in Dorchester, and it is there that he set his series of five novels featuring the unlikely pair of unlikely detectives, Patrick Kinzie and Angie Gennaro. The reality of his settings is established by the main characters' voices and attitudes: the two detectives grew up in Dorchester and are unable to escape it. In a sense, the fabric of life remains much as it was when they were schoolkids: the same gangs, the same bullies, the same stars and failures, trying desperately to play the hands that fate has dealt them. This fatalism was captured perfectly in Ben Affleck's 2007 film version of Lehane's novel *Gone Baby Gone* (1998). Angie Gennaro's family are supposedly mobsters who control crime in Boston. Interestingly, in Robert B. Parker's series featuring female ex-cop Sunny Randall, her ex's family is described as similarly controlling Boston crime: if the two families ever discover each other there could be trouble.

Mystic River, of course, was graced with a formidable adaptation by Clint Eastwood (2003), arguably his best film (*see page 103*), as Lehane played on the theme of childhood coming back to haunt characters, most of whom are as trapped in their lives as Kenzie and Gennaro and their friends. Much of the film was shot in Southie – the store where Jimmy Markum (Sean Penn) works is in reality Miller's Market at 366K Street – but the real Charlestown also figures largely as Eastwood's helicopter shots mix harbour locations, making you feel trapped on these little working class islands, cut off from the world of bars in the Four Seasons, lawyers' offices opposite the State House, and shrinks having lattes in Harvard Square. Lehane's run of first-rate film adaptations continued with Martin Scorsese's 2010 version of *Shutter Island* (2003), set in a hospital for the criminally insane on an island in Boston harbour, and filmed on Boston's Paddock Island.

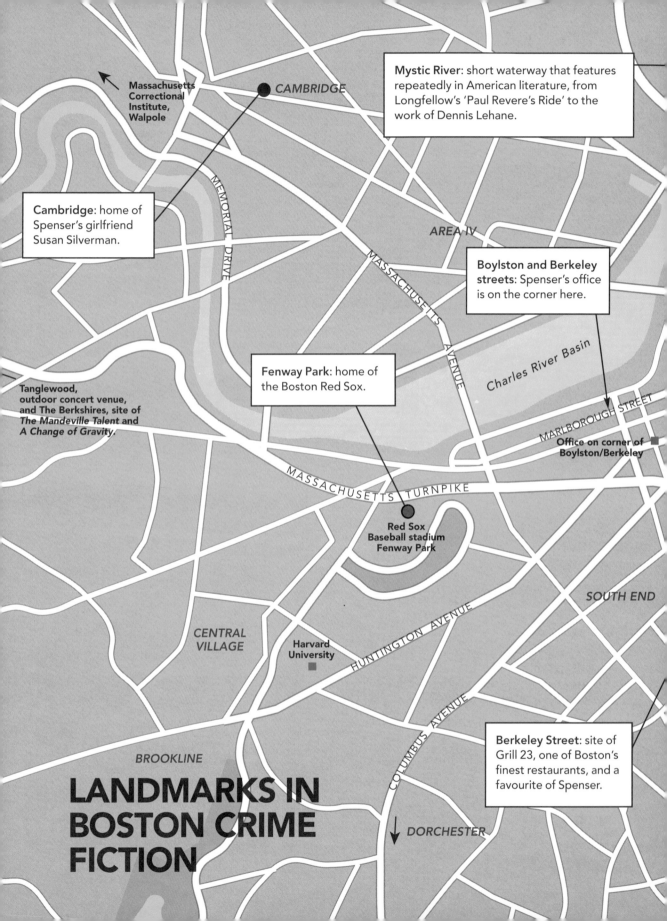

Mystic River: short waterway that features repeatedly in American literature, from Longfellow's 'Paul Revere's Ride' to the work of Dennis Lehane.

CAMBRIDGE

Cambridge: home of Spenser's girlfriend Susan Silverman.

AREA IV

MEMORIAL DRIVE

MASSACHUSETTS AVENUE

Boylston and Berkeley streets: Spenser's office is on the corner here.

Charles River Basin

Tanglewood, outdoor concert venue, and The Berkshires, site of *The Mandeville Talent* and *A Change of Gravity.*

Fenway Park: home of the Boston Red Sox.

MARLBOROUGH STREET

Office on corner of Boylston/Berkeley

MASSACHUSETTS TURNPIKE

Red Sox Baseball stadium Fenway Park

SOUTH END

CENTRAL VILLAGE

Harvard University

HUNTINGTON AVENUE

COLUMBUS AVENUE

BROOKLINE

Berkeley Street: site of Grill 23, one of Boston's finest restaurants, and a favourite of Spenser.

↓ DORCHESTER

Massachusetts Correctional Institute, Walpole

LANDMARKS IN BOSTON CRIME FICTION

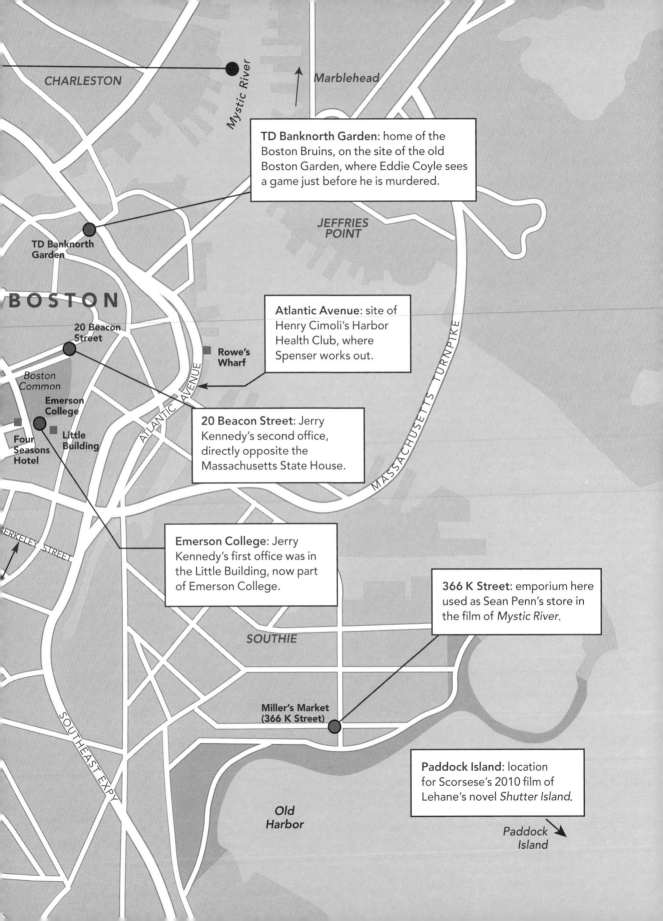

CHARLESTON

Mystic River

Marblehead

TD Banknorth Garden: home of the Boston Bruins, on the site of the old Boston Garden, where Eddie Coyle sees a game just before he is murdered.

JEFFRIES POINT

TD Banknorth Garden

B O S T O N

MASSACHUSETTS TURNPIKE

20 Beacon Street

Boston Common

Rowe's Wharf

Atlantic Avenue: site of Henry Cimoli's Harbor Health Club, where Spenser works out.

Emerson College

Four Seasons Hotel

Little Building

20 Beacon Street: Jerry Kennedy's second office, directly opposite the Massachusetts State House.

ERKELEY STREET

Emerson College: Jerry Kennedy's first office was in the Little Building, now part of Emerson College.

366 K Street: emporium here used as Sean Penn's store in the film of *Mystic River*.

SOUTHIE

Miller's Market (366 K Street)

SOUTHEAST EXPY

Paddock Island: location for Scorsese's 2010 film of Lehane's novel *Shutter Island*.

Old Harbor

Paddock Island

JOHN HARVEY & CHARLIE RESNICK'S NOTTINGHAM

Legendary 12th-century outlaw Robin Hood aside, Nottinghamshire's heroes range from Lord Byron, through football manager Brian Clough and ice-skating duo Jayne Torvill and Christopher Dean, to the mountaineer Doug Scott and up-market fashion designer Sir Paul Smith.

HP Sauce and Bramley apples originated in Nottingham, as did MRI scanning, shin guards and the Raleigh Chopper bicycle. Writers the area lays claim to include, most famously, D.H. Lawrence (1885–1930) and Alan Sillitoe (1928–2010), whose *Saturday Night and Sunday Morning* (1958) illustrates the inner city of Nottingham in all its brash working-class glory. Graham Greene (1904–91) and J.M. Barrie (1860–1937) were both, for a time, journalists on the *Nottingham Daily Journal*; children's writer Helen Cresswell (1934–2005) and novelist Stanley Middleton (1919–2009) lived and worked there all their lives, and current writers with Nottingham connections include the dramatists Michael Eaton, Billy Ivory and Stephen Lowe and the novelists Jon McGregor, Nicola Monaghan and – even though I decamped to London several years ago – John Harvey.

Nottingham, past and present

Situated in the East Midlands, about as far from the sea as it's possible in England to be, the population of the city of Nottingham is not much more than a quarter of a million people, but once the immediately surrounding areas are added, a population of almost 700,000 makes this the seventh largest urban area in the United Kingdom.

In common with many similar cities, shifts and changes in world manufacturing have seen Nottingham move from being a prosperous industrial centre to one whose economy is increasingly based on financial and business services and tourism. When I first came to the region in the mid-1960s, it was taken for granted that the majority

of the pupils in the secondary school where I was teaching would leave school at 15 and go out to work – the lads down the pit, hewing coal, and the lassies into one or other of the textile factories. Now the mines are shut down and the textile factories have been converted into either university extensions or apartments. The Raleigh bicycle factory, made famous in *Saturday Night and Sunday Morning* as the workplace of Arthur Seaton, has long closed and been swept up into the maw of one of the two ever-expanding universities.

Despite these changes, or, some might say, because of them, Nottingham is not a poor city. Yet, in common with the rest of the country, the gap between those who have and those who have not has continued to widen and sizeable pockets of quite desperate poverty remain. Where there is poverty, where there is unemployment, where educational attainment is disappointingly low you will find certain kinds of crime. Not the big business, white-collar kind of crime involving millions of pounds, but the scuffling, street-level, quick snatch, quick sell, in-at-the-back-window kind of crime that mixes opportunism with want and need.

A number of highly publicized shootings between 2000 and 2003 resulted in the city being nicknamed Shottingham in the popular media, and when it was announced that Great

THE SANDWICH MAN

Charlie Resnick's consumption of sandwiches is legendary. Here he shares a meal with one of his cats: 'The sandwich was tuna fish and egg mayonnaise with some small slices of pickled gherkin and a crumbling of blue cheese; the mayonnaise kept dripping over the edges of the bread and down on to his fingers so that Dizzy twisted and stretched from his lap in order to lick it off. Billie Holiday and Lester Young were doing it through the headphones, making love to music without ever holding hands' – *Lonely Hearts* (1989).

Britain had been successful in the bid to host the 2012 Olympics, the joke went round that the athletics would be in London, the rowing at Henley and the shooting in Nottingham. It was largely in response to this that the Nottinghamshire police force became the first in the UK where officers were routinely armed when on patrol in certain parts of the inner city. Since then, the number of reported shootings has fallen (unreported, as ever, being another matter).

The drug trade

As the most recent Resnick novel, *Cold in Hand* (2008) suggests, some of the violence is territorial and has been fuelled by rivalry between young people living on different estates; but much of the more serious violent crime, as portrayed in an earlier Resnick novel, *Last Rites* (1998), has at its heart an escalating drug trade and its own internal rivalries.

In 2006, after a three-year campaign involving more than 80 operations and 100 arrests, police finally broke the back

of a drug cartel that had been operating with seeming impunity out of the Bestwood Estate, just to the north of the city. Its leader, who despite being implicated in four murders and over 50 shootings had seemed untouchable, was finally jailed for 35 years for his involvement in a double murder, a further nine years being added to that sentence in 2007 for corrupting officers in the Nottinghamshire force.

During this police campaign, which at one stage was put on hold for budgetary reasons in favour of solving high-volume crime which would look better in the crime figures – shades of the hit television show *The Wire* – teams involved in the investigation were shielded from one another and given information on a strict need-to-know basis, and senior officers were provided with exit strategies from their homes as it was believed their lives could be in danger.

Yet Nottingham is a vibrant city, with thriving cultural and culinary scenes and more than a quarter of its population

Meadow Lane, the home ground of Notts County Football Club.

'NOTTINGHAM IS A VAST PLACE SPRAWLING TOWARDS A MILLION, AND IT IS NOTHING MORE THAN AN AMORPHOUS AGGLOMERATION. THERE IS NO NOTTINGHAM, IN THE SENSE THAT THERE IS SIENA' – D.H. LAWRENCE, 'NOTTINGHAM AND THE MINING COUNTRY' (1929)

aged between 20 and 34. Nevertheless, it's crime – or the perception of crime – that lets it down.

Harvey's Nottingham

I have lived in and just outside the city, at five different addresses, over a period of close on 20 years and have been a victim of crime on only three occasions: once, my car was broken into and items taken, once my new bicycle was stolen from my back garden and, on the last occasion, the house was broken into when I went down the road to buy a loaf of bread and everything of value spirited away. The nearest I have come to being threatened with violence was by some irate away fans during a particularly tempestuous football game at Meadow Lane. But then, as is the case with people who grow accustomed to where they live, you get to know where it's safe to go and where to avoid.

If I didn't like living in Nottingham, and feel safe at home there, I wouldn't keep coming back. And if it weren't the contradictory mixture that it is, it wouldn't be the kind of fertile terrain in which Detective Inspector Charlie Resnick could flourish, as he has now through 11 novels, two television adaptations, four radio dramas and numerous short stories. To say nothing of translation into almost 20 languages.

Resnick's origins

The idea of writing a series of police procedurals set in Nottingham first came to me when I was writing the six scripts which made up the first of a television drama series, *Hard Cases* (1988). This followed the lives and casework of a team of inner-city probation officers, taking them out onto the streets and working-class estates where a high percentage of their clients lived. Something about filming on the actual Nottingham locations made me more vividly aware of the possibilities of using the same setting for a hopefully realistic crime series, initially, at least, conceived as fiction rather than drama. The structure of *Hard Cases* had been very closely based on that of the American police series, *Hill Street Blues* (1981–87), so wasn't this simply a return to roots? What remained was, in *Hill Street* terms, to find my central character, my Frank Furillo, round whom the others would revolve. Find him and then set him in place.

The place came first. After some discussions with two senior officers in the Nottinghamshire force, I chose the small police station at Canning Circus, just on the edge of the city centre proper, as the base from which my fictional detective would operate. Away from the hubbub of Central Division, he would have a

'IF JOHN HARVEY'S NOVELS WERE SONGS CHARLIE PARKER WOULD PLAY THEM. HARVEY SINGS THE BLUES FOR PEOPLE TOO BRUISED TO CARRY THE TUNE THEMSELVES' – NEW YORK TIMES BOOK REVIEW

relatively small – and, therefore, in novelist's terms, manageable – squad under his wing; and the position of the station, between the expensive properties of the area known as The Park, and the smaller, meaner streets leading from the Alfreton Road, afforded the perfect opportunity for contrasting the two extremes of the city, the haves and the have-nots.

The station at which Resnick was based was in the inner city, far enough from the centre to feel its own identity, not so distant that it was like being in the sticks. Northeast, between the fan of arterial roads, were turn-of-the-century terraced houses, infilled here and there with modest new municipal buildings and earlier, less successful blocks of flats with linked walkways waiting to be demolished. Most of those living there were working-class poor, which meant they were lucky to be working at all: Afro-Caribbeans, Asians and whites who had clocked in at the factories producing bicycles or cigarettes or hosiery, before those factories had been torn down to make way for

superstores or turned into museums celebrating lace-and-legend heritage. To the west was an enclave of Victorian mansions and tennis courts, tree-lined hilly streets and grounds big enough to build an architect-designed bungalow below the shrubbery and still have room for badminton. Once a year these people opened up their gardens to one another and served weak lemonade they'd made themselves, a small charge, of course, for charity. The only black face ever glimpsed belonged to someone cutting through or lost – Rough Treatment (1990)

Rough treatment

Resnick himself evolved more slowly, the clue to his background and character only coming as I became more aware of the sizeable and distinctive Polish population in the city. Resnick, I decided, would have Polish ancestry and have regularly spent evenings and weekends at the Polish Club with his parents, while being educated in normal Nottingham schools. He would be native to the city and yet, at the same time, an outsider. Perfect for my purposes. Most days, on his way into the market for his morning coffee, his habits similar to my own, he would nod acknowledgement to the dozen or so ageing Poles permanently gathered around the entrance.

RESNICK ON SCREEN

Two of John Harvey's novels have been filmed for BBC Television. Tom Wilkinson – who would later star in such films as *The Full Monty* (1997) and *The Ghost* (2010) – played the leading role with a lugubriousness that befits a put-upon detective hunting a psychotic murderer but which inspired the redtops to label him 'Inspector Morose'.

Harvey hopes that there will be further screen adaptations of his work, but he is philosophical about the prospects: 'Most crime writers out there who write a few halfway decent novels tend to get their novels optioned. A handful of them get made into television. Most don't. It would be very nice if one of those scripts did get filmed, and filmed well. And if they filmed it in Nottingham, that would be great…. If things get made in other media, that's all great. But you can't afford to sit around waiting for that to happen'.

ON TELEVISION

Resnick: Lonely Hearts (1992)
Resnick: Rough Treatment (1993)

The Italian coffee stall was located among the market stalls on the upper level of one of the city's two shopping centres. Vegetables, fruit and flowers, fish and meat and bread. Afro-Caribbean and Asian specialities; the two Polish delicatessen stalls where Resnick did much of his shopping, replying to greetings offered in his family's language with the flattened vowels of the English Midlands – Wasted Years (1993).

Resnick's Nottingham

In the earlier books, there is some inconsistency about where Resnick lives, but with the filming of *Lonely Hearts* and *Rough Treatment* for the BBC in the early 1990s, an address in Nottingham's Alexandra Park, to the northeast, was settled on: a detached house, solid and dull, whose rear garden sits high above the allotments of Hungerhill Gardens and the streets of St Ann's.

The city centre now is recognizably the same as the one I myself remember from the 1960s, the one Resnick remembers from a similar time, except that the pubs in which we both used to drink, The Flying Horse and the Watson Fothergill-designed Black Boy, have been pulled down, and, in front of Nottingham City's imposing Council House with its attendant stone lions, the Old Market Square has been newly refurbished and in the summer months, thanks to several tons of imported sand, masquerades as a beach.

On one edge of the square, however, Yates's Wine Lodge, familiar from not just Sillitoe but also D.H. Lawrence, still stands, though without the sawdust on the floor or the string trio playing on the balcony. Opposite, The Bell still features lunchtime jazz on a Sunday, though, by all accounts, Resnick is more likely nowadays to find his jazz at The Five Ways in Sherwood on a Tuesday night.

Quite when Resnick transferred his footballing allegiances across the River Trent and began supporting Notts County instead of Nottingham Forest

goes unrecorded, but I suspect it was in the early 1980s, when County spent three years in the top division, only to be relegated twice in successive seasons immediately following. Knowing Resnick as well as I do, throwing in his lot with the underdog is more in keeping with his truest nature.

Visiting supporters, collected behind the far goal, chanted and jeered. A few of the home fans jeered and gesticulated back, while others, heads down, started to leave. Resnick and Millington, stoics both, waited till the bitter end: 'Nice to know some things don't change', Millington said, *as they were walking away from the ground. 'Still know how to throw three points away just this side of the final whistle.'* – Cold in Hand (2008)

Some things don't change. Some do. A little. As a city, a place to live, Nottingham is doing its best to change and change for the better. I may be back there one day to discover. As for Charlie, he's slowly, inexorably, getting older and closer to retirement and, I suspect, more and more stuck in his ways. He's never going to move, never going to leave, until, as he'd likely say, they carry him out in a wooden box. Until that time, he'll stay put, hedged in, as ever, by hope and regret.

USEFUL WEBSITES & ADDRESSES

Nottingham city breaks
www.visitnottingham.com/exec/135348/11111

D.H. Lawrence Heritage Centre
8a Victoria Street
Eastwood
Nottinghamshire
www.broxtowe.gov.uk/index.aspx?articleid=4700

Cycle tours of the places immortalized in *Saturday Night and Sunday Morning.*
http://tatehandheldconference.pbworks.com/Sillitoe+Trail

Yates's Wine Lodge
49 Long Row
Nottingham NG1 6JB
0115 947 3334
www.weareyates.co.uk

Yates's Wine Lodge: famous hostelry featured in the works of D.H. Lawrence and Alan Sillitoe, as well as Harvey.

Alfreton Road: where the well-heeled commercial centre gives way to the poorer districts of the city.

Canning Circus Police Station: Resnick's nick is small and well away from the hubbub of Central Division.

The Bell Inn: where jazz fan Resnick sometimes attends live Sunday performances.

Old Market Square: the 200 feet (60 m) tall Council House here is Nottingham's most notable landmark.

NOTTINGHAM ROAD

STOCKHILL

WOLLATON ROAD

Wollaton Park

ALFRETON ROAD

Canning Circus Police Station

The Bell Inn

THE PARK

LENTON

A52 DERBY ROAD

QUEENS DRIVE

THE
WA

HARVEY & RESNICK'S NOTTINGHAM

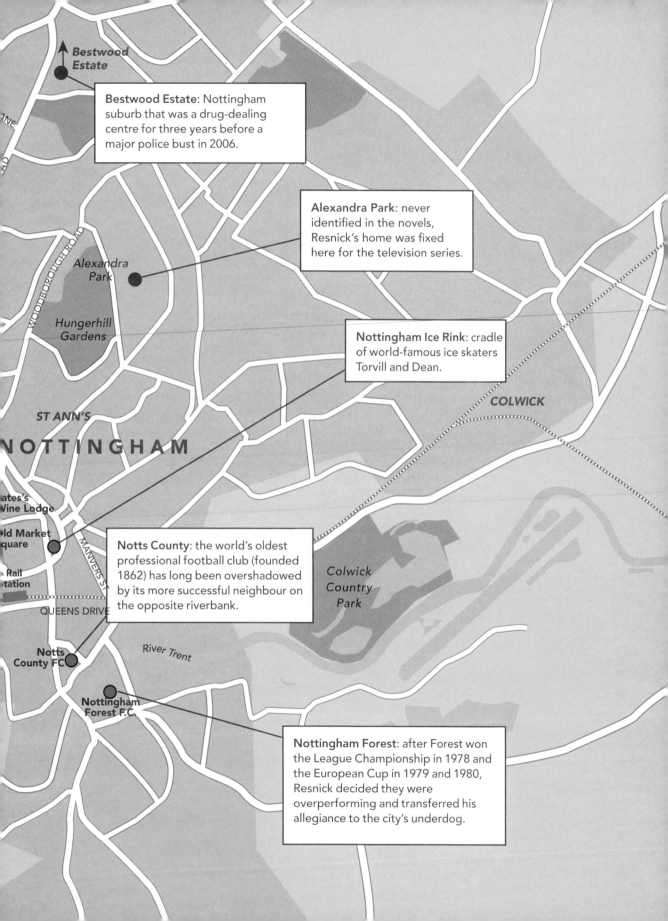

Bestwood Estate: Nottingham suburb that was a drug-dealing centre for three years before a major police bust in 2006.

Alexandra Park: never identified in the novels, Resnick's home was fixed here for the television series.

Nottingham Ice Rink: cradle of world-famous ice skaters Torvill and Dean.

Notts County: the world's oldest professional football club (founded 1862) has long been overshadowed by its more successful neighbour on the opposite riverbank.

Nottingham Forest: after Forest won the League Championship in 1978 and the European Cup in 1979 and 1980, Resnick decided they were overperforming and transferred his allegiance to the city's underdog.

Bestwood Estate

Alexandra Park

Hungerhill Gardens

WOODBOROUGH ROAD

COLWICK

ST ANN'S

NOTTINGHAM

ates's ine Lodge

ld Market quare

Rail tation

MANVERS ST.

QUEENS DRIVE

Colwick Country Park

Notts County FC

River Trent

Nottingham Forest F.C.

Peter Rozovsky

ANDREA CAMILLERI & MONTALBANO'S SICILY

Andrea Camilleri's Sicilian landscape contains no ancient ruins, though the author was born in Porto Empedocle, hard by the Valley of the Temples at Agrigento, and his creation, Inspector Salvo Montalbano, works in a town closely modelled on the author's own.

Instead, Camilleri's ruins are modern and industrial, and they stand as objective symbols of the underlying political corruption that constitutes the real landscape of Sicily.

Taking on the politicians

The Shape of Water (1994; English translation 2004), the first Montalbano novel, opens on a stretch of scrubland in the shadow of an abandoned chemical works on the island. The land, which bears a legendary, ironic relation to the name by which it is known – The Pasture – is home to an outdoor brothel. Camilleri expresses no disapproval of the women, men and in-betweens who work there, but he does serve up the first of the Montalbano series' many heapings of scorn for the politicians and their business paymasters who have ruined the land and done their best to ruin its people:

Behind [the Pasture] lay the ruins of a large chemical works inaugurated by the ubiquitous Deputy Cusumano when it seemed the magnificent winds of progress were blowing strong. Soon, however, that breeze changed into the flimsiest of puffs before dropping altogether, but in that brief time it had managed to do more damage than a tornado, leaving a shambles of compensation benefits and unemployment in its wake.

In *August Heat* (2008), the illegally concealed lower storey of a Sicilian summerhouse shelters the body of a murdered young woman and the secrets of the man who killed her. Why hide the construction? Montalbano suggests that the building's owner 'was waiting for an amnesty on code violations'; do otherwise, he says, and the owner would risk having the entire house demolished:

The fire chief started laughing. 'Demolished? Around here there are entire towns built illegally'.

The Wings of the Sphinx (2009), the 11th work in the series, has Montalbano complaining about a government that ignores the public without ever shying away from public works:

> *The inspector cursed the saints. The police stations had no gasoline, the courts had no paper, the hospitals had no thermometers, and meanwhile the government was thinking about building a bridge over the Strait of Messina.*

Comic impulse

Despite Camilleri's often grim observations, many readers love him for his humour. Camilleri will often leaven his physical descriptions with wry jokes or heroic aspiration. Montalbano generally feels better the closer he gets to the sea, and not just because the Mediterranean provides the seafood he loves so much. He escapes with long swims from the beach behind his house. He enjoys postprandial strolls to the jetty in his town of Vigàta. In Montalbano's

world humanity seems to be in better harmony with the natural world by the water's edge:

> *He opened his mouth wide and took a deep breath. He liked the smell of Vigàta's port.*
> *'What are you talking about? All ports have the same stink', Livia once said to him.*
> *It wasn't true. Every harbour has a different smell. Vigàta's combined, in perfect doses, wet cordage, fishing nets drying in the sun, iodine, rotten fish, dead and living algae and tar with, deep in the background, a hint of petrol.*
> Excursion to Tindari (2006).

Learning a language

Wise decisions by Camilleri's English translator, Stephen Sartarelli, contribute to another kind of geography in the Montalbano novels, a geography of language. Sartarelli describes Camilleri's prose as an unusual combination of slang, dialect and 'literary flourishes', among other elements. From this noisy, colourful mix, Sartarelli fashions an English version rich with malapropisms, recipes and insults, always with judiciously chosen words left in their original language, such as *cornuto*. 'Italian for "cuckold"', Sartarelli tells us in one of his informative, entertaining footnotes, '*cornuto* is a common insult throughout the country but a special favourite among southerners, Sicilians in particular'.

Words and expressions left untranslated in the text work like a suggestive seasoning, imparting their flavour to the whole. When Sartarelli gives us 'Montalbano cursed the saints', the reader is likely to hear the cursing in Italian.

To crime writers and readers from North America or from Europe's colder countries, food may indicate squalor, bachelor solitude or eccentricity. In Jean-Claude Izzo's Marseilles or Manuel Vázquez Montalbán's Barcelona or Camilleri's Sicily, food is something closer to religion, though religion of a particularly joyous kind:

'As they ate, they spoke of eating, as always happens in Italy', the narrator tells us in *The Shape of Water*. In later novels, Montalbano is more likely to eat in reverent silence; no task is more worthy of respect than eating good food. And readers are as apt to enjoy the beguiling euphony of pasta 'ncasciata, pappanozza or caciocavallo cheese as they are to salivate over the imagined pleasures of their taste and aroma.

Big men and little people

Camilleri's rich human and moral landscape includes wary peasants, lechers, wounded lovers and, above all, adroitly amoral politicians. During the 'horrific hurricane' of Italy's Clean Hands anti-corruption investigations of the 1990s, one such figure:

… had turned into a submarine, navigating underwater by means of periscope alone. He resurfaced only when he'd sighted the possibility of casting anchor in a safe port – the one just constructed by a former Milanese real-estate speculator-cum-owner of the top three private nationwide television stations-cum-parliamentary deputy, head of his own personal political party, and finally prime minister – The Paper Moon (2008).

'MONTALBANO FELT MOVED. THIS WAS REAL FRIENDSHIP, SICILIAN FRIENDSHIP, THE KIND BASED ON INTUITION, ON WHAT WAS LEFT UNSAID. WITH A TRUE FRIEND, ONE NEVER NEEDS TO ASK, BECAUSE THE OTHER UNDERSTANDS ON HIS OWN ACCORDINGLY' – ANDREA CAMILLERI, THE SNACK THIEF (2005)

At the other end of the social scale are the peasant abused by police in *August Heat*, the immigrant victims of human trafficking in *Rounding the Mark* (2006) and the *vucumprà*, African street peddlers so called for their pronunciation of '*Vuoi comprare?*' ('Do you want to buy?'). A wary woman in *Voice of the Violin* (2003) asks, 'Are you cops?' and provokes this sympathetic reflection:

> *How many centuries of police tyranny has it taken to hone this Sicilian woman's ability to detect law-enforcement officers at a moment's glance?*

One group perhaps surprisingly scarce in Montalbano's human landscape is the Mafia. Camilleri explained why in an interview with the *Independent* newspaper in 2007:

> *In literature and the cinema, more often than not, the figure of the gangster creates a relationship of total fascination. I don't believe the Mafia are worthy of this. Let's leave the literature on the Mafia as the ungrammatical report of an under-commissioner of police and the reasoning of a judge at the conclusion of a trial. That is their true literature and that's the way it should remain.*

Montalbano's treatment of the Mob reflects many of the attitudes expressed by an earlier Sicilian author, Leonardo

Cooking the books

For more than 1,000 years one of the major crossroads of Europe, Sicily bears numerous signs – architectural, cultural and linguistic – of the civilizations that visited, conquered and sometimes settled on the island. There is abundant evidence of Arab, Greek, Norman and Spanish cultures, but the most noticeable influence is that of its nearest mainland neighbour. This is particularly true of the cuisine, which is strongly Italian but with unique local modifications. The following are among the distinctively Sicilian foods described by Camilleri and enjoyed with great gusto by Montalbano:

Pasta 'ncasciata – pressed pasta – is a Sicilian variant of macaroni with meatballs in ragù sauce, with sliced hard-boiled eggs, grated pecorino (sheep's cheese), fried aubergines and garlic, all oven-baked until crispy. In a memorable passage in *The Terracotta Dog* (2004), Montalbano wolfs down two portions.

Pappanozza is a dish of onions and potatoes, boiled and mashed and seasoned with olive oil, vinegar, salt and pepper.

Caciocavallo is a cheese made of sheep or cow milk and shaped like a large tear drop.

Arancini balls are often made of meat and leftover risotto rice coated in breadcrumbs and fried or baked.

MONTALBANO ON SCREEN

In 1999 the Italian state-owned public service broadcaster RAI began an 18-episode television series based on the Camilleri novels starring Luca Zingaretti as Montalbano. Almost all the location scenes were filmed in and around Ragusa, Sicily.

 ## ON TELEVISION

Il ladro di merendine ('The Snack Thief')

La voce del violino ('The Voice of the Violin')

La forma dell'acqua ('The Shape of Water')

Il cane di terracotta ('The Terracotta Dog')

La gita a Tindari ('Excursion to Tindari')

Tocco d'artista ('The Touch of the Artist')

Il senso del tatto ('Sense of Touch')

Gli arancini di Montalbano ('Montalbano's Croquette')

L'odore della notte ('The Scent of the Night')

Gatto e cardellino ('Cat and Goldfinch')

Il giro di boa ('Rounding the Mark')

Par condicio ('The Same Condition')

La pazienza del ragno ('The Patience of the Spider')

Il gioco delle tre carte ('The Three-Card Trick')

La vampa d'agosto ('August Heat')

Le ali della sfinge ('The Wings of the Sphinx')

In 2008, two of the episodes – *Excursion to Tindari* and *Montalbano's Croquette*– were shown on BBC4 TV.

Sciascia (1921–89). Sciascia's novella *The Day of the Owl* (1961) – one of the earliest works of fiction to detail the operations of the Mafia – was loosely based on the real-life assassination of a local communist trade unionist. Its critical and commercial success inspired a follow-up, *To Each His Own* (1966), as well as a thriving literary Mob-exposé sub-genre for Italian Americans such as Mario Puzo (1920–99), author of *The Godfather* (1969), and Nicholas Pileggi (b. 1933), whose *Wiseguy* (1986) became the 1990 movie *Goodfellas*.

Camilleri is also strongly influenced by *The Leopard* (1958) by Giuseppe Tomasi di Lampedusa (1896–1957). Unfinished at the author's death, this novel about the decline of the ancient nobility and the rise to riches of a local peasant is the quintessential work of Sicilian literature and an acclaimed world masterpiece.

Among the numerous other writers who appear in Montalbano's literary landscape are Charles Baudelaire (1821–67), William Shakespeare (1564–1616), Manuel Vázquez Montalbán (1939–2003), Georges Simenon (1903–89) and the partnership of Maj Sjöwall (b. 1935) and Per Wahlöö (1926–75).

Home thoughts from abroad

Camilleri was 69 years old when he published *The Shape of Water* in Italian in 1994, and by then he had lived in Rome for many years. He has said that he tried his hand at crime fiction just for fun, after years in theatre, film and television and after having written several literary novels.

The Montalbano books reflect their author's political and social leanings, thus it is plausible to regard Montalbano as a stand-in for the author, returning as a kind of tourist to his native island after many years away. For example, at the very beginning of Montalbano's first investigation:

The inspector lit a cigarette and turned to look at the chemical factory. That ruin fascinated him. He decided he would come back one

'THE NOVELS OF ANDREA CAMILLERI BREATHE OUT THE SENSE OF PLACE, THE SENSE OF HUMOUR, AND THE SENSE OF DESPAIR THAT FILLS THE AIR OF SICILY. TO READ HIM IS TO BE TAKEN TO THAT GLORIOUS, TORTURED ISLAND' – DONNA LEON

day to take a few snapshots, which he'd send to Livia to explain some things about himself and his island that she was still unable to understand.

Some critics have denounced the Montalbano series as formulaic. While there may be some substance in this charge – all novels conform to certain conventions – it overlooks the charm of the observation, the little details. Lovers of Camilleri – and they are many; he has sold more than 2.5 million books since 1998 – are captivated above all by three facets of his work. One is the humour, which is oblique and subtle, as in the running joke about

writer's block examplified in Judge Lo Bianco's unfinished (and almost certainly never to be completed) book entitled *The Life and Exploits of Rinaldo and Antonio Lo Bianco, Masters of Jurisprudence at the University of Girgenti at the Time of King Martin the Younger (1402–09)*. Another is the slang, which, thanks to the translator, is rendered as colourfully in English as in the original Italian. But perhaps above all, the strength of Camilleri lies in his evocation of his native island, the narrative power that enables him to capture the most intimate details of traditional life on the island, as well as its colours, its tastes, its smells and – last but by no means least – its amazing cuisine.

Useful websites

The Inspector Montalbano tour from Montelusa to Vigàta
www.sicilytourguides.net/Montalbano_tour.htm

The Inspector Montalbano shooting locations tour.
www.sicilytourguides.net/Montalbano_locations-tour.htm

A complete guide to Agrigento with links to guided tours of its archaeological wonders.
www.valleyofthetemples.com/English.htm

CAMILLERI & MONTALBANO'S SICILY

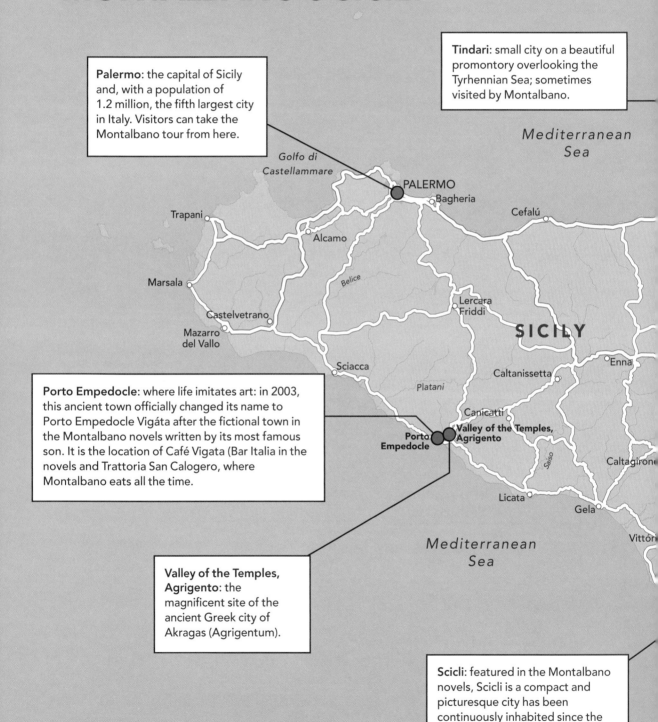

Tindari: small city on a beautiful promontory overlooking the Tyrhennian Sea; sometimes visited by Montalbano.

Palermo: the capital of Sicily and, with a population of 1.2 million, the fifth largest city in Italy. Visitors can take the Montalbano tour from here.

Porto Empedocle: where life imitates art: in 2003, this ancient town officially changed its name to Porto Empedocle Vigáta after the fictional town in the Montalbano novels written by its most famous son. It is the location of Café Vigata (Bar Italia in the novels and Trattoria San Calogero, where Montalbano eats all the time.

Valley of the Temples, Agrigento: the magnificent site of the ancient Greek city of Akragas (Agrigentum).

Scicli: featured in the Montalbano novels, Scicli is a compact and picturesque city has been continuously inhabited since the Bronze Age.

Mediterranean Sea

Golfo di Castellammare

PALERMO
Bagheria
Cefalú
Trapani
Alcamo
Belice
Marsala
Lercara Friddi
SICILY
Castelvetrano
Mazarro del Vallo
Enna
Sciacca
Platani
Caltanissetta
Porto Empedocle
Canicatti
Valley of the Temples, Agrigento
Caltagirone
Saiso
Licata
Gela
Vittór
Mediterranean Sea

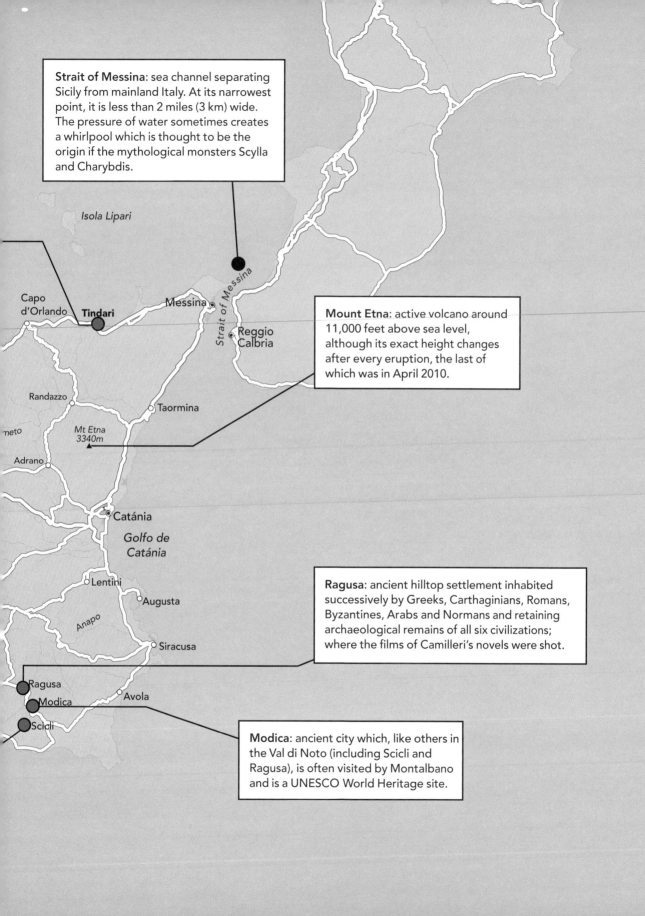

Strait of Messina: sea channel separating Sicily from mainland Italy. At its narrowest point, it is less than 2 miles (3 km) wide. The pressure of water sometimes creates a whirlpool which is thought to be the origin if the mythological monsters Scylla and Charybdis.

Isola Lipari

Capo d'Orlando

Tindari

Messina

Strait of Messina

Reggio Calbria

Mount Etna: active volcano around 11,000 feet above sea level, although its exact height changes after every eruption, the last of which was in April 2010.

Randazzo

Taormina

neto

Mt Etna 3340m

Adrano

Catánia

Golfo de Catánia

Ragusa: ancient hilltop settlement inhabited successively by Greeks, Carthaginians, Romans, Byzantines, Arabs and Normans and retaining archaeological remains of all six civilizations; where the films of Camilleri's novels were shot.

Lentini

Augusta

Anapo

Siracusa

Ragusa

Modica

Avola

Scicli

Modica: ancient city which, like others in the Val di Noto (including Scicli and Ragusa), is often visited by Montalbano and is a UNESCO World Heritage site.

Sarah Weinman

GEORGE PELECANOS'S WASHINGTON DC

When George Pelecanos's first novel, *A Firing Offense*, was published in 1992, it garnered the attention most first crime novels do – very little. Looking back, it's still hard to correlate the smart-mouthed, young-man, first-person viewpoint of Nick Stefanos in that debut with the sober social commentary, doled out in multiple-point perspectives, that infuses Pelecanos's later work.

This stylistic development would certainly have surprised the select few who bought the first edition – there were only 3,000 copies printed by St Martin's Press – hoping to get in on the ground early of an emerging talent in noir fiction. Pelecanos earned his stripes a few books in and proceeded to break free of these early constraints.

On the wrong side of the tracks

From the beginning, Pelecanos trod territory few dared to touch. Washington DC is a power broker's town, with speeches made on Capitol Hill and deals brokered behind the scenes at K Street firms. Civil servants are exiled to the barren, sterile underground malls of Crystal City and spooks of all stripes work in anonymous fortified buildings in

Virginian suburbs. The young, hungry pages for senators and congressmen meet up for drinks and dinner in upper-middle-class neighbourhoods such as DuPont Circle and Adams Morgan. And the tourists show up in throngs to gawp at the White House, the Monument or, if they are serious artistic purveyors, to admire the views on display at the Phillips Museum. That Washington DC, with its surface-sticky sweetness and the cynical, corrupt doings hardly a millimetre deep, is best chronicled in the works of Ross Thomas (1926–95), one of the thriller greats who still hasn't quite had his full due.

Crossing the divide

However, beyond George Pelecanos, never has Thomas, or any other crime writer who called Washington his or her fictional home, looked beyond the city's political echelon. They didn't venture into

Anacostia, where the drug trade turned this southeastern neighbourhood into a virtual disaster zone in the 1990s (things are better now, but the murder rate is still far higher in this part of town than others). They didn't zero in on the basketball courts where men, young and old, white or black, put aside simmering tensions to double-team or dunk over the offence. They didn't juxtapose social programmes with the hidden world of dogfighting; offer an inside look at the laughing machismo of electronics salesmen forever on the prowl – for another sale or another chick – or pan away from the Independence Day Bicentennial to those Superfly-emulating hipsters about to get in big trouble in the wrong places.

But George Pelecanos did. He continues to do so. And even in *A Firing Offense* there were clues to his eventual mission to chronicle

the real Washington DC and provide a window on the working class, the poor, the blacks and, of course, the Greeks to whose community he himself belongs. Already, at just 31 years of age, George Pelecanos had the dichotomy that would dictate his subsequent career nailed in a single paragraph:

We pulled up to Malone's rowhouse on Harvard Street, a darkish block lit by old-style DC lampposts. This was a real

PELECANOS'S PIS

George is of Greek American descent and worked as a teenager in his father's diner.

He once shot his best friend in an accident as a youth.

His PI Nick Stefanos appears in *A Firing Offense* (1992), *Nick's Story* (1993) and *Where the Dead Men Go* (1995).

The investigating duo of Derek Strange and Terry Quinn appear in *Right As Rain* (2001), *Hell to Pay* (2002), *Soul Circus* (2003) and *Hard Revolution* (2004).

neighborhood, a mix of Latins, blacks, and pioneer whites. There was just enough of a violent undercurrent here to keep the aspiring-to-hipness young professionals away and on the fringe of their beloved Adams Morgan, which had become an artificially eclectic mess of condos, 'interesting' ethnic restaurants, Eurotrash discos, and parking lots.

The music man

In *The Night Gardener* (2006), Pelecanos captures the essence of 1985, when the US capital was on the brink of an eruption caused by a crack cocaine boom – which he chronicled in greater detail in *The Sweet Forever* (1998), set a year later – and when young teenagers were being murdered with startling frequency in the poorer parts of the city:

> Across town, at the same time the father cried out over his daughter's body, young Washingtonians were in their homes, tuning in to Miami Vice, doing lines of coke as they watched the exploits of two hip undercover cops and their quest to take down the kingpins of the drug trade. Others read bestselling novels by Tom Clancy, John Jakes, Stephen King,

and Peter Straub, or sat in bars and talked about the fading playoff prospects of the Jay Schroeder-led Washington Redskins. Others watched rented VCR tapes of Beverly Hills Cop and Code of Silence, the top picks that week at Erol's Video Club, or barely sweated to Jane Fonda's Workout, or went out and caught the latest Michael J. Fox at the Circle Avalon or Caligula at the Georgetown. Mr Mister and Midge Ure were in town, playing the clubs.

> As these movers of the Reagan generation entertained themselves west of Rock Creek Park and in the suburbs, detectives and techs worked assiduously at the crime scene at 33rd and E, in the neighborhood of Greenway, in Southeast DC.

Pelecanos's world constantly bumps up against the moneyed class but never quite breaches that unseen divide. His characters, be they cops or drug dealers, crooked or honourable, or somewhere in between, take a spin along Georgia Avenue looking for adventure, running from problems or crashing headlong into truths they thought they could avoid.

It's a world, as has often been pointed out, that comes with a soundtrack. Pelecanos's characters listen to Curtis

The Capitol, seat of the US Supreme Court, the Senate and the House of Representatives.

'I WANT TO LEAVE A RECORD. HOPEFULLY IF YOU READ A BOOK SET IN 2004 AFTER I'M DEAD AND GONE, IT WILL PROVIDE YOU WITH AN ACCURATE PICTURE OF THE WAY DC WAS IN 2004' – GEORGE PELECANOS, GUARDIAN (2008)

Mayfield (one of the author's favourite soul men) while tapping their fingers on the dashboard in souped-up 1970s-era cars, or groove to Freddie Fender's 'Wild Side of Life' just before hitting the hotel bars for a night on the town. Whatever the decade, whatever the locale, Pelecanos has a playlist ready for mixing – and invariably it includes a little bit of Miles Davis, too.

But always, Pelecanos's work is a love song to his home city, the one he's vowed never to leave. Love is complicated, never blind, and doesn't whitewash, and Pelecanos's brand of city love makes sure the reader knows how much wounds cut deep and that people feel pain and suffer consequences. Washington is the one constant of his work as it's moved from the small world of the early Stefanos novels to the larger, bat-swinging reach of The DC Quartet – *The Big Blowdown* (1996); *King Suckerman* (1997); *The Sweet Forever* (1998) and *Shame the Devil* (2000) – to the socially conscious (though somewhat dismal) contemporary trilogy featuring private eyes Derek Strange and Terry Quinn, to the post-*Night Gardener* opuses, honed and toned after years of working on hit US-televison series *The Wire* alongside crime-story masters David Simon, Richard Price and Dennis Lehane.

The rise of Little Voice

As he ages, George Pelecanos seems less concerned with making grand, sweeping statements about Washington. Instead, there's a subtler examination of specific themes, like father-son relationships or how young men are too often designated as society throwaways, placed against the necessary, but not show-stealing, backdrop of the city. Where The DC Quartet, with its bravura and pizzazz, makes a point that the 'other Washington' merits examination in the same way that James Ellroy and David Peace mined Los Angeles and Yorkshire for their respective criminal quartets, Pelecanos is now more content to spend time, as he does in *The Way Home* (2009), describing the inner conflicts and moral dilemmas of his characters. He's also moving away even more from the constraints of genre conventions towards more literary examinations of how one act creates a domino effect upon family, society and race. In *The Way Home*, the Flynn family – comprised of ex-cop turned construction- firm owner Thomas, his born-again wife Amanda and their rather wayward, pot-smoking son Chris – live in the middle-class northwest DC neighbourhood of Friendship Heights, a result of Flynn's hard work and desire to give his son a better, college-bound life. So no wonder,

'GEORGE PELECANOS IS PERHAPS AMERICA'S GREATEST CRIME WRITER' – STEPHEN KING, NOVELIST

PELECANOS ON SCREEN

Between 2002 and 2008, George Pelecanos worked in various capacities on 17 episodes of *The Wire*, the acclaimed 5-season HBO TV series set in Baltimore, Maryland. Later he co-produced the first three episodes of *The Pacific* (2010), a 10-part TV series about the experiences of three US Marines in the Pacific during World War II.

 ## IN FILM

Executive producer, with Jim Pedas, Bill Durkin and Ted Pedas, of:

Joel and Ethan Coen's *Blood Simple* (1984) starring John Getz and Frances McDormand.

Raising Arizona (1987), with Nicolas Cage, Holly Hunter, John Goodman and Frances McDormand.

Miller's Crossing (1990), featuring Gabriel Byrne, John Turturro and Albert Finney.

Caught (1996), directed by Robert M. Young and starring Edward James Olmos and Maria Conchita Alonso.

Shops in Friendship Heights.

when Chris blows it and ends up in juvenile detention at the end of his teenage years, it's a major setback for the whole family. A few years later, Flynn takes stock of his son's prospects:

'Chris is

twenty-six. No college, time in prison, his days spent on his knees laying carpet…. Thirty-five grand a year, tops'.

The supporting players in Pelecanos's later works, too, get their moments to convey the division between classes and neighbourhoods. In *The Way Home*, one well-to-do woman's habit of ordering the same dish (with the same exact tip) for lunch at a Thai restaurant in Wheaton, off

University Boulevard – 'where nothing was upscale and fast-food wrappers and cigarette butts littered the streets' – infuriates her young server:

She couldn't stand this weathered shrew with the stupid haircut, who would never round up the tip one penny to an even one-fifty, who asked about her family but never really listened to the reply or looked into her eyes. But this is what you put up with every day. It was work.

shrug off entire swaths of generations or classes as hopeless. As one of the young men on the road to redemption says:

'They talk about the negative impact on the community when you let jailed boys out and put them under supervision, But when you lock up kids without looking at other alternatives, you destroy communities. There's gonna be some failures, naturally. But there's gonna be some success stories, too' (The Way Home).

Capital chronicler

These casual moments are the backbone of why human behaviour goes terribly awry – but they are also why there's good reason to hope. The Washington that the moneyed classes are too busy or blind to pay attention to is easily dismissed as a lost cause, still rendered a victim because of high crime rates, drug problems and poverty. Yet George Pelecanos refuses to see Washington as a lost cause, and won't

It is this viewpoint, ultimately, that marks George Pelecanos as the bard of Washington, the font of a wellspring of stories about real people facing real problems that tell readers what they desperately need to know, not what they think they already know. And thus he is set fair to achieve his stated ambition to provide a record of how Washington – not just the political centre, but the whole city – was during his lifetime.

USEFUL WEBSITES

Washington DC TV and Movie Sites Tour
www.destination-store.com/tour/washington+dc/washingtondctvandmoviesitestour

Official website of the American football team based at FedExField, Landover, Maryland
www.redskins.com/gen/index.jsp

Civic guide to George Pelecanos's home town of Silver Spring, Maryland, a suburb of Washington
www.discoverourtown.com/MD/Silver%20Spring/Attractions-1673.html

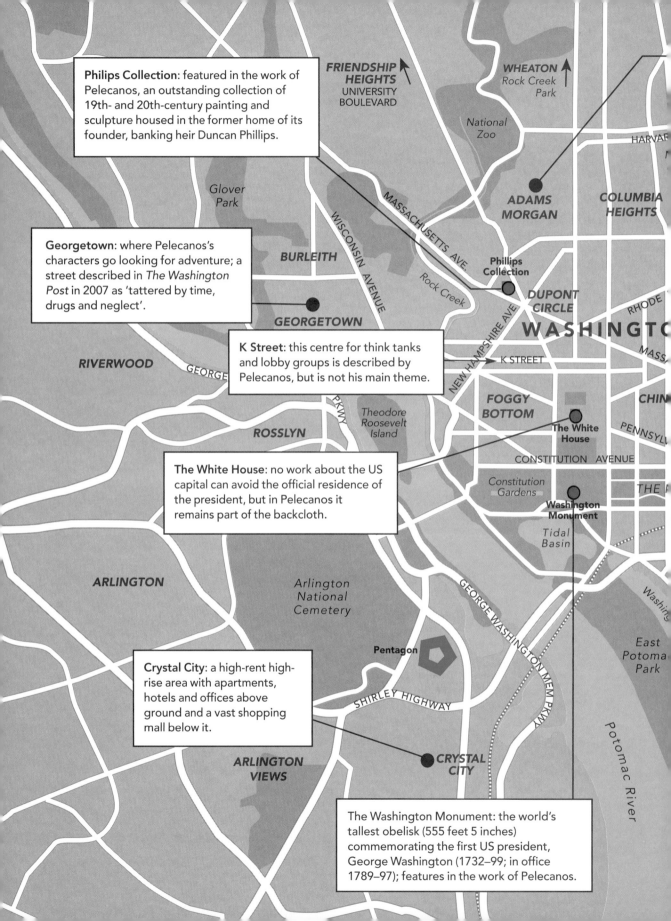

Philips Collection: featured in the work of Pelecanos, an outstanding collection of 19th- and 20th-century painting and sculpture housed in the former home of its founder, banking heir Duncan Phillips.

Georgetown: where Pelecanos's characters go looking for adventure; a street described in *The Washington Post* in 2007 as 'tattered by time, drugs and neglect'.

K Street: this centre for think tanks and lobby groups is described by Pelecanos, but is not his main theme.

The White House: no work about the US capital can avoid the official residence of the president, but in Pelecanos it remains part of the backcloth.

Crystal City: a high-rent high-rise area with apartments, hotels and offices above ground and a vast shopping mall below it.

The Washington Monument: the world's tallest obelisk (555 feet 5 inches) commemorating the first US president, George Washington (1732–99; in office 1789–97); features in the work of Pelecanos.

FRIENDSHIP HEIGHTS
UNIVERSITY BOULEVARD

WHEATON
Rock Creek Park

National Zoo

HARVAR

Glover Park

ADAMS MORGAN

COLUMBIA HEIGHTS

WISCONSIN AVENUE

BURLEITH

MASSACHUSETTS AVE.

Rock Creek

Phillips Collection

DUPONT CIRCLE

RHODE

WASHINGTO

MASS

GEORGETOWN

RIVERWOOD

GEORGE

NEW HAMPSHIRE AVE.

K STREET

FOGGY BOTTOM

CHIN

PKWY

Theodore Roosevelt Island

ROSSLYN

The White House

PENNSYLV

CONSTITUTION AVENUE

Constitution Gardens

THE

ARLINGTON

Arlington National Cemetery

Washington Monument

Tidal Basin

GEORGE WASHINGTON MEM PKWY

Washin

East Potoma Park

Pentagon

SHIRLEY HIGHWAY

ARLINGTON VIEWS

CRYSTAL CITY

Potomac River

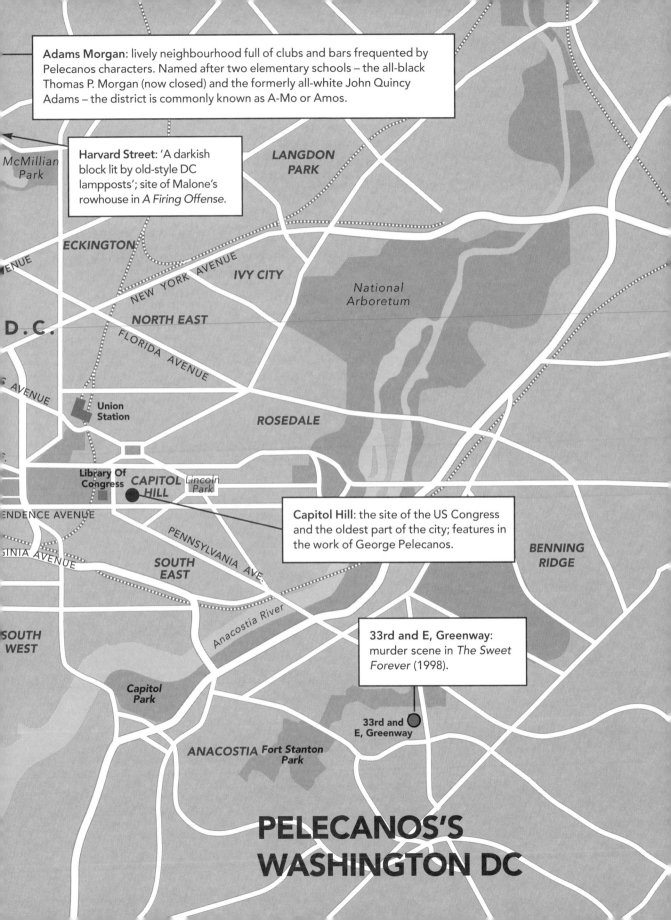

Adams Morgan: lively neighbourhood full of clubs and bars frequented by Pelecanos characters. Named after two elementary schools – the all-black Thomas P. Morgan (now closed) and the formerly all-white John Quincy Adams – the district is commonly known as A-Mo or Amos.

Harvard Street: 'A darkish block lit by old-style DC lampposts'; site of Malone's rowhouse in *A Firing Offense*.

McMillian Park

LANGDON PARK

ECKINGTON

AVENUE

NEW YORK AVENUE

IVY CITY

NORTH EAST

National Arboretum

D.C.

FLORIDA AVENUE

Union Station

ROSEDALE

Library Of Congress

CAPITOL HILL

Lincoln Park

Capitol Hill: the site of the US Congress and the oldest part of the city; features in the work of George Pelecanos.

BENNING RIDGE

ENDENCE AVENUE

PENNSYLVANIA AVE.

GINIA AVENUE

SOUTH EAST

Anacostia River

33rd and E, Greenway: murder scene in *The Sweet Forever* (1998).

SOUTH WEST

Capitol Park

33rd and E, Greenway

ANACOSTIA *Fort Stanton Park*

PELECANOS'S WASHINGTON DC

Barry Forshaw

PETER JAMES & ROY GRACE'S BRIGHTON

In literary terms, criminal Brighton was once Graham Greene (1904–91). In the 21st century, Greene's heir apparent is Peter James.

For all that it is a snapshot of a vanished era (Britain in the 1930s) and a celebrated portrait of a quintessential seaside town, Graham Greene's *Brighton Rock* (1938) remains one of the most trenchant evocations of urban criminality ever written. Greene's main preoccupations were, of course, guilt (both Catholic and secular), and he was eternally concerned with the worst excesses of human behaviour. In this book, he created one of the most fascinating criminal protagonists in the teenage gangster Pinkie, bloodily brandishing a razor in the dark backstreets behind tourist Brighton. Pinkie is a monster, struggling in his barely literate manner with the Catholic faith, which grants him no comfort and promises only a grim posthumous retribution. Greene is nonpareil on both the specifics of gang warfare in Brighton and the geography of the town itself, and the savage murder of one of Pinkie's victims in the early chapters establishes the character's utter amorality. However, contrasted with malevolent Pinkie is the sympathetic Ida Arnold, overblown and brassy but kind-hearted, who decides to exact justice for the killing of a man she met briefly. Non-believers are sometimes daunted by the reputation of Greene's work for espousing Catholic values, but he is never a proselytizer for the faith.

A murky past

These days, our guide to the favourite weekend getaway of Londoners is the writer Peter James. James first made a mark thanks to his great success as a horror novelist, but his more recent career as a writer of adroitly written and highly compelling crime novels has – perhaps unfairly – eclipsed his earlier work. (The author has said that he was, in any case, always essentially a crime writer – even in the days of his earlier acclaim.) Interestingly, his horror novels have resurfaced, disingenuously repackaged to appeal to his new crime-fiction audience.

To the outsider, Brighton, where Peter James was born and raised, is a hip, beautiful seaside city, but it has a long history of darkness – right back to its roots as a smugglers' village. In Regency times

(1811–20) it gained a reputation as a fashionable bathing resort, but in 1841, when the London to Brighton railway line opened, criminals flooded down from London, finding rich pickings and a much pleasanter environment than in their native city. They brought cockfighting, prostitution, pickpockets, muggers, smugglers, burglars, gangs and protection rackets. Simultaneously, with the railway enabling quick access from London, many wealthy Londoners brought their mistresses to Brighton and it became known as the key place for 'dirty weekends'.

In the early 1930s, after a series of dismembered female bodies was discovered in different left-luggage lockers, Brighton became known first as 'Queen of Slaughtering Places' and then acquired the soubriquet of both 'the crime capital of England' and 'the murder capital of Europe'. It is a reputation that it has never been able to shake off.

A criminal paradise

As befits the only town in England where a serving Chief Constable has ever been murdered (Henry Solomon in 1844), three past Chief Constables of Sussex Police have (according to James) noted that Brighton is the favoured place in the UK for first-division criminals to live. The reasons are clear: firstly, it has major seaports on either side – Shoreham and Newhaven, perfect for importing drugs and exporting stolen cars, antiques and cash. Secondly, it has a lot of escape routes, very important to all criminals: it has the Channel ports and Eurotunnel relatively nearby,

PETER JAMES

Before his popular Roy Grace crime series (soon to be filmed), Peter James had a highly successful career as horror writer with such books as *Host* and *Prophecy* - all now reissued.

He is also a successful film producer, with such credits as the Al Pacino version of Shakespeare's *The Merchant of Venice* under his belt.

James's mother, Cornelia, was a glovemaker to Queen Elizabeth II.

James is a fan and owner of vintage racing cars and actually holds a racing driver's licence.

James is a die-hard fan of Biggles.

as well as Gatwick Airport just 25 minutes away. London is 50 minutes by train. It is the town with the largest number of antique shops in the UK – perfect for laundering stolen goods and cash. It has a wealthy young middle-class population combined with the largest gay community in the UK, two universities and a huge number of nightclubs, all providing a big market for recreational drugs. It also has a large, transient population, which makes it hard for the police to keep tabs on villains.

James has noted that (to his good fortune) Brighton has not been over-covered by other writers. Patrick Hamilton, in *The West Pier* (1952), and Greene (*Brighton Rock* is James's favourite novel) are the only writers to have delved into its criminal underbelly. Yet playwright Noël Coward (1899–1973) spotted it: 'Ah, dear Brighton – piers, queers and racketeers!' And so did its late resident, the columnist, novelist and playwright Keith Waterhouse (1929–2009): 'Brighton has the air of a town that is permanently helping the police with their inquiries'.

The Palace Pier, Brighton.

An unusual tourist guide

James's books featuring the urbane and resourceful copper Roy Grace (their considerable merits as crime fiction aside) are an unbeatable guide to the city and its environs. Grace is a strongly realized character, developed (in subtle and unspectacular fashion) by his creator from book to book, and his verisimilitude is shored up by James's close relations with the real Brighton police. Grace's criss-crossing of the area makes him the perfect conduit to Brighton and its environs.

With Grace, one has the pleasure of discovering some of the area's less noted attractions. For example, *Dead Simple* (2005), the first Roy Grace novel, takes the reader to one of the detective's favourite buildings. Grace travels up a steep hill to All Saints Church in Patcham village. It is a classic early English parish church – intimate, simple, with unadorned grey stonework, a small tower, a fine stained-glass window behind the altar and tombstones going back centuries in the overgrown graveyard in front and along the sides.

In *Looking Good Dead* (2006), one of the strongest of James's novels, we learn about the route of Grace's morning run – and some aspects of Brighton. His run takes him straight down to the Kingsway, a wide dual carriageway running along Hove seafront. On one side are houses, which give way in half a mile or so to continuous mansion blocks and hotels – some modern, some Victorian, some Regency – that continue the full length of the seafront. Opposite are two small boating lagoons and a playground, lawns, and then the promenade with stretches of beach huts, and the pebble beaches beyond. Just over a mile to the east is the wreck of the old West Pier. Grace loves being out early at the weekend, feeling as if he has the whole city to himself. The tide is out and he can see the orb of the rising sun already well up in the sky. A man walks, far out on the mudflats, swinging a metal detector. A container ship, barely more defined than a smudge, sits on the faraway horizon, looking motionless.

Grace's six-mile (10 km) run is to the start of the marina and back again. For the final mile he always turns inland, running up the busy shopping thoroughfare of Church Road in Hove to an open-all-hours grocery store to pick up some milk and a newspaper.

It is also in *Looking Good Dead* that we learn about Grace's own modest three-bedroom semi in a street that leads directly down to the Kingsway. We also hear of one of the constant highlights of his childhood: the Palace Pier. The big lure of the pier for Roy as a child had been the attractions, particularly the bumper cars and the ghost train, and most of all the old wooden glass-fronted slot machines that contained moving tableaux. He had one favourite, and was always cajoling his father into giving him more pennies for the slot. It was a haunted house, and for a full minute, as gears cranked and pullies whined, doors would fly open, lights would go on and off, and all kinds of skeletons and ghosts would appear, as well as Death itself, a hooded figure all in black holding a scythe.

Double lives

Not Dead Enough (2007), with the series now fully in its stride, has Grace

'I'M DEEPLY FASCINATED BY THE
MANY FACETS OF POLICE WORK, AND
PARTICULARLY HOW IT IS CHANGING
WITH THE TIMES, AND MY RESEARCH
FOR THE GRACE NOVELS TAKES ME
THROUGH ALMOST ALL OF IT'
– PETER JAMES

investigating the grotesque murder of a member of Brighton's social elite, Katie Bishop. Her husband, Brian, appears to be in the clear – he was in another town at the time, sound asleep. But Grace begins to suspect the presence of a doppelgänger: is someone else – nigh-identical to Bishop – involved? As in his previous cases, Grace's diligent exhumation of murky secrets soon demonstrates that the Bishops' outwardly settled lives had darker corners.

Featured in the novel is Sussex House. Like many of the products of the early postwar building boom, Sussex House, a sleek, rectangular two-storey building, is not ageing particularly well. The original architect had clearly been influenced by Art Deco, and from some angles the place looks like the superstructure of a small, tired cruise liner. Originally constructed in the early 1950s as a hospital for contagious diseases, at that time it had

occupied a commanding, isolated position on a hill on the outskirts of Brighton, just beyond the suburb of Hollingbury, and the architect could no doubt have seen his vision in its full, detached glory.

The areas around Brighton afford some spectacular sights. The celebrated view from the South Downs features in *Not Dead Enough*. The views from up here give the impression of standing on the top of the world. To the south is the whole vista of Brighton and Hove – the rooftops, the cluster of high-rises around the Brighton end of the seafront, the single chimney stack of Shoreham power station and the normally grey water of the English Channel beyond looking as blue as the Mediterranean. Farther to the southwest, one can make out the silhouette of the genteel seaside town of Worthing, fading away, like so many of its elderly inhabitants, into the distant haze. To the north stretches a view virtually unbroken, apart from a few pylons, of green downland grass and fields of wheat, some freshly harvested with square or cylindrical bales laid out like pieces in a vast board game, others criss-crossed by combine harvesters looking as small as Dinky toys.

Dead Man's Footsteps (2008) is one of the most visual of the author's novels. But it's a

SCREEN & STAGE CONNECTIONS

Although the Roy Grace novels have yet to be transferred to television or cinema – much to the surprise of fans who regard the books as some of the most filmable of modern detective series – author Peter James has strong links with the screen: he has produced more than 20 movies, most famously *The Merchant of Venice* (2004), starring Al Pacino as Shylock and Jeremy Irons as Antonio.

 IN FILM

A lifelong admirer of the adventure stories of Capt. W.E. Johns (1893–1968) about RAF pilot James Bigglesworth, Peter James was also associate producer of the film *Biggles* (1986) with Neil Dickson in the title role. The novelist has also directed several stage plays, including Harold Pinter's *Landscape* and *A Slight Ache* for the Royal Shakespeare Company in London.

The classic film version of *Brighton Rock* (1947) was directed by Roy Boulting and starred Richard Attenborough as Pinkie. The local council opposed the project on the grounds that it would bring the town into disrepute.

Trafalgar Street, Brighton.

safe bet that no television adaptation can match James's skills on the page. During the chaos after the terrorist bombings of New York on 11 September 2001, a shady Brighton businessman has taken advantage of events to disappear and start a new life in another country. But when the remains of a woman's body are discovered in a storm drain, Roy Grace finds himself on a dangerous quest across the globe. Closer to home, however, the book takes Grace to Brighton's Pelham Square, a small, elegant square of Regency terraced houses with a railed-off park in the centre. The benches near the Trafalgar Street entrance have always been a popular lunch spot for local office workers on fine days. Now (as James notes), with the workplace smoking ban, they seem even more popular.

'ROSE: PEOPLE CHANGE.
IDA: I'VE NEVER CHANGED. IT'S LIKE THOSE STICKS OF ROCK. BITE ONE ALL THE WAY DOWN, YOU'LL STILL READ BRIGHTON. THAT'S HUMAN NATURE' – BRIGHTON ROCK (FILM, 1947)

The sea with the hills behind

James's narrative skills are at full throttle in *Dead Tomorrow* (2009). A body is found off the coast of Sussex, mutilated to remove its organs. Other macabre discoveries ensue. While this is happening, young Caitlin Beckett is in a Brighton hospital, desperately in need of a liver transplant. Her mother is convinced she has to help her daughter by going to secret sources, while Grace, searching for the killers, runs into sinister Eastern European child traffickers.

In this book we learn that Roy Grace's favourite walk is underneath the chalk cliffs east from Rottingdean. As a child it was almost a Sunday ritual with his parents; he loved the sense of drama, particularly on rough days, when there was a blustery wind and the tide was high, and occasionally the sea surged right up the beach and sent spray and pebbles crashing over the low stone wall. And the signs that warned of the danger of falling rocks added to that drama. Grace loves the smells here too, the salty tang and the seaweed and the occasional whiff of rotting fish that would be gone in an instant. And the sight of cargo ships and tankers out on the horizon, and sometimes yachts closer in.

Dead Tomorrow focuses sharply on the local topography. James observes that the city of Brighton and Hove straddles several low hills, with Whitehawk sprawled over one of the highest. A council development of terraced and semi-detached houses and low- and high-rise blocks of flats, started in the 1920s to rehouse residents of the city-centre slums, Whitehawk has long – and somewhat unjustly – had a name for violence and crime. A few of its warrens of streets, many with fabulous views across the city and the sea, are inhabited and dominated by some of the city's roughest crime families, and their reputation has infected that of everyone else on the estate.

Should any TV series featuring Roy Grace be commissioned, we will be able to experience on screen the sights so lovingly evoked by Peter James in his striking series of books. Yet it is the author's descriptive skill that affords most pleasure – and the sequence of novels (thankfully) continues to showcase that skill along with James's powerful storytelling gifts.

USEFUL WEBSITES

A choice of conducted walks, including one with a *Brighton Rock* theme.
www.brightonrockwalks.co.uk

The official tourist guide to the city, with up-to-date information about what's on and where to stay.
www.visitbrighton.com

Peter James's website
www.peterjames.com

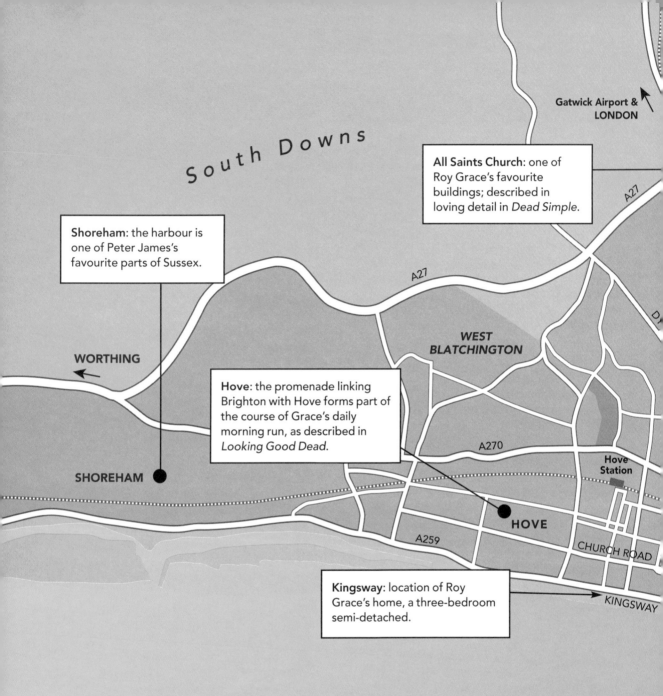

Gatwick Airport & LONDON

All Saints Church: one of Roy Grace's favourite buildings; described in loving detail in *Dead Simple*.

Shoreham: the harbour is one of Peter James's favourite parts of Sussex.

S o u t h   D o w n s

A27

A27

WEST BLATCHINGTON

WORTHING

Hove: the promenade linking Brighton with Hove forms part of the course of Grace's daily morning run, as described in *Looking Good Dead*.

A270

Hove Station

SHOREHAM

HOVE

A259

CHURCH ROAD

Kingsway: location of Roy Grace's home, a three-bedroom semi-detached.

KINGSWAY

English Channel

JAMES & GRACE'S BRIGHTON

West Pier: now derelict, even in its heyday this pier lacked the appeal of its eastern neighbour, but it did provide the title of a work by Patrick Hamilton described by Graham Greene as 'the best novel about Brighton'. Peter James said: 'I pray the West Pier will be brought back to life'.

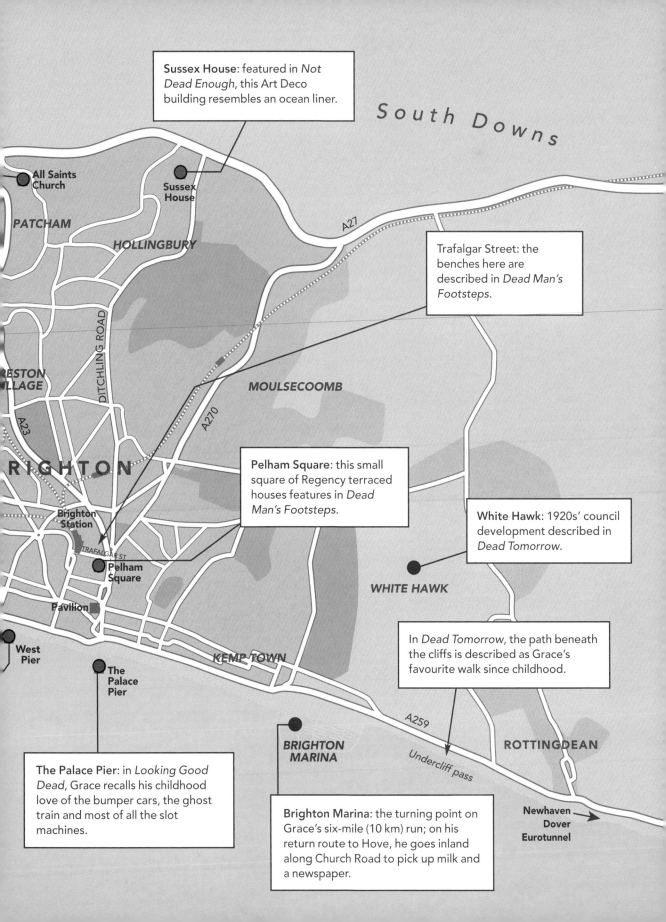

Sussex House: featured in *Not Dead Enough*, this Art Deco building resembles an ocean liner.

S o u t h   D o w n s

All Saints Church

Sussex House

PATCHAM

HOLLINGBURY

A27

Trafalgar Street: the benches here are described in *Dead Man's Footsteps*.

DITCHLING ROAD

RESTON ILLAGE

A23

A270

MOULSECOOMB

Pelham Square: this small square of Regency terraced houses features in *Dead Man's Footsteps*.

White Hawk: 1920s' council development described in *Dead Tomorrow*.

RIGHTON

Brighton Station

TRAFALGAR ST

Pelham Square

Pavilion

WHITE HAWK

In *Dead Tomorrow*, the path beneath the cliffs is described as Grace's favourite walk since childhood.

West Pier

The Palace Pier

KEMP TOWN

A259

Undercliff pass

ROTTINGDEAN

The Palace Pier: in *Looking Good Dead*, Grace recalls his childhood love of the bumper cars, the ghost train and most of all the slot machines.

BRIGHTON MARINA

Brighton Marina: the turning point on Grace's six-mile (10 km) run; on his return route to Hove, he goes inland along Church Road to pick up milk and a newspaper.

Newhaven Dover Eurotunnel

Maxim Jakubowski

JAMES LEE BURKE & DAVE ROBICHEAUX'S NEW ORLEANS

If you are seeking atmosphere, whether in real life or fiction, New Orleans seldom disappoints. It is a city unlike any other. Seductive architecture, smells and fragrances, a marked contrast between affluence and poverty, a climate that sticks to your skin, a sense of history that permeates every single street and alley, the lethal combination of spice, food and heavy drinking literally litters the air alongside the sounds of jazz, zydeco, the blues and country music.

New Orleans lends itself like few other urban sprawls to the romance of noir fiction.

A rich and varied past

Paradoxically, New Orleans is the least American of all US cities. It was initially colonized by the Spanish, owned by the French, and then occupied over the passing centuries by a subtle blend of Acadians from Canada, followed by waves of economic immigration from the Caribbean, Latin America, Ireland and other parts of the compass, as well as attracting a high proportion of artists and writers enticed by

its sheen of Southern abandon, sin and easy, laid-back living. Of strategic importance to the Southern Confederacy during the American Civil War (1861–65), New Orleans later became one of America's largest ports, thanks to the dominating presence

of the Mississippi River, and throughout its history it has been synonymous with both beauty and violence as the haves and the have-nots have danced a seesawing waltz across its lush and often quaint streets. Successive hurricanes have had a terrible impact on New Orleans, with Katrina in 2005 almost bringing the city to its knees. The damage it wreaked is still vivid in the memory and stands out like scars across many of the city's districts.

It's against such a background that James Lee Burke introduced the character of Dave Robicheaux in *The Neon Rain* in 1987. Robicheaux is a recovering alcoholic and Vietnam veteran who was once a detective with the New Orleans Police Homicide Department. He resigned following a particularly harrowing case during which he also met Bootsie, a social worker who would become his next wife, and he later operates as a sheriff's deputy in New Iberia in nearby Bayou country (Burke himself is based in New Iberia, although he also spends part of the year in Montana). Dave is a man with a trigger temper who, literally, lives with the ghosts of his past, with

supernatural elements and voices from beyond the grave often conversing with him in his dreams or even his waking state, both abetting and confusing his investigations. As such, he is one of the most haunted characters in modern crime fiction, a beautifully sketched human being full of frailties; he is emotionally conflicted, torn between family and friendship and a deep-seated desire to do the right thing and redeem himself by avenging the

DAVE ROBICHEAUX

Favourite drink:
Ice-cold Dr Pepper

Wives:
1st: Annie (deceased),
2nd: Bootsie

Daughter:
Alafair (adopted)

Past activity:
Vietnam veteran

Sidekick:
Cletus Purcel

innocent victims whom he so regularly stumbles across in his righteous path.

Homage to Don Quixote

Robicheaux's unorthodox style and inner turmoil, which are ultimately responsible for the failure of his first marriage and the ensuing murder of his second wife, combined with, later, the death by illness of his third spouse, make him something of a brooding loner. This is particularly true following his departure from the sheriff's office at the end of *Last Car to Elysian Fields* (2003), since when he has been a maverick do-righter, albeit assisted by his ex-NOPD cohort, 'big man' Clete Purcell. Purcell is now a private investigator in New Iberia, and one of the most politically incorrect sleuths on the map. Burke sees the two men as descendants of Don Quixote and his sidekick Sancho Panza, loyally devoted to each other and both in turns regularly tilting at windmills, whether they be political corruption, racism or the local Mafia. On another occasion, Burke compared his hero not with the main character in the work of Spanish novelist Miguel Cervantes (1547–1616) but with an older English model:

> *Robicheaux is the Everyman from the morality plays of the Renaissance. He tries to give voice to those who have none. He is possessed of an awareness of events that will occur, but he can't control the outcome.*

Robicheaux the gourmet

However, beyond the angst, the blood and the fury, Burke is first and foremost a Louisiana writer and evokes the magic of the place like no other. Robicheaux is constantly popping in and out of local eateries and bars throughout his journeys, both in the big city and the bayou-hugging

'IF YOU PUT SOMEBODY ON A CRACK PIPE AND GIVE THEM A 9MM BARETTA, YOU DON'T HAVE TO BE A ROCKET SCIENTIST TO FIGURE OUT WHAT'S GOING TO HAPPEN NEXT' – JAMES LEE BURKE

151

James Lee Burke &
Dave Robicheaux's New Orleans

country roads, and following in his footsteps can prove a variable feast of the senses. A popular oyster bar Robicheaux visits on several occasions throughout the novels in the series is The Pearl, on Iberville, just off Canal Street, where Dave always enjoys a beer and some oysters on the half shell. The owners of the bar have, as a result, now devoted part of a wall in the eating area of the bar to copies of book covers and the pages in which The Pearl appears, not only in Burke's novels but also in the work of other authors who have followed in his footsteps (including myself, as I insisted on having a character walk into the place in a short story with the unashamed intention of landing myself on that wall; it worked). Just a few blocks away, also on Iberville, stands the legendary Acme Oyster Bar, again immortalized not just by Burke but also many others. But then New Orleans is the sort of place where eateries become the stuff of legend.

In the words of Burke:

A person cannot pass up the beignets in the French Market. We used to go to mass early in the morning and go across the street from St Louis Cathedral. They have 12-step groups for beignet addiction, because you simply cannot eat just one of them. It's difficult enough to stop at two dozen – Daily Telegraph (2008).

By far the most celebrated beignet outlet in the French Quarter is the world-famous Café du Monde (*see image, page 150*) on Jackson Square, a most colourful area of the city, where musicians and fortune-tellers abound. As he added in the same interview:

Jackson Square is a medieval panorama rather than a Renaissance kind of place – you get people on unicycles, jugglers, musicians playing for free there in front of the cathedral – it's really out of Victor Hugo's portrayal of Europe.

Celebrating the exotic

The exotic beauty and inescapable seediness of New Orleans become a sensual fulcrum for Robicheaux and his fellow fictional travellers. Here, in *Dixie City Jam* (1994), he ambles through the French Quarter at the break of day:

The streets were still deep in shadow and the water from the previous night's rain leaked from the wood shutters down the pastel sides of the buildings, and you could smell coffee and fresh-baked bread in the small grocery stores and the dank, cool odour of wild spearmint and old brick in the passageways. Every scrolled-iron balcony along the street seemed overgrown with a tangle of potted roses, bougainvillea, azaleas, and flaming hibiscus, and the moment could be so perfect that you felt you had stepped inside an Utrillo painting.

Beyond the Vieux Carré, as the French Quarter is also known, lie the lush opulence and antebellum mansions of New Orleans' Garden District. The Garden District can still be reached on the fabled surviving tramway, which is still one of the Crescent City's (so named because of the course taken through it by the Mississippi River) most favoured modes of transport. Burke again, this time in *Heaven's Prisoners* (1988):

> At one time New Orleans was covered with streetcar tracks, but now only the St. Charles streetcar remains in service. It runs a short distance down Canal, the full length of St. Charles through the Garden District, past Loyola and Tulane and Audubon Park, then along what is probably one of the most beautiful streets in the world. St. Charles and the esplanade in its center are covered by a canopy of enormous oak trees and lined on each side by old, iron-scrolled brick homes and antebellum mansions with columned porches and pike-fenced

yards with hibiscus, blooming myrtle and oleander, bamboo and giant philodendron.

This is a journey Robicheaux repeats often, moving from the bustle of the French Quarter, with its hundreds of restaurants and ten times as many bars, towards the quiet, residential haven of civilization and corruption hidden behind closed doors, before regularly crossing the Mississippi and finding himself in the industrial suburb of Algiers, home of criminals, dark alleys and festering nests of crime.

Feeding the senses

New Iberia, where Robicheaux now tends his bait-shop business between cases (an imaginary company, of course, but you can purchase Robicheaux tee-shirts and fishing paraphernalia on Burke's website www.jamesleeburke.com) is two hours away from New Orleans and feels like a throwback to an earlier, genteel era away from the frenzy of the city. Once again, Burke punctuates Robicheaux' home life there with regular visits to local restaurants and often lyrically evokes the local food with as much talent as he has for landscape. Life in Louisiana can be particularly hedonistic and a feast for the senses. From the *Daily Telegraph* again:

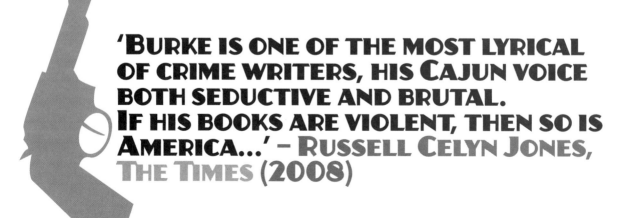

'BURKE IS ONE OF THE MOST LYRICAL OF CRIME WRITERS, HIS CAJUN VOICE BOTH SEDUCTIVE AND BRUTAL. IF HIS BOOKS ARE VIOLENT, THEN SO IS AMERICA...' – RUSSELL CELYN JONES, THE TIMES (2008)

NEW ORLEANS IN FILM

The Crescent City is a popular film destination. The following are just some of the classic movies that were shot or set there:

 IN FILM

Panic in the Streets (1950), directed by Elia Kazan, with Richard Widmark, Paul Douglas and Barbara Bel Geddes.

A Streetcar Named Desire (1951), based on the play by Tennessee Williams; directed by Kazan and starring Vivien Leigh and Marlon Brando.

Suddenly, Last Summer (1959), directed by Joseph L. Mankiewicz, with Elizabeth Taylor, Katharine Hepburn and Montgomery Clift.

Walk on the Wild Side (1962), directed by Edward Dmytryk, with Laurence Harvey, Capucine and Jane Fonda.

The Cincinnatti Kid (1965), directed by Norman Jewison and starring Steve McQueen, Ann-Margret and Karl Malden.

Easy Rider (1969), directed by Dennis Hopper, who also co-starred with Peter Fonda.

Pretty Baby (1978), directed by Louis Malle, with Brooke Shields, Keith Carradine and Susan Sarandon.

Tightrope (1984), directed by Richard Tuggle and starring Clint Eastwood.

The Big Easy (1986), directed by Jim McBride, with Dennis Quaid, Ellen Barkin.

Angel Heart (1987), directed by Alan Parker, with Mickey Rourke and Robert De Niro

The Pelican Brief (1993), directed by Alan J. Pakula, with Julia Roberts and Denzel Washington

The Runaway Jury (2003), directed by Gary Fleder, with John Cusack, Gene Hackman and Dustin Hoffman.

Where to eat in New Iberia? Cajun food is like the music, it's hard to find bad. Etouffee, gumbo and all the traditional things like dirty rice – it's the best seafood I have ever tasted. The Patio is a great spot, or Clementine's, or the Little River Inn in the old Tabasco factory …. You should also try Mulate's Cajun Restaurant in Breaux Bridge. Back in the 1960s, when all the vice was run by the mob, that was a gambling joint and all the bartenders there were sheriffs.

One of Robicheaux's most regular eating and drinking haunts is Victor's Cafeteria on Main Street, where many a meeting with friends, foes, witnesses and acolytes tends to take place when he is in town and investigating a case.

Such a focus on food and places is an important aspect of James Lee Burke's sense of place. However, so too is the plush Southern landscape that surrounds Robicheaux; it becomes a character in its own right in the sometimes convoluted plots, in which layers of betrayal and evil sandwich each other until the mind reels and an explosion of cathartic violence is often required to cauterize the soul. And no one can evoke place more sensually than Burke:

That night I dreamed of South Louisiana, of blue herons standing among flooded cypress trees, fields of sugarcane beaten with purple and gold light in the fall. The smell of smouldering hickory and pork dripping into the ash in our smokehouse, the way billows of fog rolled out of the swamp in the morning, so thick and white that sound – a bass flopping, a bullfrog falling off a log into the water – came to you inside a wet bubble, pelicans sailing out of the sun over the breakers out on the Gulf, the palm trees ragged and green and clacking in the salt breeze, and the crab and crawfish boils and fish fries that went on year-round, as though there were no end to a season and death had no sway in our lives' – Black Cherry Blues (1989).

And no more attractive paean to the magic of New Orleans' fever dream and unforgettable features is there than at the conclusion of *Dixie City Jam*, as Robicheaux and his family, cleansed through violence, enjoy the noisy peace afforded by the annual Jazz and Heritage Festival:

'IT'S BEEN A LONG TIME SINCE A CRIME NOVELIST MADE ME CRY. IT'S BEEN A LONG TIME SINCE A CRIME NOVEL MADE EVERY HAIR ON MY BODY STAND ON END. THE TIN ROOF BLOWDOWN DID BOTH' – MARK TIMLIN, INDEPENDENT (2007)

NEW ORLEANS SLEUTHS

What with the plethora of fictional sleuths who have roamed the evocative streets of New Orleans in the footsteps of other literary predecessors, such as Mark Twain (1835–1910), Tennessee Williams (1911–83) and Anne Rice (b. 1941), visitors may wonder why there actually isn't a 'Mystery Street' in the city. Indeed, Dave Robicheaux is far from the only sleuth operating in New Orleans. Others include:

Julie Smith's Skip Langdon, a local New Orleans policewoman who appears in nine novels.

Tony Dunbar's Tubby Dubonnet, a pudgy, would-be easy-going attorney.

O'Neil De Noux's Lt Dino La Stanza, a hard-headed policeman (De Noux was himself a Lieutenant in the NOPD for 15 years).

Chris Wiltz's Neil Raffertry, a tough but sensitive gumshoe.

J.M. Redman's lesbian sleuth Micky Knight.

Tony Fennelly's aristocratic lawyer Matt Sinclair and the colourful local stripper-cum-involuntary sleuth Margo Fortier.

David Fulmer's Valentin St Cyr, who investigates during the golden age of the jazz record label Storyville.

Robert Skinner's nightclub-owner Wesley Farrell.

Other crime writers who have used a New Orleans setting on a regular basis include the legendary king of the locked-room novel, John Dickson Carr, who situated a trilogy there; John Grisham, who has frequently used the city as a setting; and John and Joyce Corrington. And, as if New Orleans hadn't enough of a claim to mystery fame, novelist and screenwriter Elmore Leonard was also born there.

The music rose into the sky until it seemed to fuse with the gentle and pervasive light spreading far beyond the racetrack, over oak-lined streets, paintless wood houses with galleries and green window shutters, elevated highways, the Superdome, the streetcars and palm-dotted neutral ground of Canal, the scrolled-iron balconies, colonnades, and brick chimneys in the Quarter, Jackson Square and the spires of St. Louis Cathedral, the Café du Monde, the wide, mud-churned sweep of the Mississippi, the shining vastness of the wetlands to the south, and eventually the Gulf of Mexico, where later the moon would rise like an enormous pearl that had been dipped in a glass of burgundy.

USEFUL WEBSITES & ADDRESSES

Guide to walking tours of New Orleans' literary landmarks
www.ehow.com/how_4500120_take-literary-tour-new-orleans.html

St Louis Cathedral
615 Pere Antoine Alley
New Orleans
www.stlouiscathedral.org

Café du Monde
http://www.cafedumonde.com/frenchMarket.html

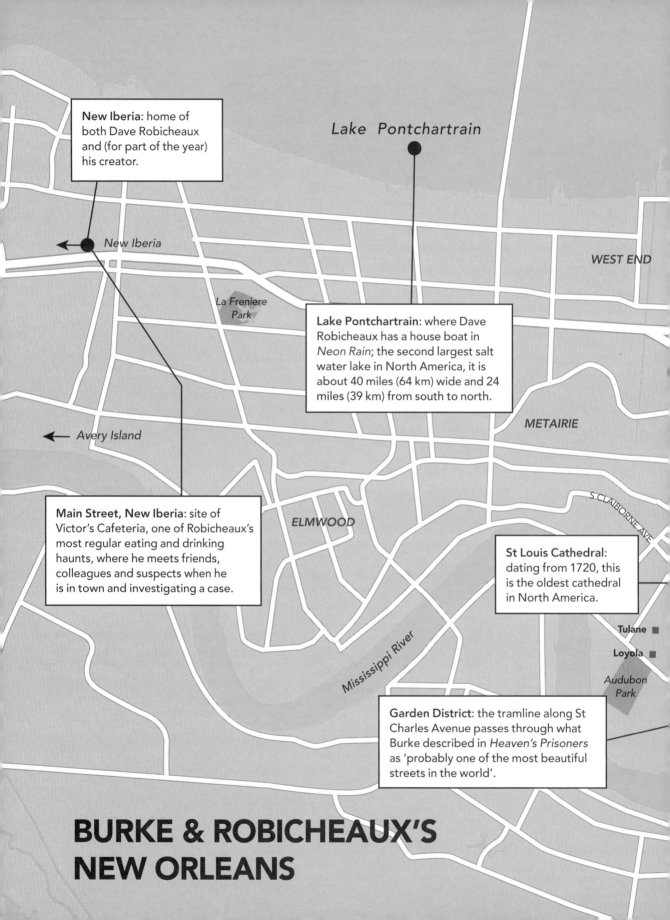

New Iberia: home of both Dave Robicheaux and (for part of the year) his creator.

Lake Pontchartrain

New Iberia

WEST END

La Freniere Park

Lake Pontchartrain: where Dave Robicheaux has a house boat in *Neon Rain*; the second largest salt water lake in North America, it is about 40 miles (64 km) wide and 24 miles (39 km) from south to north.

← *Avery Island*

METAIRIE

S CLAIBORNE AVE

ELMWOOD

Main Street, New Iberia: site of Victor's Cafeteria, one of Robicheaux's most regular eating and drinking haunts, where he meets friends, colleagues and suspects when he is in town and investigating a case.

St Louis Cathedral: dating from 1720, this is the oldest cathedral in North America.

Tulane ■

Loyola ■

Mississippi River

Audubon Park

Garden District: the tramline along St Charles Avenue passes through what Burke described in *Heaven's Prisoners* as 'probably one of the most beautiful streets in the world'.

BURKE & ROBICHEAUX'S NEW ORLEANS

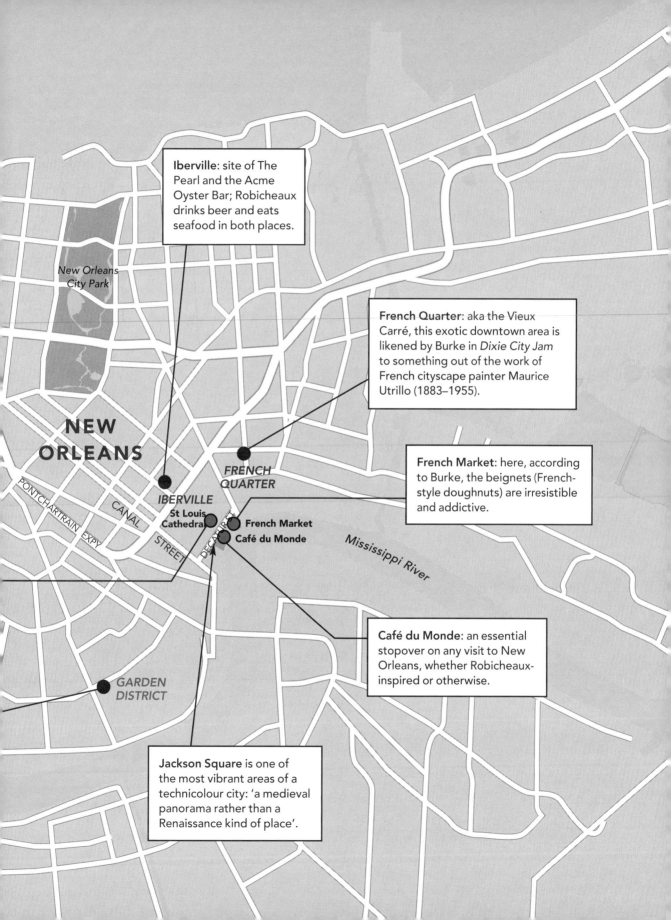

Iberville: site of The Pearl and the Acme Oyster Bar; Robicheaux drinks beer and eats seafood in both places.

French Quarter: aka the Vieux Carré, this exotic downtown area is likened by Burke in *Dixie City Jam* to something out of the work of French cityscape painter Maurice Utrillo (1883–1955).

French Market: here, according to Burke, the beignets (French-style doughnuts) are irresistible and addictive.

Café du Monde: an essential stopover on any visit to New Orleans, whether Robicheaux-inspired or otherwise.

Jackson Square is one of the most vibrant areas of a technicolour city: 'a medieval panorama rather than a Renaissance kind of place'.

New Orleans City Park

NEW ORLEANS

PONTCHARTRAIN EXPY

CANAL STREET

IBERVILLE

St Louis Cathedral

FRENCH QUARTER

DECATUR ST

French Market

Café du Monde

Mississippi River

GARDEN DISTRICT

Barry Forshaw

GEORGES SIMENON & INSPECTOR MAIGRET'S PARIS

The name Georges Simenon is synonymous with the very finest French crime fiction, and his tenacious copper Jules Maigret is one of the iconic figures of the genre.

Georges Simenon was born in Liège, Belgium, on 13 February 1903. As a young man, his life was affected by his father's poor health. Simenon had to face the fact that (as with Charles Dickens in England before him) he would be forced to give up his studies to work off his father's debts.

Simenon's early beginnings

A period working in a bookshop was more to Simenon's liking than many of the other short-term positions he held when he was young, as he was deeply immersed in the world of books. His first job as a writer was as a journalist for the *Gazette de Liège*, during which period he polished the taut and pared-down use of language that was to become his signature style.

As a teenager, Simenon published an apprentice novel and engaged with an organization known as *La Caque* (The Cask). This 'artistic' group of painters and writers adopted a transgressive approach to life, and the distractions of alcohol, drugs and sex were par for the course. This was perfectly acceptable to Simenon, who had always been a keen appreciator of women (and healthily indulged this appreciation over the years). In 1923 he married a young artist called Régine Renchon, but the marriage was short-lived.

Much as he enjoyed the indulgences of the Cask group, Simenon finally broke free and made the de rigueur journey to Paris in 1922 to forge a career as a journeyman writer. He wrote many novels and stories under a great variety of noms de plume, and began his career as one of the great chroniclers of Paris, City of Light.

Paris and beyond

Simenon's immersion in the artistic life of Paris was total, at a time when the city was in its cultural ascendancy, a magnet for émigré writers and artists from all over the world. He demonstrated a particular predilection for the popular arts, becoming a friend of the notorious American dancer Josephine Baker (1906–75) after seeing her many times in her well-known showcase 'La Revue Nègre'. Baker was celebrated for dancing topless, and this note of sensuality chimed with author's enthusiastic leanings towards the erotic.

He was also a keen traveller, and in the late 1920s made many journeys on the canals of France and Europe, an experience he was later to draw on in books such as *Lock 14* (1931), with its vivid descriptions of the world of bargees and lock-keepers in the area around Épernay.

As the 1930s progressed, Simenon began writing the groundbreaking police procedural novels featuring the doughty Inspector Maigret. This series was his principal legacy to the literary world and one that continues to influence other writers to this day. However, he did not neglect his travels, considering that the more experience of other countries he accrued, the better a writer he would become. Yet Paris was the centre of his universe, both as a man and as a writer.

Ups and downs

As it was for so many Frenchmen, Simenon's life was to change as the war years approached. In the late 1930s, he became Commissioner for Belgian refugees at La Rochelle. When France fell to the Germans in 1940, the writer travelled to Fontenay in the German-occupied zone. His wartime experiences have always been a subject of controversy. Under the occupation, he added a new string to his bow when a group of films was produced (under the Nazis) based on his writings. It was, perhaps, inevitable that he would later be branded a collaborator, and this stain was

Maigret

Maigret appears in 75 novels and 28 short stories.

Maigret almost always is seen wearing an overcoat during his investigations, even in hot weather or on the Côte d'Azur, and is as a result always recognized as a policeman.

Maigret lives at 132 Boulevard Richard Lenoir.

A statue of Maigret was unveiled in 1966 in Delfzijl in the Netherlands, sculpted by Pieter d'Hont.

Maigret's tipples of choice are beer and cider, although he is also partial to pastis and wine at dinner.

MAIGRET

to stay with him for the rest of his career. To avoid French hostility, he spent much of the first decade after the war in the United States and Canada. Exile had no adverse effect on productivity: he wrote prolifically throughout this period, and his output included *Maigret in Retirement* (1945) and *Maigret in New York* (1946).

The trajectory of Simenon's success continued unabated for many years, and by the 1970s it was clear that he was the most successful writer of crime fiction in a language other than English, and that his character Maigret had become as much of an institution as the author himself. Simenon created something of a stir with his autobiography, *Quand J'étais Vieux* (1970; published in English in 1971 as *When I Was Old*), in which he made the controversial claim that he had had sexual relations with more than 10,000 women. This astonishing number was met with both scepticism (how had he managed to be such a prolific author if his entire time seems to have been spent in libidinous pursuits?) as well as a certain distaste at what seemed like boastfulness.

Leaving such things aside, by the time of his death in 1989, it was clear that the author had created a writing legacy quite as substantial as many more 'serious' French literary figures. And Simenon now seems like the Trojan horse for the explosion of interest in translated crime fiction that has since taken place in both Britain and America.

Introducing Inspector Maigret

The Georges Simenon novels that can be described as stand-alones (that is, books in which no continuing detective figure features) are among the most powerful in the genre. Regardless of this, there is absolutely no debate as to which

'SIMENON'S KNOWLEDGE OF THE STREETS OF THE CITY SHOWED AN INTIMACY THAT HIS READERS COULD FOLLOW ALMOST LIKE A GUIDEBOOK' – OBITUARY, *NEW YORK TIMES* (1989)

of his creations is most fondly remembered: the pipe-smoking Jules Maigret, Commissaire in the Paris police.

The detective first appeared in the novel *Pietr-le-Letton* (*The Case of Peter the Lett*) in 1931 (translated as *Introducing Inspector Maigret*), and the author has stated that he utilized characteristics that he had observed in his own great-grandfather. Considering this, it is not surprising that all the elements that made the character so beloved were finely honed almost immediately by the author.

Maigret's office is at 36 Quai des Orfèvres, the headquarters of the Parisian judicial police at the Grande Maison, on the banks of the Seine on the Île de la Cité – a place of pilgrimage for the Simenon enthusiast. Venturing inside the building, it is still possible to see the famous 148 steps that Maigret ascended to his office. The cast-iron stove and worn linoleum that Simenon described are not to be found, but looking through the windows one can see boats moving slowly down the Seine, just like those that Maigret gazed upon.

The stand-alone novel *The Man Who Watched the Trains Go By* (1938) – one of Simenon's most accomplished books – is virtually a travelogue of Paris, as the protagonist (Kees Popinga) wanders aimlessly around from district to district, sleeping (but not having sex) with a variety of prostitutes. The novel contains an evocative description of an elderly woman

selling flowers in the Rue de Douai, an image not impossible to conjure up in modern-day Paris. The book also features a vividly rendered trip to a neighbourhood at the opposite end of town – Les Gobelins – which Maigret finds one of the 'saddest sections of Paris', with wide avenues of depressing flats laid out like army barracks and cafés crowded with 'mediocre people' who are neither rich nor poor.

Simenon wrote what he planned as the last Maigret novel, *Maigret Returns*, in 1934. (He had by now written six novels in a more 'literary' style.) In many of the Maigret books, the Pigalle district is where Maigret encounters denizens of the underworld, drug addicts, pimps and prostitutes. As described by Simenon, this was a sleazy but curiously attractive area – in fact, it might be said to have had a better class of sleaze in that era, as more downmarket (and more sordid) distractions have since replaced those that Simenon

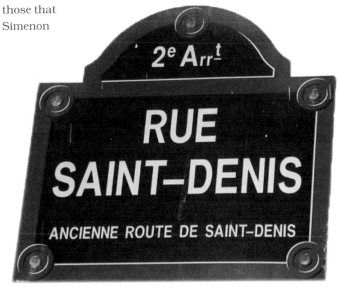

wrote about: prostitutes still haunt the red-light bars, but they seem very unlike those described in the Maigret novels. Similarly, Rue Saint-Denis is much more a tourist hotspot in the 21st century than the more exotic (and atmospheric) locale described by Simenon.

Although Simenon is best known in Britain as the writer of the Maigret books, his prolific output of over 400 novels made him a household name and institution in Europe. Simenon was and is acclaimed for his astute psychological portrayals of loneliness, guilt and innocence. *Maigret Sets A Trap* (1955) sees the inimitable Inspector facing a seemingly unstoppable serial killer, and explores the author's central theme of the individual forced to act in extraordinary ways in the face of adversity. The Parisian underworld conjured by Simenon has few equals in French fiction.

The author was not above being playful with the conventions of the detective novel – and with the identity of the author. In *Maigret's Memoirs* (1951), Maigret talks about meeting a strange young man called 'Georges Sim' – not hard to guess who this is – who arrives to study him and his working methods, reproducing them (Dr Watson-like, with embellishments) in a series of books. Just as Sherlock Holmes would have done (*see pages 216–227*), Maigret ruefully remarks on these embellishments and laments their inaccuracy.

Maigret landmarks

Maigret's Memoirs features a location familiar to many visitors, the Gare de l'Est, which always evokes for the detective scenes of mobilization for war (the main lines from this station lead towards the German frontier). In contrast, Maigret notes, the Gare de Lyon and the Gare Montparnasse – from which trains head south to the Mediterranean coast – always make him think of people going away on holiday. Meanwhile, the Gare du Nord, the gateway to the industrial and mining regions of the Pas de Calais, prompts thoughts of the harsh struggle people once had for their daily bread.

The omnibus *Maigret Right and Wrong* (1954) included *Maigret in Montmartre* and *Maigret's Mistake* and featured the detective reminiscing about a striptease in the Picratt's nightspot in Montmartre (he remembers the stripper wriggling out of her dress with nothing underneath and standing there 'as naked as a worm' – and, as in the American burlesque, 'the moment she has nothing left on all the lights go out'). The sort of discreet striptease act that Simenon described here seems quaintly historical now, and

'... SOME ASPECTS OF [SIMENON'S] BIOGRAPHY... ARE FAMILIAR FROM PROFILES OF MURDERERS AND WE SHOULD PERHAPS BE THANKFUL THAT HE WAS A BALANCED ENOUGH MAN TO RESPOND TO HIS PSYCHOLOGICAL PROBLEMS BY PICKING UP A PEN RATHER THAN A GUN' – MARK LAWSON, *GUARDIAN* (2002)

MAIGRET ON SCREEN

The character of Jules Maigret is uncommon insofar as he has been portrayed on the screen by actors of diverse nationalities, and has had more incarnations than Arthur Conan Doyle's Sherlock Holmes.

 ## IN FILM

Pierre Renoir in *La Nuit du Carrefour* (1932)

Abel Tarride in *Le Chien Jaune* (1932)

Harry Baur in *La Tête d'un Homme* (1933)

Albert Prejean in *Picpus* (1943); *Cecile est Morte* (1944); and *Les Caves du Majestic* (1945)

Charles Laughton in *The Man on the Eiffel Tower* (1949)

Michel Simon in *Brelan d'As* (1952)

Maurice Manson in *Maigret Dirige L'Enquête* (1956)

Jean Gabin in *Maigret Tend un Piège* (1958); *Maigret et L'Affaire du Saint Fiacre* (1959); and *Maigret voit Rouge* (1963)

Heinz Ruhmann in *Maigret Und Sein*

ON TELEVISION

Basil Sydney in *Maigret and the Lost Life* (1959 UK)

Louis Arbessier in *Liberty Bar* (1960 France)

Rupert Davies in *Maigret* (1960–69 UK)

Kees Bruisse in *Maigret: de Kruideniers* (1964 Netherlands)

Gino Cervi in *Maigret à Pigalle* (1966) and *Le Inchieste del Commissario Maigret* (1964–72 Italy)

Jan Teulings in *Maigret* (1964–69 Belgium)

Boris Tenin in *Megre I Staraya Dama* (1974 USSR)

Jean Richard in *Les Enquêtes de Commissaire Maigret* (1967–90) and *Signe Furax* (1981)

Richard Harris in *Maigret* (1968 UK)

Bruno Cremer in *Maigret* (1991–2005 France)

Michael Gambon in *Maigret* (1992–3 UK)

Sergio Castellito in *Maigret* (2004 Italy)

it is necessary to travel to Montmartre at very specific times of the day to avoid its tourist-trap atmosphere. Nevertheless, it is not impossible to mentally recapture the world Simenon evokes.

Simenon aficionados were particularly pleased with *Maigret and the Idle Burglar* (1961), in which Maigret must disobey instructions in order to investigate the murder of an unlikely gang member whose battered corpse has been found in the Bois de Boulogne. The novel was a classic example of Simenon's skill at devising ingenious plots and situations. The book features the Palais de Justice (the law court), which is next to the Conciergerie on the Île de la Cité at the south corner of the Pont-au-Change. Now a museum, the Conciergerie was used as a prison during the French Revolution

(1789–99) and was much feared – among those held there were Thomas Paine (1737–1809), the English-born American revolutionary, and Marie Antoinette (1755–93), Queen of France (1774–92), while she waited to follow her husband, Louis XVI (1754–93; reigned 1774–92), to the guillotine.

Maigret's Special Murder (1948) takes the reader to the Boulevard Richard-Lenoir, where the detective speculates on the reason for the area's bad reputation. He talks about its unfortunate proximity to the Bastille (hardly a disincentive for the Parisian visitor these days, of course, now that the area features an opera house and numerous restaurants) and, he continues, the area is surrounded by 'miserable slummy little streets'. (Again, this is not quite as true of the district in the 21st century.) Maigret notes, however, the friendly atmosphere and the fact that those who live here grow to love it.

Plus ça change…

Much of Paris has changed since Simenon's day, but the beautiful Place des Vosges, where the author lived (and where, at one time, he located his detective's own home, although Maigret is more often described as living in the Boulevard Richard-Lenoir), is still very much the area that Simenon evoked, in terms of both its elegant atmosphere and its beauty. The upmarket art galleries and haute-cuisine restaurants still nestle under the historic arches, and (more so than in many Parisian locations) it is possible to imagine oneself retracing the footsteps of the author's pipe-smoking copper. In addition to Maigret and his prolific creator, famous inhabitants of the square have included the authors Victor Hugo (1802–85) and Théophile Gautier (1811–72).

One particularly striking memory of Georges Simenon may be found at a watering hole in the Rue des Victoires, the Taverne Henri IV (13 Place du Pont-Neuf); the owner was, in fact, a friend of the author, and various photographs on the wall show Simenon enjoying himself at this very location. So, this could be considered as good a place as any to start and/or finish a tour of the City of Light in the company of messieurs Simenon and Maigret.

Once visitors have ticked off all the capital locations, they may wish to range further afield into provincial France, where there are numerous other settings used by Simenon as Maigret locations. Guido de Croock's website (address below) provides a comprehensive list of these places, many of which are in some of the most beautiful parts of the country and easily accessible from central Paris by road or rail.

Useful websites

'The Official Maigret Website'
www.maigret.com/inspector_maigret/paris.php

Maigret forum
www.trussel.com/f_maig.htm

List of Maigret locations in provincial France
www.trussel.com/maig/buiten.htm

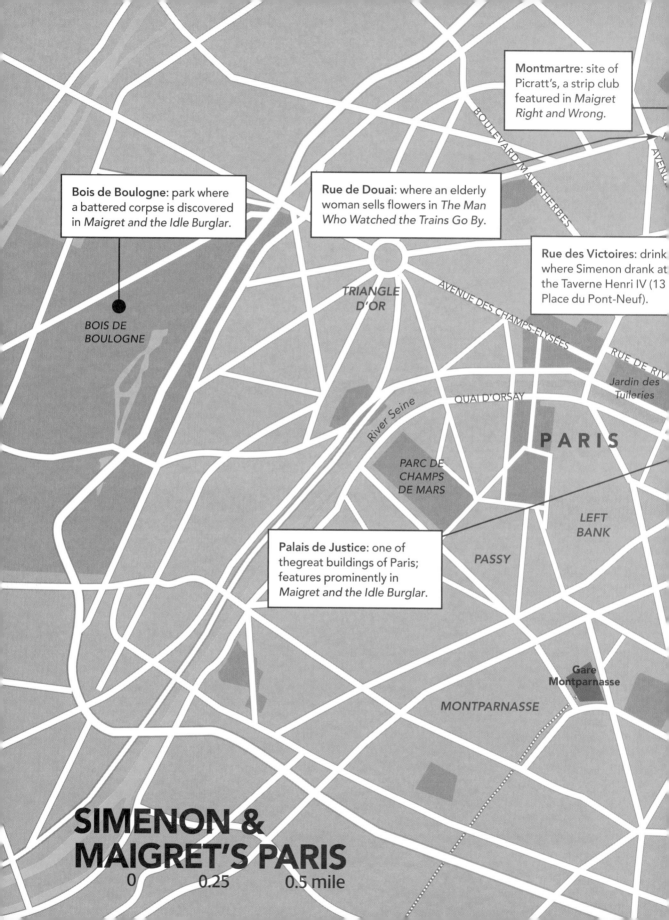

Montmartre: site of Picratt's, a strip club featured in *Maigret Right and Wrong.*

Bois de Boulogne: park where a battered corpse is discovered in *Maigret and the Idle Burglar.*

Rue de Douai: where an elderly woman sells flowers in *The Man Who Watched the Trains Go By.*

Rue des Victoires: drink where Simenon drank at the Taverne Henri IV (13 Place du Pont-Neuf).

BOULEVARD MALESHERBES

AVENUE

BOIS DE BOULOGNE

TRIANGLE D'OR

AVENUE DES CHAMPS-ELYSÉES

RUE DE RIV

Jardin des Tuileries

QUAI D'ORSAY

River Seine

PARIS

PARC DE CHAMPS DE MARS

LEFT BANK

PASSY

Palais de Justice: one of thegreat buildings of Paris; features prominently in *Maigret and the Idle Burglar.*

Gare Montparnasse

MONTPARNASSE

SIMENON & MAIGRET'S PARIS

0   0.25   0.5 mile

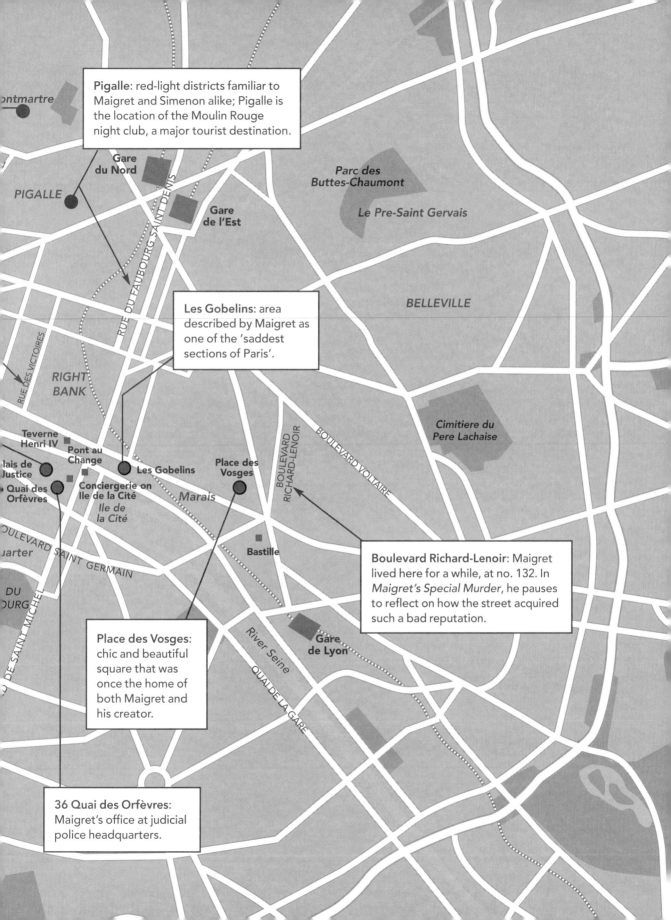

Pigalle: red-light districts familiar to Maigret and Simenon alike; Pigalle is the location of the Moulin Rouge night club, a major tourist destination.

Montmartre

Gare du Nord

PIGALLE

Gare de l'Est

Parc des Buttes-Chaumont

Le Pre-Saint Gervais

Les Gobelins: area described by Maigret as one of the 'saddest sections of Paris'.

BELLEVILLE

RUE DU FAUBOURG SAINT DENIS

RUE DES VICTOIRES

RIGHT BANK

Cimitiere du Pere Lachaise

Teverne Henri IV

Pont au Change

lais de Justice

Quai des Orfèvres

Conciergerie on Ile de la Cité

Les Gobelins

Ile de la Cité

Marais

Place des Vosges

BOULEVARD RICHARD-LENOIR

BOULEVARD VOLTAIRE

BOULEVARD SAINT GERMAIN

uarter

DU OURG

Bastille

Boulevard Richard-Lenoir: Maigret lived here for a while, at no. 132. In *Maigret's Special Murder*, he pauses to reflect on how the street acquired such a bad reputation.

DE SAINT MICHEL

Place des Vosges: chic and beautiful square that was once the home of both Maigret and his creator.

River Seine

QUAI DE LA GARE

Gare de Lyon

36 Quai des Orfèvres: Maigret's office at judicial police headquarters.

Martin Edwards

ELLIS PETERS & BROTHER CADFAEL'S SHROPSHIRE

The green and pleasant county of Shropshire seems an unlikely setting for multiple crimes, and yet a born-and-bred Salopian (as Shropshire folk are often called), Edith Mary Pargeter (1913–95), better known to readers by her pen name Ellis Peters, was responsible for ensuring that her home ground will forever be associated with murder mysteries – ranging from the 12th century to the 20th century.

Pargeter produced a series of sound contemporary whodunnits featuring policeman George Felse, the first being *Fallen into the Pit* (1951). However, she was to find fame and fortune through the creation of a herbalist-sleuth, Brother Cadfael. Cadfael made his first appearance in *A Morbid Taste for Bones* (1977) and became the protagonist in 19 further crime books, all set in her beloved home county, but primarily in Shrewsbury Cathedral.

Few areas of the English countryside have inspired so much of a single author's work, especially in the crime genre. Ellis Peters proclaimed that inspiration with pride:

> I have used this landscape, native and familiar to me, in all my books; sometimes in its veritable shape and by its own names, sometimes with its

edges diffused into a topography between reality and dream, but just as recognizable, for those who know it as I do, as if it had been mapped with the precision of an Ordnance Survey sheet. I did not set out deliberately to make use of my origins. Shropshire is simply in my blood, and in the course of creation the blood gets into the ink, and sets in motion a heartbeat and a circulation that brings the land to life – Cadfael Country by Robin Whiteman and Rob Talbot (1990).

Shropshire connection

Pargeter was born in 1913 in the small village of Horsehay, which is today absorbed within the boundaries of the new(ish) town of Telford. Her birthplace was close to the Ironbridge Gorge, which

carries the River Severn south towards the Bristol Channel. The valley is beautiful, despite the disfiguring presence of a vast power station. Although Shropshire's economy has long been centred on agriculture, paradoxically Ironbridge and neighbouring Coalbrookdale can claim to have formed the cradle of the Industrial Revolution. This is where, in 1779, the iron-master and engineer Abraham Darby III (1750–91) raised the world's first cast-iron arch bridge to provide local industries with a more satisfactory means of carrying goods across the river than the old ferry. The bridge was closed to traffic in 1934, but tolls continued to be collected from pedestrians until 1950. The bridge remains a much-visited tourist attraction, and the gorge has been designated a UNESCO World Heritage Site.

The Pargeter family had close connections with the local ironworks: Edith's father was head clerk and timekeeper, her brother worked there as an engineer. Growing up in such proximity to historical landmarks must have fired her interest in the past, while her early life in tranquil rural surroundings prompted a lifelong fascination with landscape. A third factor to influence her writing was the nature of life on the borders between England and Wales. Edith's maternal

grandmother was Welsh, and she was conscious of the long history of tension between the two nations, dating back to the turbulent times when Anglo-Saxons and Celts engaged in repeated conflict. Until it became absorbed within the Kingdom of Mercia, a process completed by the eighth-century king Offa (builder of the famous dyke that served both as a line of demarcation and a defence against invasion), Shropshire formed part of the Welsh kingdom of Powys.

BROTHER CADFAEL

Full name
Cadfael ap Meilyr ap Dafydd

Key dates
1096: embarks on First Crusade, during which he fathers a son, Olivier de Bretagne, by Mariam, a Muslim woman in Antioch
1114: returns to England where he discovers that his fiancée, Richildis Vaughan, has left him for another man; later serves for a while in the army of King Henry I before putting down his sword and taking holy orders

*The magnificent
interior of
Shrewsbury
Abbey.*

'IF EDITH PARGETER HAD A MESSAGE IN HER OEUVRE… IT WAS THAT BY AND LARGE MANKIND WAS NOT ENTIRELY IRREDEEMABLE' – OBITUARY, *INDEPENDENT* (1995)

Peters often spoke of her love for her native county. This was where she spent most of her life, other than during World War II (1939–45), when she worked in Liverpool at the Royal Navy's Western Approaches Command. She even wrote (with Roy Morgan) a book called *Shropshire: A Memoir of the English Countryside* (1992). In it, she commented:

> Shropshire has left images in my books as indelibly as in my memory and imagination. I am well aware that my writing is very visual, I paint in words. The landscape, the townscape, weather and season are all there within and between the lines…. Shropshire is present as a pervasive sense of place, never fully revealed, but strongly felt.

From Pargeter to Peters

Despite her attachment to Shropshire, Pargeter was not a parochial woman. She first visited Czechoslovakia in 1947 and became fascinated by the language (which she quickly learned) and the culture. She formed a deep attachment to the Czech people, and translated no fewer than 16 novels from Czech, including Jan Neruda's *Tales of the Little Quarter* (1957) and Joseph Bor's *The Terezn Requiem* (1963) about a Verdi concert at Auschwitz. Some of her books – starting with *Hortensius, Friend of Nero* (1936) and including a

few of her mysteries and short stories – are set overseas.

Pargeter already had a long list of novels to her credit by the time she created the amiable, if rather bland, Detective Inspector George Felse. However, after his first appearance in *Fallen into the Pit* – published under Pargeter's own name – as a sergeant investigating the murder of an unrepentant Nazi land-worker, Felse did not return in book form for a decade, when *Death and the Joyful Woman* (1961) was published under the byline of Ellis Peters. Previously, the author had from time to time used other pseudonyms (among them Jolyon Carr, John Redfern and Peter Benedict) and had only flirted with the genre of crime fiction, with her most successful work falling outside of that genre. *Death and the Joyful Woman* was a huge success and represented a breakthrough for Pargeter, winning an Edgar Allan Poe award from the Mystery Writers of America in 1962. Morale duly boosted, Pargeter turned out 11 more Felse novels between 1964 and 1978.

The arrival of Brother Cadfael

The creation of Brother Cadfael was a coalescence of Pargeter's twin passions: for the county she knew so well, and also for history, which goes some way to explaining the character's success.

Cadfael's debut in *A Morbid Taste for Bones* was originally intended as a one-off. At first, the book was not even produced in a paperback edition; a smallish print run was targeted mainly at the library market,

'CADFAEL SPRANG TO LIFE SUDDENLY AND UNEXPECTEDLY WHEN HE WAS ALREADY APPROACHING 60, MATURE, EXPERIENCED, FULLY ARMED AND 17 YEARS TONSURED' – ELLIS PETERS, A RARE BENEDICTINE (1989)

and Pargeter, writing as Peters, followed the book up with another Felse novel, *Rainbow's End* (1978), which proved to be the last.

In 1979, Cadfael returned in *One Corpse Too Many*, and for the author (by now 66 years old) there would be no turning back from a journey that was to transform her into an international bestseller. *Monk's Hood* (1980) was awarded the Crime Writers' Association Silver Dagger in 1980, and Pargeter received the ultimate acclaim in 1993 when the Crime Writers' Association's Cartier Diamond Dagger was bestowed upon her in recognition of her outstanding contribution to the genre.

Cadfael's world

Protagonist Cadfael is possibly an unlikely sleuth, being a member of the Benedictine Order based at Shrewsbury Abbey. The abbey was founded in 1083 by Roger de Montgomery, who had been responsible for the establishment of the town's castle a few years earlier. The first entry in the Cadfael Chronicles sees the monk despatched to Wales to help bring back from Gwytherin the bones of Saint Winifred. Cadfael is himself a Welshman, born in Trefriw, and is able to act as an interpreter on behalf of the monks. He benefits from an exotic background, having left the service of a wool merchant in Shrewsbury to join the army of the First Crusade (1095–99), after which he became a ship's captain. He learned a great deal

about herbs before taking monastic vows, and his knowledge of plants and their medicinal properties plays a significant part in the Chronicles.

One Corpse Too Many takes its starting point from historical fact: the siege of Shrewsbury Castle and its town walls in 1138. When the forces of King Stephen (reigned 1135–54) broke through, he ordered that the 94 defenders be hanged from the castle walls. In this novel, Cadfael – given the melancholy task of assisting with the burials – discovers that there is a 95th corpse. The extra body belongs to someone who has been strangled by an unknown killer.

The novels of Ellis Peters display an acute sense of the way in which people interact with each other within and between communities, and depict the 12th-century equivalent of office politics with skill and insight. In *Saint Peter's Fair* (1981) we are told that:

> *Relations between the town of Shrewsbury on one side of the river and the abbey on the other, if never exactly cordial – that was too much to expect, where their interests so often collided – were always correct.*

The eponymous fair takes place over three days, the busiest of the year, when 'all shops in the town must be shut and nothing sold but ale and wine'. All boats, as the Provost complains at the start of the story, tie up at the abbey's jetty and pay

CADFAEL ON SCREEN

The first adaptations of the Cadfael Chronicles were for BBC Radio, with Glyn Houston in the leading role. The novels were later adapted by Central Television in the UK. Thirteen episodes, all based on actual novels by Ellis Peters, were filmed between 1994 and 1998. The celebrated British actor Derek Jacobi played the monk and botanist, and he was joined in all filmed episodes by Michael Culver as Prior Robert and Julian Firth as Brother Jerome. Other notable actors who appeared in the series included Sean Pertwee, Hugh Bonneville, Steven Mackintosh, Jonny Lee Miller, Julian Glover and Anna Friel. One of Cadfael's Executive Producers, Ted Childs, was also responsible for the Morse television series.

ON TELEVISION

Series One (1994)
'One Corpse Too Many'
'The Sanctuary Sparrow'
'The Leper of Saint Giles'
'Monk's Hood'

Series Two (1995–96)
'The Virgin in the Ice'
'The Devil's Novice'
'Saint Peter's Fair'

Series Three (1997):
'The Rose Rent'
'The Raven in the
   Foregate'
'A Morbid Taste for Bones'

Series Four (1998):
'The Holy Thief'
'The Potter's Field'
'The Pilgrim of Hate'

their dues to the abbot. But the abbot refuses to share the proceeds with the town's merchants. Tempers fray, and when a merchant is found dead, Cadfael investigates. Throughout the Cadfael Chronicles, people pursue their everyday lives against a background of simmering civil strife.

A Medieval setting

The old Abbey Foregate in Shrewsbury – described in *A Morbid Taste for Bones* as 'bustling with life… a constant traffic of housewives, urchins, dogs, carters and pedlars on the move, or gathered in gossiping groups' – is the hub of the town's activities and features regularly in the Chronicles. In *The Raven in the Foregate* (1986), Abbot Radulfus returns from London accompanied by a priest called Father Ailnoth for the vacant living of Holy Cross. Father Ailnoth is the 'Raven in the Foregate' – a man 'with every virtue except humility and human kindness'. Ailnoth is soon found drowned in the Abbey millpond; the question for Cadfael is whether his death was an accident or the result of a murderous attack.

The passage of the years has been kinder to Shrewsbury and its environs than to many other parts of England, as

visitors to the area will see. Despite the destruction of most of the abbey's monastic buildings in Henry VIII's Dissolution of the Monasteries (1536–41), a good deal has survived, including four of the massive drum-shaped columns from the Norman church and fragments of the shrine of St Winifred. The modern foregate is relatively quiet, bypassed by much of the traffic that teems through the town. Many other places described in the Chronicles remain identifiable to this day. An example is Maerdol, a street which was once the main approach from the town centre to the medieval Welsh Bridge. In *The Rose Rent* (1986), the Vestier family, the biggest and best clothiers in the town, have premises at the head of Maerdol, 'a right-angled house, with wide shop-front on the street, and the long stem of the hall and chambers running well back behind, with a spacious yard and stables'. Today, although there is no trace of any such building, the street remains, but it is now spelled Mardol.

In her introduction to *The Cadfael Companion* by Robin Whiteman (1991), Ellis Peters wrote of having created 'not merely a sequence of individual stories, but an unfolding history of England, and especially of Shropshire and the Marches'. It is a notable achievement and one for which the tourist authorities of the county must be enduringly grateful. Certainly, they acknowledge on their website that it is partly because of the success of the books that Shrewsbury Abbey attracts thousands of visitors from all over the world. There is now a range of car trails inspired by the Cadfael books, including 'The Hermit of Eyton Forest Trail', which passes by Buildwas Abbey and Much Wenlock, and 'The Virgin in the Ice Trail', which travels through attractive towns such as Ludlow and Bridgnorth and over the rolling hills of south Shropshire.

The Cadfael Chronicles were eventually very successfully adapted for television and featured a stellar cast led by Derek Jacobi, whose gifts were well suited to the title role.

Edith Pargeter died in 1995. Late in life, thanks to her creation of Cadfael, she achieved considerable wealth and international renown, yet she remained to the end modest and devoted to the county she knew so well.

She said that to stand on top of any of the western hills in Shropshire:

> *... is to look round on an apparently unpeopled world, and yet it is there that you may suddenly experience this conviction of having a place in the continuity of tenure of this earth that makes you securely one in a chain longer than history.*

Even though the Cadfael novels are deeply steeped in the past and an England that no longer existed when she wrote the brave monk's adventures, Edith Pargeter's undying love for the British landscape shines through its pages, and shows how well a writer can evoke place, not just in geography, but in atmosphere, colour and even smells. Add a handful of mysterious crimes and you have a perfect recipe (or should that be a potion?) for a resonant sense of place.

USEFUL WEBSITES

Brother Cadfael Car Trails in the Shropshire Countryside
www.shropshiretourism.co.uk

Coach and walking tours of Pargeter/Peters territory
http://www.shrewsburyforgroups.com/guides.htm

The Abbey is little changed since the years of the Cadfael Chronicles (1135–50)
www.shrewsburyabbey.com

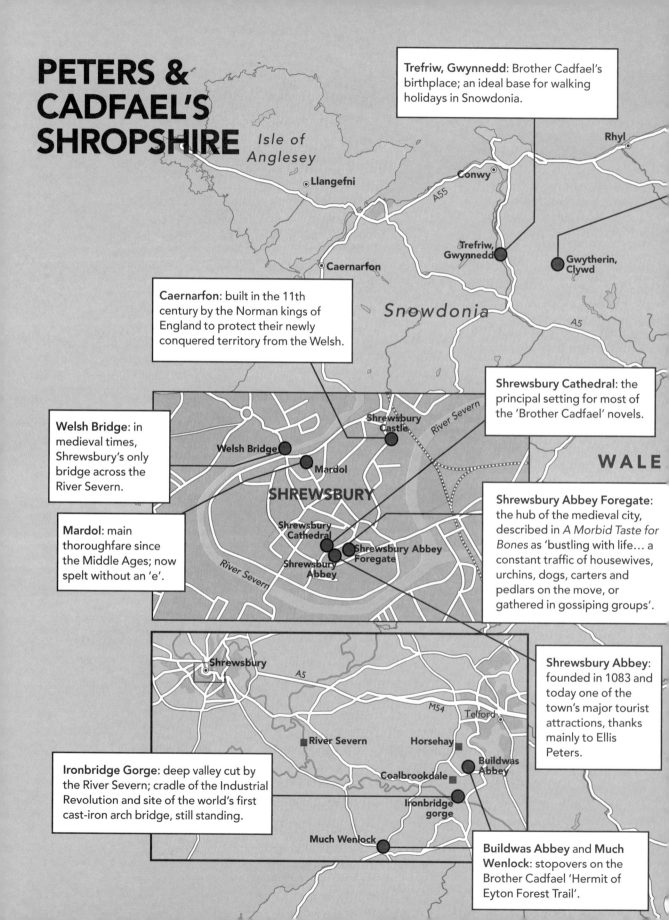

PETERS & CADFAEL'S SHROPSHIRE

Isle of Anglesey

Trefriw, Gwynnedd: Brother Cadfael's birthplace; an ideal base for walking holidays in Snowdonia.

Caernarfon: built in the 11th century by the Norman kings of England to protect their newly conquered territory from the Welsh.

Welsh Bridge: in medieval times, Shrewsbury's only bridge across the River Severn.

Mardol: main thoroughfare since the Middle Ages; now spelt without an 'e'.

Shrewsbury Cathedral: the principal setting for most of the 'Brother Cadfael' novels.

Shrewsbury Abbey Foregate: the hub of the medieval city, described in *A Morbid Taste for Bones* as 'bustling with life… a constant traffic of housewives, urchins, dogs, carters and pedlars on the move, or gathered in gossiping groups'.

Shrewsbury Abbey: founded in 1083 and today one of the town's major tourist attractions, thanks mainly to Ellis Peters.

Ironbridge Gorge: deep valley cut by the River Severn; cradle of the Industrial Revolution and site of the world's first cast-iron arch bridge, still standing.

Buildwas Abbey and **Much Wenlock:** stopovers on the Brother Cadfael 'Hermit of Eyton Forest Trail'.

Rhyl

Llangefni

Conwy

Trefriw, Gwynnedd

Gwytherin, Clywd

Caernarfon

Snowdonia

A55

A5

Shrewsbury Castle

River Severn

WALE

Welsh Bridge

Mardol

SHREWSBURY

Shrewsbury Cathedral

Shrewsbury Abbey Foregate

Shrewsbury Abbey

River Severn

Shrewsbury

A5

M54

Telford

River Severn

Horsehay

Buildwas Abbey

Coalbrookdale

Ironbridge gorge

Much Wenlock

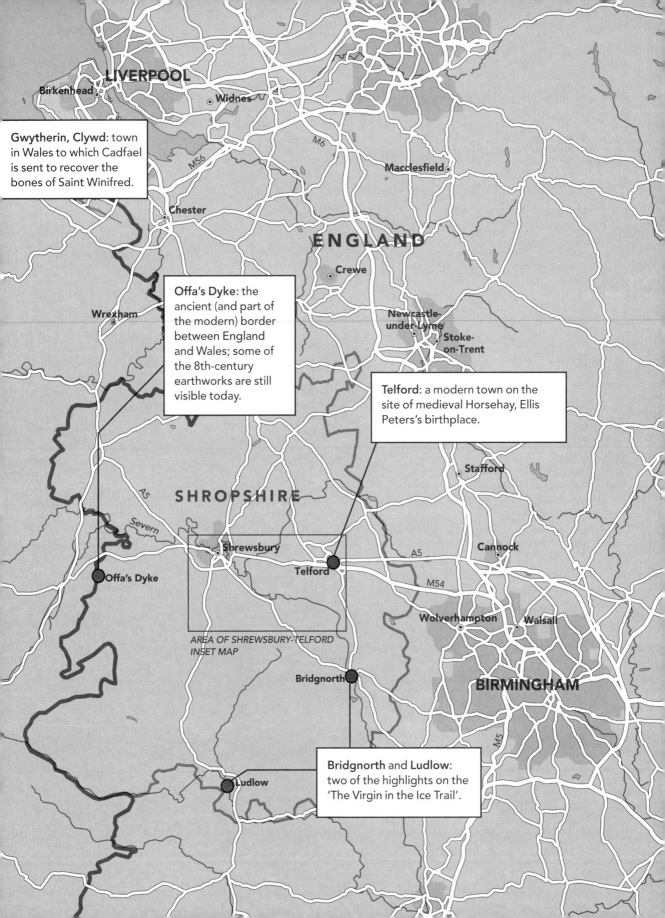

Gwytherin, Clywd: town in Wales to which Cadfael is sent to recover the bones of Saint Winifred.

Offa's Dyke: the ancient (and part of the modern) border between England and Wales; some of the 8th-century earthworks are still visible today.

Telford: a modern town on the site of medieval Horsehay, Ellis Peters's birthplace.

AREA OF SHREWSBURY-TELFORD INSET MAP

Bridgnorth and **Ludlow:** two of the highlights on the 'The Virgin in the Ice Trail'.

J. Kingston Pierce

DASHIELL HAMMETT & SAM SPADE'S SAN FRANCISCO

Somebody hoping to reinvent himself in the early 20th century might have found no town more conducive to helping him than San Francisco – a place that, after booming with fortune and fame, was suddenly flattened, seemingly by nature's wrath, and thus had also to make itself anew.

Dashiell Hammett's transformation was achieved with considerably fewer fireworks, but equally memorable results. In 1921 he arrived in northern California's richest and most colourful city a private detective. He left eight years later as an author – the creator of sleuths Sam Spade and the Continental Op – and as a man credited with imparting greater realism to the growing American school of detective fiction. To quote his fellow novelist, Raymond Chandler (1888–1959), Hammett was 'the ace performer', a guy who seemed destined for a robust and prolific future in the world of letters.

The making of Hammett

Few people who knew Samuel Dashiell Hammett as an impatient, red-headed youth would have expected him to become such a literary trailblazer. He was born on his grandfather's tobacco farm in

southern Maryland on 27 May 1894 but soon moved with his family to Philadelphia, Pennsylvania, and then on to Baltimore, Maryland. Although he thrived on education, he spent less than a year in high school before having to drop out and pick up some of the income slack left by his sick father. He worked without enthusiasm as a railroad messenger, a stevedore and a nail-machine operator in a box factory. He described himself as an 'unsatisfactory and unsatisfied employee'. The jobs young Sam took he didn't fight to hold; 'Usually I was fired', he once confided.

And then, in 1915, Sam Hammett answered an enigmatic advertisement for men 'free to travel and respond to all situations'. It led him to the Continental Building (now One Calvert Plaza) in downtown Baltimore and the local headquarters of the Pinkerton National Detective Agency. Pinkerton, with its 'We Never Sleep' slogan and logo of an unblinking eye (which inspired the term 'private eye'), had been founded in the 1850s by a former Chicago police detective, Scottish immigrant Allan Pinkerton (1819–84). The agency gained acclaim in 1861 by foiling an alleged attempt on the life of

President-elect Abraham Lincoln (1809–65; President 1861–65) and by pursuing western outlaws. It was eventually criticized for undermining labour unions and quashing strikes. However, such disrepute didn't stop Hammett from applying for a Pinkerton post and loving the one he was given – even though it meant his being shot at, clubbed and knifed ('I was never bored', he would say of the job).

Pegged as a crackerjack, Hammett was soon sent as a Pinkerton operative, or 'op', all over the United States. If the tales he passed down were true – and Hammett often demonstrated

HAMMETT ON SPADE

'He is a dream man in the sense that he is what most of the private detectives I worked with would like to have been and in their cockier moments thought they approached. For your private detective... wants to be a hard and shifty fellow, able to take care of himself in any situation, able to get the best of anybody he comes in contact with, whether criminal, innocent by-stander or client' – Introduction to *The Maltese Falcon* (1934 edition).

a gift for glamorizing his own back-story – he once nabbed a check forger in the Pacific Northwest, trailed a supposed German spy through Washington DC, captured a guy who had filched a Ferris wheel and, as a strikebreaker, was offered US$5,000 to murder a man in Montana.

However, during World War I (1914–18) he left 'the Pinks' to join the US Army Motor Ambulance Corps. His year-long military career was short on glory, as during most of it he lay flat on his back in an army hospital outside Baltimore having succumbed to the 1918 influenza pandemic that killed tens of millions of people; he then contracted tuberculosis, which would bedevil him for years to come. During one of his early returns to medical care, he met Josephine Dolan, a nurse from Montana, who thought him witty and handsome, and admired his military mien. Hammett saw 'Jose' (pronounced 'Joe's') as fun, and she smiled a lot, and the trip from there to sweating up bedsheets wasn't particularly protracted. Soon afterwards, his illness went into remission and Pinkerton assigned him to strikebreaker duty in San Francisco. He was there when a letter reached him, telling him Jose was pregnant.

Life in San Francisco
The pair swapped 'I do's' on 7 July 1921 in the rectory of St Mary's Cathedral on Van Ness Avenue (a building destroyed by fire in 1962). Prior to their wedding, Jose

hadn't known Hammett well enough to realize he was Roman Catholic.

They'd considered settling in Baltimore, but stayed in the Bay Area instead. San Francisco in those days was brushing off its rowdy past, courting sophistication. It had sprung up from near nothing in the mid-19th century, fertilized by greed and growing gaudy in the wake of the California Gold Rush (1848–55). Crime had attended the boom. San Francisco's Barbary Coast – a sort of diabolical Disneyland, all bright lights and dim prospects, centred on Pacific Avenue – drew gamblers, thieves, prostitutes and con men, as well as slumming young heirs who hungered after its watering holes and ribald delights. Other quarters held

'HAMMETT WAS THE GREAT POET OF THE GREAT AMERICAN COLLISION – PERSONAL HONOUR AND CORRUPTION, OPPORTUNITY AND FATALITY' – JAMES ELLROY, GUARDIAN (2007)

dangers, too: Chinatown, for instance, was a highly segregated warren of squalid alleyways with hired killers, shops curtained with duck carcases and fetid basement opium dens.

When the earthquake of 18 April 1906 walloped San Francisco, it ignited a three-day firestorm and destroyed more than 28,000 buildings. It also, however, gave planners a blank slate on which to recreate the town, this time taller and more elegant, with fewer unsavoury elements. San Francisco celebrated its

phoenix-like comeback with the Panama-Pacific International Exposition of 1915, a World's Fair that covered what's now the Marina District at the north end of town.

By the time the Hammetts moved into a US$45-a-month furnished apartment at 620 Eddy Street (just north of Civic Center) in 1921, cable cars and electric trolleys criss-crossed downtown, and there was talk of someday bridging the scenic Golden Gate at the mouth of San Francisco Bay, though many folks deemed such a feat impossible.

Private eye view

It's interesting, the picture one gleans of San Francisco from reading the many yarns Hammett set there, most of which he batted out in his Eddy Street flat. There are lots of references to specific places in Hammett's book – the old Hall of Justice on Kearny Street, where gumshoes and police detectives swapped sarcasm; Telegraph Hill, which the Continental Op climbed to give an egg-yellow house 'the up-and-down'; and Portsmouth Square, on the edge of Chinatown, where a suspect 'stretched himself out on the grass face-down, lit a black pipe, and lay looking dejectedly at the [Robert Louis] Stevenson Monument, probably without seeing it'. Visitors can also eat at John's Grill, at 63 Ellis Street, the chop house where Sam Spade stopped to refuel himself in *The Maltese Falcon* (1930), and eat the chops, baked potato and sliced tomato that Spade ate. Today, marked with a plaque and a falcon silhouette, John's Grill is the only place where Spade ate that still exists. However, Hammett provides little insight into the city's history, or how it came to be the way it was in his time. Hammett's San Francisco reflects what one might have learned by walking its streets, chatting up its cabbies and footsore waitresses and elevator operators, rather than studying it in books. It's the city as seen through the eyes of a private dick, which is exactly what Hammett was during his early days there.

He worked out of the Pinkerton offices on the third floor of the James Flood Building, an imposing 12-story edifice (built in 1904) at Market and Powell streets, with its main entrance right round the corner from John's Grill. During his time as an op in San Francisco, Hammett investigated the theft of US$125,000 in gold specie from the ocean liner *Sonoma* (riches that, to his disappointment, were recovered prior to his boarding the ship for a sail to Hawaii, during which he'd continue the search). He claimed, too, that he'd gathered information for the legal defence of world-famous silent-screen funnyman Roscoe 'Fatty' Arbuckle (1887–1933). Arbuckle was accused in September 1921 of manslaughter after a young model-actress named Virginia Rappe fell ill during a 'wild party' in his suite at the St Francis Hotel on Union Square, and subsequently perished from peritonitis brought on by a ruptured bladder. Three sensational trials were held before the comic finally won acquittal (but lost his career as a result of the scandal). Hammett's verdict was that Fatty had been framed 'by some of the corrupt local newspaper boys', together with San Francisco District Attorney Matthew Brady, who has been cited as Hammett's inspiration for the bullying DA Bryan in *The Maltese Falcon*. 'Arbuckle was good copy', Hammett later wrote, 'so they set him up for a fall'.

A new career

But Hammett was really too weak to work any more as a strikebreaker or to participate in lengthy surveillances; and the murky fogs that stretched over San Francisco did his lungs no good at all.

SAM SPADE ON SCREEN

Sam Spade was tall and blond. Humphrey Bogart was neither, but his film portrayal of Hammett's hero has become the definitive version: the actor became synonymous with the role, and vice versa.

 IN FILM

The Maltese Falcon (1931), directed by Roy Del Ruth starring Ricardo Cortez (an Austrian actor né Jacob Krantz)

The Maltese Falcon (1941), directed by John Huston, who also collaborated with Hammett on the script, and starring Humphrey Bogart as Sam Spade. This is widely regarded as the definitive film noir version.

Satan Met a Lady (1936) was also based on the Hammett novel, but loosely – it was a comedy. Sam Spade's name was changed to Ted Shane; the part was played by Warren William, who co-starred opposite Bette Davis.

ON STAGE

The first authorized stage version of *The Maltese Falcon* was staged in 2005 by The Long Beach Shakespeare Company. Two years later, the same company mounted a second adaptation. Also in 2007, the Alpha Stage of the Renaissance Theatre produced another version at Huntsville, Alabama.

ON RADIO

In 2009, the BBC broadcast a radio adaptation with Tom Wilkinson as Sam Spade.

So, at age 27, he quit the Pinks for the last time, and in early 1922 he enrolled in a secretarial school on Sutter Street, where he learned to type. He also began frequenting the San Francisco Public Library's neoclassical main branch (today's Asian Art Museum), a 1917 pile at Larkin and McAllister streets, across from City Hall, where he spent hours with his nose in one volume or another.

'Uneducated, he had no grounds for choosing this book over that', Diane Johnson recalled in *Dashiell Hammett: A Life* (1983). 'He chose them all, read everything, and when he struck something good, he knew it, and thrilled to it.'

Having won praise for the quality of his case reports, Hammett was encouraged to embark on the more sedentary life of a writer. He'd read the detective stories of his day, by the likes of Carroll John Daly (1889–1958) and S.S. Van Dine (1888–1939), and thought them pretty ridiculous. He speculated that his real-life experiences might give him a leg up. And, indeed they did. After seeing some of his work published in 1922 in *The Smart Set*, a literary magazine, he started peddling fiction to another periodical more

interested in adventure and mystery stories: *Black Mask*. It was there, in a series of stories beginning with 1923's 'Arson Plus' (which he published under the pseudonym 'Peter Collinson'), that Hammett introduced the Continental Op, a short, 'fat, middle-aged, hard-boiled, pig-headed guy' of 40. Hammett admitted the character was based on James Wright, his Pinkerton boss in Baltimore, who'd taught him how to be vigilant and self-reliant, how to assume false identities and how to tail a suspect covertly. ('Keep behind your suspect as much as possible; never try to hide from him; act in a natural manner no matter what happens; and never meet his eye', the Continental Op advises in the 1924 story 'Zigzags of Treachery'.)

Hammett wasn't a well man; his tuberculosis flared up periodically, sometimes so badly that he sent Jose and their two daughters out of town for their own good. He was drinking too much, and smoking like a train engine, and sometimes he was too weak to cross his apartment without gripping a lineup of chairs. He had to supplement his fiction-writing income by penning advertising copy for a downtown jewellery store. However, goaded on by *Black Mask*'s editor, Captain Joseph T. Shaw (1874–1952) – and despite urges to write more 'serious' fiction – Hammett continued

'IN ALL MY EXPERIENCE I HAVE NEVER READ A STORY AS INTENSE, AS GRIPPING, AS POWERFUL AS THIS LAST INSTALLMENT. IT IS A MAGNIFICENT PIECE OF WRITING' – BLACK MASK EDITOR JOSEPH T. SHAW OF THE MALTESE FALCON

plugging away at detective tales. In November 1927 *Black Mask* began serializing his first novel, *Red Harvest*, a bloody saga in which the Continental Op tries to clean up a corrupt imaginary western mining town – Personville, aka 'Poisonville'. He followed that up with the novelettes he'd later gather to form *The Dain Curse*, a character-crowded suspense story combining murder, robbery and a sinister San Francisco cult. Both were published in book form in 1929.

The Maltese Falcon

In 1930, Hammett published *The Maltese Falcon*, which won him his most fervid plaudits. Critic Alexander Woollcott (1887–1943) called it 'the best detective story America has yet produced'. *The New Republic* extolled its 'glittering and fascinating prose', while the American national humour magazine *Judge* delivered one of the cleverest ovations, declaring that Hammett 'writes with a lead pipe and poisoned arrows as coups de grâce. He stands alone as ace shocker. Hereafter even S.S. Van Dine [creator of the intellectual and foppish amateur sleuth, Philo Vance] must lower his monocle, cough up the encyclopedia and eat some humble pie'.

For *The Maltese Falcon*, Hammett ditched the first-person narration of his previous novels, writing instead from a third-person limited point of view that left readers to discover the turns of the story as his protagonist, Sam Spade, experienced them himself, and to discern what the private eye thought of the action and his fellow players only from his words and facial expressions. (That perspective change would make the Falcon easier to transfer onto the big screen.)

The story was a thriller, all about the pursuit of a gold-and-jewel-encrusted, falcon-shaped statuette, and how such a storied prize will bring out the desperate and homicidal depths of people. Lured unwittingly into looking for the falcon by Brigid O'Shaughnessy, acting under a false name, Spade and his partner, Miles Archer, trail Floyd Thursby, who, she claims, has helped her sister disappear. It's all a lie as O'Shaughnessy, Thursby and three others are all looking for the falcon themselves.

The Maltese Falcon was Hammett's most personal tale yet. Sam Spade, the Satan-faced, morally suspect San Francisco gumshoe, is willing to sleep with Archer's wife, but won't sit still for that same partner's murder. He was certainly much more like the author than the Continental Op had been. Not only did Spade have his creator's appetite for the ladies (Hammett wasn't faithful to

'IT'S BEEN A LONG TIME SINCE I BURST INTO TEARS BECAUSE A POLICEMAN DIDN'T LIKE ME' – SAM SPADE, THE MALTESE FALCON

Jose during their years together), but he was also given Hammett's real first name. Hammett even gave Spade the home address at which he actually wrote *The Maltese Falcon* – 891 Post Street, where he lived from 1926 to 1929. He also wrote *Red Harvest* and *The Dain Curse* while living there. Visitors can take a four-hour tour of Dashiell Hammett's San Franscisco run by Don Herron, cabbie and Hammett fan, which takes in John's Grill and the Flood Building among other sites.

Other places of interest on the Hammett trail include Burritt Street, the alley south of Bush Street, just west of Stockton Street, where Miles Archer was murdered, his body tumbling down to the Stockton Tunnel, where a plaque now marks the spot.

CINEMATIC SAN FRANCISCO

While Dashiell Hammett immortalized San Francisco in its historical heyday, there is no end to the contemporary crime and mystery writers who use the city as a setting in their books. Of particular note are Edgar-winning novelist Domenic Stansberry (creator of Dante Mancuso), Stephen Greenleaf (Marsh Tanner series), Laurie M. King (the Kate Martinelli novels), Marcia Muller (Sharon McCone series), Perry O'Shaughnessy (Nina Reilly series), Meg Gardiner (author of the Evan Delaney novels) and Sheldon Siegel (Mike Daley and Rose Fernandez series), among a horde of others.

However, the primary image many people have in mind is, of course, of San Francisco on the silver screen. Who can forget Steve McQueen's Ford Mustang racing up and down the hilly streets of the city in the iconic *Bullitt* (1968), James Stewart's hapless and romantic search for a woman in Hitchcock's *Vertigo* (1958) or Clint Eastwood as Inspector Callahan in Don Siegel's *Dirty Harry* (1971) and the numerous sequels? All these very different views of the city lodge in the mind for eternity. Also worthy of mention is the American television series *Streets of San Francisco*, whose 120 episodes ran from 1972 to 1977.

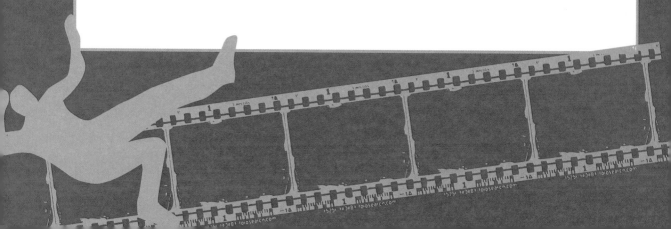

Hammett's last years

Hammett worked on one other novel while living in San Francisco, a stand-alone story of political corruption called *The Glass Key*. But by the time it began its *Black Mask* serialization in the spring of 1930, he had left the city, going to New York, then heading to Hollywood, which was showing interest in his fiction – at last. In 1930, he encountered an MGM script reader and aspiring playwright named Lillian Hellman (1905–84), a dozen years his junior. Although the pair never wed, they spent what Hellman termed '31 on and off years' together, until his demise in 1961 at age 66. (Hammett had gotten a quick-and-easy Mexican divorce from his wife in the mid-1930s, though he continued to send his family money). He went on to encourage Hellman's playwriting ambitions and based the character of Nora Charles, the wealthy, witty heroine of his last published novel, *The Thin Man* (1934), on her.

Sadly, the author's creative spark seemed then to go out. With artist Alex Raymond (1909–56), he created a comic strip called 'Secret Agent X-9' (which continued to be syndicated until the mid-1990s) and developed a world-weary private eye character, Brad Runyon – aka 'The Fat Man' – for radio. Meanwhile, Sam Spade took on a new life over the airwaves and on celluloid – three cinematic adaptations were made of *The Maltese Falcon*. Dashiell Hammett's days as a novelist were done, but he'd accomplished enough to cement his association with San Francisco as well as his renown as a father of the American detective novel. As Chandler remarked in his famous 1940s' essay, 'The Simple Art of Murder', Hammett 'gave murder back to the kind of people that commit it for reasons, not just to provide a corpse; and with the means at hand, not hand-wrought dueling pistols, curare and tropical fish'.

Or, to quote Ross Macdonald (1915–83), another author who benefited from Hammett's lead, 'We all came out from under Hammett's black mask'. Legacies don't come much better than that.

USEFUL WEBSITES

Dashiell Hammett tour
leaves daily at noon from the corner of Fulton and Larkin
www.donherron.com

John's Grill
for impromptu drinks, full meals à la Spade or formal occasions
www.johnsgrill.com

The Asian Art Museum
This magnificent building was formerly the main branch of San Francisco Public Library, where Hammett taught himself to write bestsellers
www.asianart.org

HAMMETT & SPADE'S SAN FRANCISCO

San Francisco Bay

Telegraph Hill: it was from the high ground here that the Continental Op recced a house in the short story 'The Scorched Face'.

St Mary's Cathedral: where Hammett married. The building was destroyed by fire in 1962.

Pacific Avenue: in Hammett's time, a red light district and a hotbed of lowlifes.

Sutter Street: site of the secretarial school where Pinkerton agent Hammett learned to type, a skill he later used to alter the course of literary history.

Burritt Street: the alley where Miles Archer was murdered in *The Maltese Falcon*.

Post Street: Hammett wrote *The Maltese Falcon* at # 891 and gave the address to the hero of the work, Sam Spade.

MARINA DISTRICT

LOMBARD STREET

VAN NESS AVENUE

GOUGH STREET

LARKIN STREET

SAN FRANCISCO

BROADWAY STREET

PACIFIC AVENUE

FRANKLIN ST

PACIFIC HEIGHTS

GOUGH STREET

CALIFORNIA STREET

CALIFORNIA STREET

BUSH STREET

891 Post Stre

POST STREET

SUTTER STREET

620 Eddy Street

LARKIN STREE

CIVIC CENTER PLAZA

MCALLISTER STREET

City Hall

Asian Art Muse

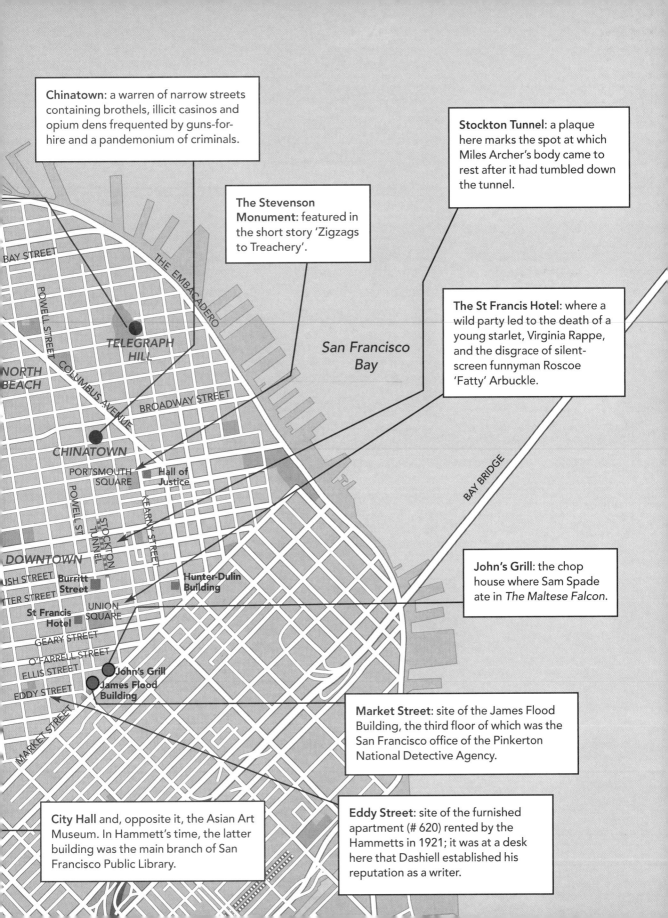

Chinatown: a warren of narrow streets containing brothels, illicit casinos and opium dens frequented by guns-for-hire and a pandemonium of criminals.

The Stevenson Monument: featured in the short story 'Zigzags to Treachery'.

Stockton Tunnel: a plaque here marks the spot at which Miles Archer's body came to rest after it had tumbled down the tunnel.

The St Francis Hotel: where a wild party led to the death of a young starlet, Virginia Rappe, and the disgrace of silent-screen funnyman Roscoe 'Fatty' Arbuckle.

John's Grill: the chop house where Sam Spade ate in *The Maltese Falcon*.

Market Street: site of the James Flood Building, the third floor of which was the San Francisco office of the Pinkerton National Detective Agency.

City Hall and, opposite it, the Asian Art Museum. In Hammett's time, the latter building was the main branch of San Francisco Public Library.

Eddy Street: site of the furnished apartment (# 620) rented by the Hammetts in 1921; it was at a desk here that Dashiell established his reputation as a writer.

BAY STREET

THE EMBACADERO

POWELL STREET

COLUMBUS AVENUE

TELEGRAPH HILL

San Francisco Bay

NORTH BEACH

BROADWAY STREET

CHINATOWN

PORTSMOUTH SQUARE

Hall of Justice

POWELL ST

KEARNY STREET

STOCKTON TUNNEL

BAY BRIDGE

DOWNTOWN

USH STREET

Burritt Street

TER STREET

Hunter-Dulin Building

St Francis Hotel

UNION SQUARE

GEARY STREET

O'FARRELL STREET

ELLIS STREET

EDDY STREET

John's Grill

James Flood Building

MARKET STREET

Declan Burke

DECLAN HUGHES & ED LOY'S DUBLIN

'Dubh Linn', the Gaelic translation of the Anglicized 'Dublin', means 'the black pool'. Despite its resonances, Irish crime writers have yet to use 'The Black Pool' as the title of a private detective novel, although Declan Hughes, creator of private eye Ed Loy and the Irish heir to the tradition of Dashiell Hammett, Raymond Chandler and Ross Macdonald, may yet oblige.

The settlement that grew into the city of Dublin was first established in AD 841 by raiding Viking warriors near the mouth of the Liffey, the river that runs from west to east and divides Dublin in two. Today, the city proper is a relatively small affair, bounded north and south by the Royal and Grand canals, respectively, beyond which the capital of the Republic of Ireland dissipates into sprawling suburban housing estates. The city centre extends for no more than five or six miles (8–9 km) from east to west, but Greater Dublin, with a population of around 1.2 million, stretches from Swords in the north to Bray in the south, a distance of some 20 miles (32 km).

Irish private eyes

For a city its size, Dublin has not been blessed with an abundance of private eye detectives. This may be because, until relatively recently, Dublin was less of a city

and more an agglomeration of joined-up villages, in which the anonymity of a large city was largely absent. Generally speaking, when a serious crime was committed, everyone knew who was responsible. The trick, in a post-colonial country in which the national mantra was Seamus Heaney's 'Whatever you say, say nothing', was to prove what everyone already knew – a job for a police force rather than a private eye.

Nonetheless, there are two notable precursors to Declan Hughes's Ed Loy. Vincent Banville's John Blaine, prowled the mean streets of north inner-city Dublin. Based in Cabra, with an office 'on a side street off the main thoroughfare' of O'Connell Street, Blaine was a humorous homage to Chandler's Philip Marlowe. He first appeared in *Death by Design* (1993), some years before the Celtic Tiger economic boom hit its stride, and

subsequently in *Death: The Pale Rider* (1995) and *Cannon Law* (2001).

Arlene Hunt's *False Intentions* (2005) introduced the private eye team of Sarah Quigley and John Kenny, a pairing based in Dublin's inner-city Southside, with an office on the top floor of a 'dilapidated old building on Wexford Street'. Hunt plays a straighter bat than Banville, being less concerned with paying homage, and her detectives, appearing at the height of the economic boom, are much more mobile. Where John Blaine only occasionally ventured beyond his Northside domain, Quigley and Kenny are required to criss-cross the city in the course of their investigations as the economic boom brings with it illicit wealth, greater anonymity and an increasing disrespect for human life. Their horizons are broader, too: while Blaine eventually (and tentatively) ventures as far south as rural County Wicklow during the course of *Cannon Law*, John Kenny thinks nothing of hopping on a plane to London for the sake of an investigation in Hunt's *Missing, Presumed Dead* (2008).

Loy's Southside

Declan Hughes's Ed Loy first appeared in *The Wrong Kind of Blood* (2006), which is set for the most part in the fictional south Dublin suburbs of Bayview, Castlehill and Seafield (these roughly correspond to the well-heeled real-life suburbs of Dalkey, Killiney and Dun Laoghaire). Loy is a character in which Ireland's past, present and future collide. Named for the weapon which Christy Mahon used to 'kill' his father in J.M. Synge's 1907 play *The Playboy of the Western World* – a 'loy' is a kind of spade used for cutting turf – Ed Loy returned to Dublin from Los Angeles at the height of Ireland's Celtic Tiger boom, one of a wave of Irish economic exiles returning

DECLAN HUGHES

Declan Hughes read English and Philosophy at Trinity College, Dublin.

His first play, *I Can't Get Started*, was about the relationship between Lillian Hellman and Dashiell Hammett, whom he describes as 'the J.S. Bach of the genre'.

His great master is Ross Macdonald; others influences include Ian Rankin, George Pelecanos, Dennis Lehane and James Lee Burke.

Favourite composers: Sibelius, Mahler, Vaughan Williams, Shostakovich, Bruckner… and Warren ('Werewolves of London') Zevon.

to the 'oul' sod' in the first experience of reverse emigration the country had ever known.

The Dublin Loy had once known has changed dramatically, however, and nowhere as dramatically as in the city's southern suburbs. Five or six miles out from the city centre, the area is almost another country entirely; that country is not the past, but the future. The north/south divide of the city created by the Liffey is a crucial one. The Northside is commonly perceived as working-class and

Leinster House on Kildare Street, Dublin.

underprivileged by comparison with the more middle-class, prosperous Southside. The National Parliament of Ireland is housed in Leinster House, on Kildare Street, on the south of the River Liffey. When James Fitzgerald, Earl of Kildare, ordered Leinster House built in 1745, however, the south side of the river was the unfashionable part of Dublin. The earl, no stranger to self-satisfaction, announced that the fashion would follow him, and so it did: fashion, wealth and prestige attached themselves to the Southside of Dublin, and have remained there ever since, even if the wealth has tended to migrate ever farther south with each passing generation.

Declan Hughes uses the settings of the fictional suburbs of Bayview,

'IMAGINE ROSS MACDONALD WITH BLOOD ON HIS HANDS. NOT FOR THE FAINT OF HEART, BUT HIGHLY RECOMMENDED' – REVIEW OF HUGHES ON WWW.THRILLINGDETECTIVE.COM

Castlehill and Seafield to investigate the consequences that generations of wealth have had on the moral, spiritual and psychological fibre of the affluent families of south County Dublin. These consequences, as you might imagine, are for the most part sapping and debilitating. Although situated far from the urban ghettoes of conventional criminality, those who reside in the plushly upholstered areas, 'the great Georgian houses, the Victorian castles of Castlehill' (*The Wrong Kind of Blood*, 2006), are revealed to be no less vicious, ruthless and homicidal than their inner-city peers when it comes to acquiring and protecting wealth.

Loy has returned to Dublin after a long absence in order to bury his mother, and takes over the family home in Quarry Fields. Quarry Fields is, again, a fictionalized version of where the upmarket suburb of Sandycove merges with Glasthule, the private houses of which are of a modest scale, and one step up from the local authority housing of Glasthule proper. Thus Loy straddles many intersecting social and geographic lines: he is a returned emigrant, a local with an outsider's eye; the scion of an upwardly mobile family, he has an appreciation of both working-class and middle-class mores and contacts in both camps: being

socially mobile himself, he is adaptable enough to move with the ebb and flow of new money as it washes against the ever-eroding landmarks of old wealth.

When Loy does venture into Dublin's city centre, to meet with his mother's solicitor, it is a brief visit during which he remains on the Southside: Trinity College (Hughes's and Loy's alma mater) and St Stephen's Green – all within a stone's throw of Leinster House – are part of an older, more genteel Dublin, while adjacent Leeson Street – a 'broad tree-lined street of detached Victorian and Edwardian villas' (*The Wrong Kind of Blood*) – runs south across the Grand Canal in the direction of Ballsbridge and the Royal Dublin Society.

The Irish Los Angeles
Back in south County Dublin, Loy finds himself at home roaming from one interconnected suburb to another, dependent – as he would be in LA – on a car for transport, and specifically in his father's Volvo, an Amazon 122S, 'an old saloon car, racing green with curved

'HUGHES IS NOT AFRAID TO TAKE HIS REFERENCES AND RUN WITH THEM, HE IS NOT AFRAID TO HAVE A GOOD TIME. ABOVE ALL, HE IS NOT AFRAID OF WRITING WELL' – ANNE ENRIGHT, *GUARDIAN* (2008)

lines, tail fins and a tan leather interior' (*The Wrong Kind of Blood*). His investigation takes him into totems of wealth, such as the Royal Seafield Yacht Club and the Castlehill Golf Club, and

The coast near Dalkey (Hughes's Bayview.

... the upscale Bayview-Castlehill 'Top People's Seaside Suburb', where the luxury homes of top Irish rock stars, film directors, barristers and CEOs formed the exclusive enclave the reporter claimed was nicknamed 'Bel Eire' (ibid.).

The 'Bel Eire'/Bel Air reference is no throwaway pun. To Loy, although he does not make the comparison explicitly, south County Dublin has become an Irish version of Los Angeles, in which the previously distinct villages of Bayview (Dalkey), Castlehill (Killiney) and Seafield (Dun Laoghaire) have merged into a homogeneous, anonymous mini-city. The 'broad tree-lined streets' may not be as mean as Raymond Chandler's celebrated thoroughfares, but in *The Wrong Kind of Blood* Hughes took

DECLAN HUGHES ON SCREEN AND STAGE

The creator of Ed Loy was co-writer, with John Brown and Simon Rose, of *The Flying Scotsman* (2006), Douglas Mackinnon's film about Graeme Obree, the cyclist who twice broke the world one-hour distance record on a home-made bike.

Before establishing himself as a detective novelist, Declan Hughes was Writer-in-Association with Dublin's Abbey Theatre. He continues to work for the stage and has had seven original plays performed by the Rough Magic Theatre Company.

 ## ON STAGE

I Can't Get Started (1990)
Digging for Fire (1991)
Love and A Bottle (1991)
New Morning (1993)

Halloween Night (1997)
Boomtown (1999)
Shiver (2003)

murder out of the alleyways and dropped it into the drawing rooms.

To be precise, given that *The Wrong Kind of Blood* turns on a murder victim discovered in the concrete underpinning Seafield Town Hall, Hughes dropped murder into the very foundations of said drawing rooms. The social mobility of those made wealthy by the economic boom, and thus empowered to reside in the most desirable areas of Dublin, is shown to be built on constantly shifting sands. 'It looked,' as Loy acidly observes, on coming across yet another building development, 'like they had just dug up the Parthenon, and were laying the foundations for another shopping mall.

Questions of sport

Croke Park today.

In *The Colour of Blood* (2007), Loy remains based in south County Dublin, although his investigations take him farther south.

The theme remains the same, however: delusions of grandeur fostered by illicit gains. Loy finds himself calling on Rowan House, in the Dublin Mountains south of Sandyford, which 'looked like a Victorian merchant's idea of a baronial castle'. Here, the totem of wealth becomes the Seafield Rugby Club, a 'religion' to replace or – more often – reinforce the religions of sailing and golf.

In *The Dying Breed* (2008), the religion becomes horse-racing, as Loy ranges even farther south, and west into 'the open plains of Kildare', the spiritual heart of Ireland's horsey set. The totem here is the fictional Tyrrellscourt Country Club (which may or may not have been modelled on the real-life 'Bel-Air Riding Club' in Wicklow), which nestles cheek-by-jowl with a village hosting 'a variety of misfits and ne'er-do-wells of one kind or another who couldn't cut it in the new thrusting entrepreneurial Ireland'.

'[I'VE] JUST READ *THE COLOUR OF BLOOD* BY DECLAN HUGHES. I'M A NEW FAN' – PETE TOWNSHEND, LEAD GUITARIST, THE WHO

Changing tack

This tacit acknowledgement that the ostensible success of the Irish economy was in fact a façade papering over a multitude of cracks is amplified in *All the Dead Voices* (2009), in which the direction of Ed Loy's investigations abruptly about-turn and take him north, back into the heart of Dublin city proper. The novel even opens on the Northside, in Tolka Park, the home of football team Shelbourne F.C., when a man armed with a machine gun runs onto the pitch and lets fly with the kind of volley not generally associated with the sport of soccer – although the random shooting does bring to mind, for those aware of their Irish history, the horrific incident known as Bloody Sunday, when British forces opened fire on the crowd attending a Gaelic football match in Croke Park on 21 November 1920, killing 14 civilians.

The massacre was in retaliation for the murder by the Irish Republican Army (IRA) of 12 British agents and two auxiliary soldiers earlier that morning, and it's surely no coincidence that *All the Dead Voices* concerns itself in large part with the fallout from Northern Ireland's 'Troubles', in which former Republican paramilitaries have parlayed their ill-gotten gains into the kind of socially acceptable wealth that allows them to dine in long-established restaurants favoured by the rich and famous:

The wheels might have been coming off the economy at a frantic rate, but you wouldn't have known a thing about it if the only place you ate your dinner was Shanahan's on the Green. Mind you, if you could afford to dine in Shanahan's Steakhouse every night, you probably didn't care: you'd stored up enough nuts to get you through however long the winter lasted.

It's not only the geographical direction of Loy's investigations that have changed, however (and *All the Dead Voices* takes Loy back out to the southern suburb of Blackrock, and farther south again, to the Wicklow Hills). Loy, who has until the fourth novel operated out of the family home in Quarry Fields, has made the conscious decision to move into an office in the heart of Dublin city, on Holles Street, near Merrion Square. It appears that the migratory Loy has finally dropped anchor. But the permanence is illusory.

'I lived in my car', Loy says, 'on the move, depending on momentum to yield results, postponing as long as possible the moment I had to go home'.

The harsh truth for the insider/outsider Loy is that the Dublin he has returned to is no longer his home, with the implicit extension that the city itself, recently propelled into a state of physical and financial flux, is 'depending on momentum to yield results, postponing as long as possible the moment' when it has to admit that it is no longer a home but has instead become a battleground on which the struggle to keep up with the O'Joneses has degenerated into a poignant scuffle for the Celtic Tiger's few remaining scraps.

Heading home

Recognizing this, Ed Loy leaves Dublin behind in *The City of the Lost Girls* (2010), travelling to Los Angeles to investigate the possibility that a film producer friend is a psychopathic killer of young women. Loy's journey has come full circle, from Bel Air to 'Bel Eire' and back again to the real 'LA-LA Land', of which the Dublin of the economic boom era, despite its self-aggrandizing aspirations, revealed itself as only the palest of imitations.

Perhaps it was inevitable that Loy, the digger of dirt named for a spade, would eventually return to the city of Spade, Marlowe and Archer: contemporary Dublin, for all its sprawling breadth and length, has proven itself built on very shallow foundations. Perhaps Loy will come back to Dublin some day. But if he does not, then Declan Hughes, if we can paraphrase George Bernard Shaw (1856–1950), not only exhumed the skeletons from the foundations of the Celtic Tiger's building frenzy, but made them dance a merry jig. In the process the author has done the Irish state some considerable service and established a formidable literary reputation. Michelle Peckham in *Euro Crime* was one of many who praised Hughes's *All the Dead Voices* (2009) for the way it 'weaves together the different threads of the story expertly, and every word counts. So, read and enjoy, but pay attention or you might miss something!'

USEFUL WEBSITES & ADDRESSES

Literary walking tour that starts at the Dublin Writer's Museum in Parnell Square
www.dublintourist.com/walks_around_dublin/literary_dublin.shtml

Tours of the Irish capital's literary watering holes
www.dublinpubcrawl.com

One of Dublin's top eateries
www.shanahans.ie

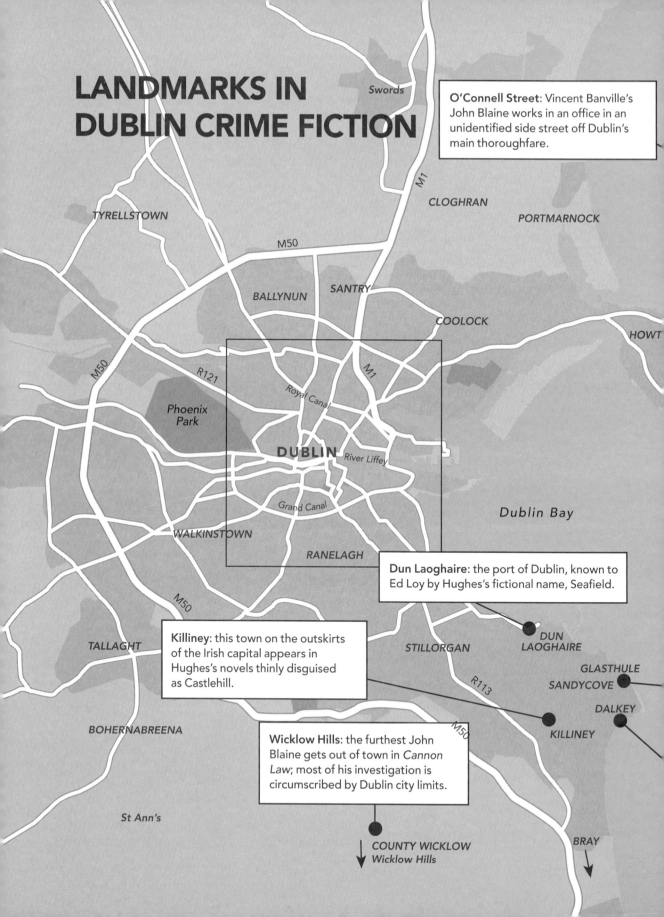

LANDMARKS IN DUBLIN CRIME FICTION

Swords

O'Connell Street: Vincent Banville's John Blaine works in an office in an unidentified side street off Dublin's main thoroughfare.

M1

CLOGHRAN

PORTMARNOCK

TYRELLSTOWN

M50

BALLYNUN

SANTRY

COOLOCK

HOWT

M50

R121

M1

Phoenix
Park

Royal Canal

DUBLIN   River Liffey

Dublin Bay

Grand Canal

WALKINSTOWN

RANELAGH

Dun Laoghaire: the port of Dublin, known to Ed Loy by Hughes's fictional name, Seafield.

M50

Killiney: this town on the outskirts of the Irish capital appears in Hughes's novels thinly disguised as Castlehill.

STILLORGAN

DUN
LAOGHAIRE

GLASTHULE

SANDYCOVE

R113

TALLAGHT

DALKEY

KILLINEY

BOHERNABREENA

M50

Wicklow Hills: the furthest John Blaine gets out of town in *Cannon Law*; most of his investigation is circumscribed by Dublin city limits.

St Ann's

COUNTY WICKLOW
Wicklow Hills

BRAY

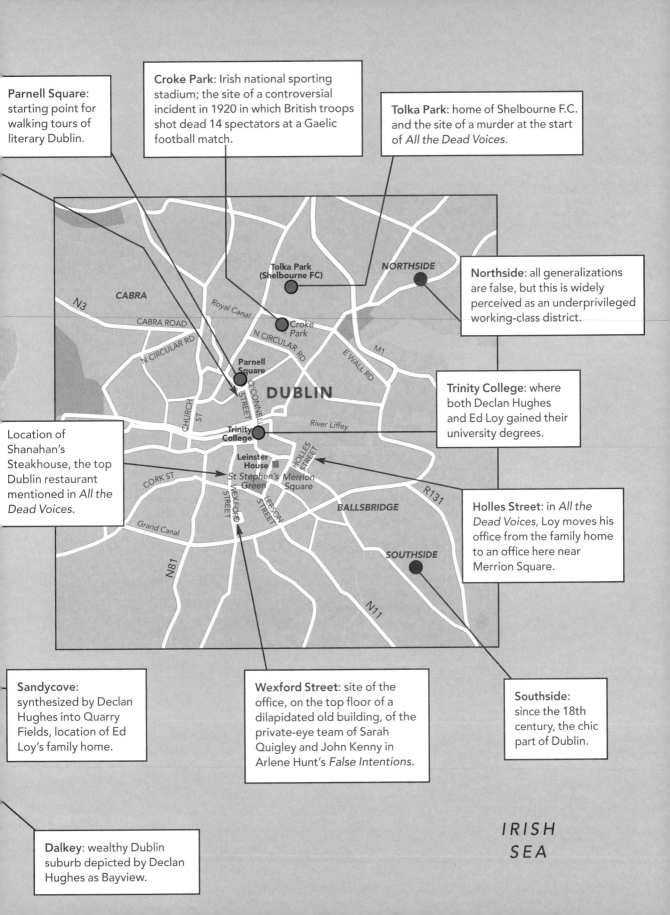

Parnell Square: starting point for walking tours of literary Dublin.

Croke Park: Irish national sporting stadium; the site of a controversial incident in 1920 in which British troops shot dead 14 spectators at a Gaelic football match.

Tolka Park: home of Shelbourne F.C. and the site of a murder at the start of *All the Dead Voices*.

Northside: all generalizations are false, but this is widely perceived as an underprivileged working-class district.

Trinity College: where both Declan Hughes and Ed Loy gained their university degrees.

Holles Street: in *All the Dead Voices*, Loy moves his office from the family home to an office here near Merrion Square.

Southside: since the 18th century, the chic part of Dublin.

Wexford Street: site of the office, on the top floor of a dilapidated old building, of the private-eye team of Sarah Quigley and John Kenny in Arlene Hunt's *False Intentions*.

Sandycove: synthesized by Declan Hughes into Quarry Fields, location of Ed Loy's family home.

Location of Shanahan's Steakhouse, the top Dublin restaurant mentioned in *All the Dead Voices*.

Dalkey: wealthy Dublin suburb depicted by Declan Hughes as Bayview.

IRISH SEA

NORTHSIDE

Tolka Park
(Shelbourne FC)

CABRA

N3

Royal Canal

CABRA ROAD

N CIRCULAR RD

Croke Park

N CIRCULAR RD

E WALL RD

M1

Parnell Square

CHURCH ST

O'CONNELL STREET

DUBLIN

River Liffey

Trinity College

Leinster House

St Stephen's Green

HOLLES STREET

Merrion Square

R131

BALLSBRIDGE

CORK ST

WEXFORD STREET

LEESON STREET

SOUTHSIDE

Grand Canal

N81

N11

Michael Carlson

ROSS MACDONALD & LEW ARCHER'S SOUTHERN CALIFORNIA

California has always been the ultimate destination of the American Dream. In 1865, newspaper editor Horace Greeley (1811–72) famously told Americans to 'Go West', but once they got to the Pacific Ocean there was nowhere left to go, so they turned and spread up and down the California coastline.

The American detective story followed much the same trail from the Eastern Seaboard to the shores of the Pacific Ocean. Although its roots lie in Westerns, the genre developed in the ghettos of New York and the streets of gangland Chicago before reaching its apotheosis in California. It's surely no coincidence that the two greats of American detective writing, Dashiell Hammett (1894–1961) and Raymond Chandler (1888–1959), both chose California for their settings. San Francisco is where Hammett's Continental Op does most of his work, and where Sam Spade chases the Maltese Falcon. Hammett absorbed the conventions of the rough-edged detective operating among the upper crust, but his dicks relish the contrast between the foggy alleys of the waterfront and Chinatown and the rich of Nob Hill, and relish even more their similarities. For Chandler,

California was where second acts were built over failed lives, an experience he knew at first hand.

Hollywood created a new aristocracy in Los Angeles, with a very thin veneer of respectability; it is the contrast between that veneer and the corruption underneath which provides the framework for the best of California writing. As migration flowed to the land where the sun always shines, egged on by Hollywood dreams that can be located on the maps sold by street vendors, Los Angeles expanded, and the ethos that drove its growth spread as well – the concept of a city with no centre, expanding like an alien being, its roads snaking into arid areas newly granted fresh water. Fresh water may have brought the area alive, and the newly burgeoning highways became its skeleton, but the ocean remained its soul, the reflection of its dreams. And the very

best of California detective fiction seems to take place in a murky area between the freeways and the surf.

Capitalizing LA

In the Forties and Fifties, Hollywood's conceit was to grant the rather sleepy city of Los Angeles the stature of New York or Chicago. Ross Macdonald described LA during this period as:

> ... in a sense, our national capital, alas... the place where our children learn how and what to dream and where everything happens just before, or just after, it happens to us.

This notion is reflected in the great detective films and fictions of the period, which are full of country settings, disconnected from the city, into which the lost and damned retreat, escape, or just vacation. Robert Mitchum and Burt Lancaster hide out and try to remake

their lives in small-town garages, waiting to be spotted by someone from their past who happens to be travelling back to LA.

Chandler saw places like Santa Monica, only 15 miles (24 km) from downtown Los Angeles, as distinct, even distant, cities. Santa Monica was then where LA people kept summer houses, and boarded boats to pursue gambling in international waters. Chandler's version, disguised as Bay City, was deeply corrupt and festering, a place where Marlowe could be waylaid and dumped on the long empty road back to LA. It looked

LEW ARCHER

Divorced; smokes; drinks ('but not before lunch'); favours a .38 police special but often doesn't carry a gun.

Hobbies include fishing and chess, lonely pastimes for someone described (in *Black Money*, 1966) as 'a middle-aged man lying alone in darkness while life fled by like traffic on the freeway'.

pretty but, like many of the people who flocked to settle in California, its dark secrets were never very far below the shiny surface.

It was this aspect of Southern California that Ross Macdonald used as a springboard to a series in which Lew Archer both examines the two-dimensional nature of the new California culture and reveals how easily the past may come back to haunt those who think they've somehow escaped it. Although Archer's office is in the 8400 block of Sunset Boulevard, a few blocks past the intersection with Harper Avenue – the street name was given to the Archer-like hero of the 1966 movie *Harper*, starring Paul Newman – and he lives in a nondescript apartment in West LA, Archer himself is an immigrant to the City of Angels; he was born elsewhere and raised in Long Beach, where he surfed and got in trouble with cars. This is an interesting inversion of Macdonald's own life story: born in Los Gatos, California, but raised in Canada, the author later settled in Santa Barbara. This city – just under 100 miles (160 km) north of Los Angeles – lay at the heart of

Lew Archer's beat, a broad area of Southern California that inspired the title of *The Barbarous Coast* (1956), the sixth novel in the 18-novel series.

The heart of Macdonald's *The Drowning Pool* (1950) is the stark contrast between the town (Venice) where offshore oil drilling takes place, and the town (Pacific Point) where the wealthy live, unaffected by the pollution. *The Drowning Pool* took Archer as far south as Palm Springs (Chandler's caustically renamed 'Poodle Springs') and as far north as San Francisco, where Macdonald had first lived before moving to Santa Barbara. The theme of offshore oil would recur in *Sleeping Beauty* (1973), where a leaking derrick is central to the story and based on the 1969 blowout of Union Platform A off the coast of Santa Barbara. By this time, Macdonald had become deeply involved in California's ecological movement. He writes movingly of being unable to cycle into town on the now busy roads. At the same time, Disneyland had grown up in Anaheim. This engineered amusement park reflected the sense that life

Sleeping Beauty's Castle at the heart of Disneyland, Anaheim.

itself could be perfectly programmed into an American dream of suburban house, cars in the garage, Mom and Dad and two kids and their bikes and surfboards. In this sense, if the ocean is Southern California's soul, Walt Disney is its heart.

SoCal status

The best of the later Southern California crime writers work the freeways that connect theme park developments such as Disneyland itself and Universal Studios. Of necessity, they moved away from the Marlowe/Archer tradition of a wisecracking private eye whose roots are more urban and urbane. This makes sense, because as the population expands farther and farther from its nexus, the old idea of a PI in an office in West LA actually receiving clients from far-off areas becomes less and less likely. As LA expanded and homogenized this became a small artistic problem

for Macdonald. For example, in *The Goodbye Look* (1969), a college, which is recognizably Loyola Marymount, is presented as being far outside LA when, in reality, it is close to LAX airport in an area that has long been subsumed by the widening conurbation.

But distances present no problems for the new breed of SoCal writers, one of the most interesting of whom is T. Jefferson Parker, born in 1953 and raised in the area. His books reflect the special status of those who've grown up there, even as it has expanded.

If LA reflects the Hollywood dream, Orange County, which was Parker's original beat, and then San Diego County farther south, reflect a different population, one which feels the pressure of having seen itself reflected in Hollywood's distorting mirror for decades. Parker's debut novel, *Laguna Heat* (1985), was a stunning update of Macdonald, drawing on the idea of the past being inescapable but set in the beach town where Parker himself then lived and reflecting his familiarity with the more suburban ethos of Orange County: towns and cities with no discernible centres, held together merely by shared assumptions of the Disney version of the American Dream.

The quintessential spirit of California lies at the heart of Parker's *LA Outlaws* (2008), in which Suzanne Jones, an eighth-grade history teacher in the Los Angeles school system, lives an hour and forty minutes outside the city (when driven at the right time and in the right muscle car) in Valley Center, midway between the Avocado Highway (a section of Highway 15) and Hellhole Canyon. She becomes a 21st-century highwaywoman by transforming herself into Allison Murietta, direct descendant of Joaquin Murietta (1829–53), Gold Rush bandit sometimes known as the Mexican Robin Hood. The book opens with a killing in East LA, where the 10 and 710 join, and it speeds onward like a car on the open road, through a backdrop of faceless hotels, the Airport Marriott, the Torrance Residence Inn, junkyards and junk food. It's a tour de force, made more interesting by Parker's spinning off LA County Sheriff's deputy Charlie Hood into what could

become a series of his own – the county sheriffs are responsible for crimebusting outside the LA (and certain other) city limits; it's like patrolling the area between London and Brighton, only far more developed.

Anyone interested in California car culture should also seek out Philip Reed's kaleidoscopic novels *Bird Dog* (1997) and *Low Rider* (1998) featuring ex-car salesman Harold Dodge; the latter work opens on the 405 Freeway, with Dodge getting the thumbs up from gangbangers admiring his lime-green 300 horsepower '64 Impala. Californians define their material world by the cars they drive, and Dodge winds up seeing greed and crime at their most venal and comical.

What goes around…

Parker's best book may be *California Girl* (2004), which flashes back to tumultuous 1968 when Nick Becker, the aging cop protagonist, has to revisit his first-ever homicide investigation. The story then goes back even further, to 1954, when Becker and his brother were growing up in San Clemente (site of Richard Nixon's 'Western White House') and illustrates the aphorism about life being an endless repetition of high school. Parker is at his best detailing the changes five decades

'MACDONALD OUTGREW HIS LITERARY PREDECESSORS AND SURPASSED THEM… HE BEGAN… TO PLUMB THE METAPHYSICAL DEPTHS, WRITING NOT JUST ABOUT LEGAL TRANSGRESSIONS BUT ALSO ABOUT, IN HIS WORDS, "SORROWS"'
– TOBIAS JONES, GUARDIAN (2009)

MACDONALD ON SCREEN

The works of Ross Macdonald have inspired some memorable films and performances, notably from Paul Newman.

 ON TELEVISION

The Underground Man (1974) (TV), with Peter Graves as Lew Archer
Archer (1975) six-part TV series , with H. Jon Benjamin and Jessica Walter

 IN FILM

Harper (1966) based on *The Moving Target (1949)*, with a screenplay by William Goldman and Paul Newman and Lauren Bacall in the leading roles
The Drowning Pool (1975), with Paul Newman

Double Negative (1980) based on The Three Roads (1948), with Michael Sarrazin and Anthony Perkins
Blue City (1986), starring Judd Nelson and David Caruso
Criminal Behavior (1992) made-for-television move based on The Ferguson Affair (1960), starring Farrah Fawcett as a lawyer stalked by a killer
The Wolf of the West Coast (2002), based on 'Guilt-Aged Blonde', a short story in The Name Is Archer (1955) , with James Faulkner as the detective, here renamed Lew Millar

have brought, but he also excels at revealing the persistence of class differences that are not allowed for in the American Dream. The murder takes place in an abandoned packing house for a fictional farming produce company, SunBlesst, whose trademark – a smiling girl and her orange – become a metaphor of telling weight for the whole area.

Territorial disputes

Class distinctions are very much at the core of John Shannon's series about the child-finder Jack Liffey. In *Palos Verdes Blue* (2009), one of the best of the series, Liffey lives in East LA with his Latina cop girlfriend, but his ex-wife still lives in their house in Redondo Beach, and she sends him to help a friend who lives where Liffey grew up, in San Pedro. As Liffey searches for the friend's missing daughter, he revisits all the old turf wars between the inhabitants of the posh Palos Verdes peninsula, the rougher San Pedro proper, and the newer element, illegal Mexican workers living on the hillsides, out of sight, out of mind until one of their

youngsters decides that he too wants to surf Lunada Bay. What could be more one-dimensionally part of the smiling American dream than surfing? The Beach Boys, Dick Dale, Gidget, Beach Blanket Bingo, drag racers – American culture concentrated like frozen orange juice with sunshine and smiles on the packaging.

Boone Daniels, the surfing ex-cop turned private eye (when the waves are no good) made his first appearance in Don Winslow's *The Dawn Patrol* (2008), in which illegal immigrants live in a similar shanty area and attract a similar response from some of the more sensitive locals. The story, which begins with the murder of a stripper scheduled to testify, is another which updates the classic LA detective, but Daniels, surfing Pacific Beach, turns it into something home-grown, a new-generation dick with a new definition of hard-boiled. Winslow had already produced an amalgam of genre elements in *The Winter of Frankie Machine* (2006), whose title character is a retired hit man running a bait shop on San Diego's Ocean Beach Pier. It's no surprise Robert DeNiro got the title role in the forthcoming film adaptation. Winslow, whose Neal Carey series was set in New York, and whose *Isle of Joy* (1996) is an exceptional *hommage* to 1950s' New York City, hit southern California with a bang in the excellent and unjustly overlooked

'NOTHING IS WRONG WITH CALIFORNIA THAT A RISE IN THE OCEAN LEVEL WOULDN'T CURE' – LEW ARCHER

California Fire and Life (1999), which was hard-boiled and encapsulated everything about the materialism of a culture with no culture at its heart. Winslow reached his current peak with *The Power of The Dog* (2005), a sweeping and powerful epic covering three decades of the war on drugs, whose epicentre is Southern California and its border with Mexico. Art Keller, the book's protagonist, ex-CIA now DEA, grew up in San Diego's Barrio Logan and realizes that the border is merely a line on the map. Which brought us back to the cowboy days, when getting across the border with stolen cattle, or money to fund revolutions, had a more romantic twinge. Winslow doesn't shy away from the politics of the drug wars, the Nicaraguan Contras and the involvement of governments in the very

crimes they purport to be trying to stop, but he also anchors the story in the Southern California filled with people looking for material success, for the American Dream.

It is the collapse of that dream which preoccupies Ross Macdonald and the other Southern California crime writers mentioned here. All influenced by Raymond Chandler, they are perhaps less romantic than the master, but they are no less acute in their charting of the petty failures and the bigger ones in the cityscape that surrounds Disneyland.

USEFUL WEBSITES

Coach tours from Anaheim into undiscovered Southern California
www.graylineanaheim.com

Discover Lew Archer's home town
www.longbeachtours.net

Trips round Chandler's Poodle Springs and one of the settings for Macdonald's *The Drowning Pool*
www.palmspringstours.net

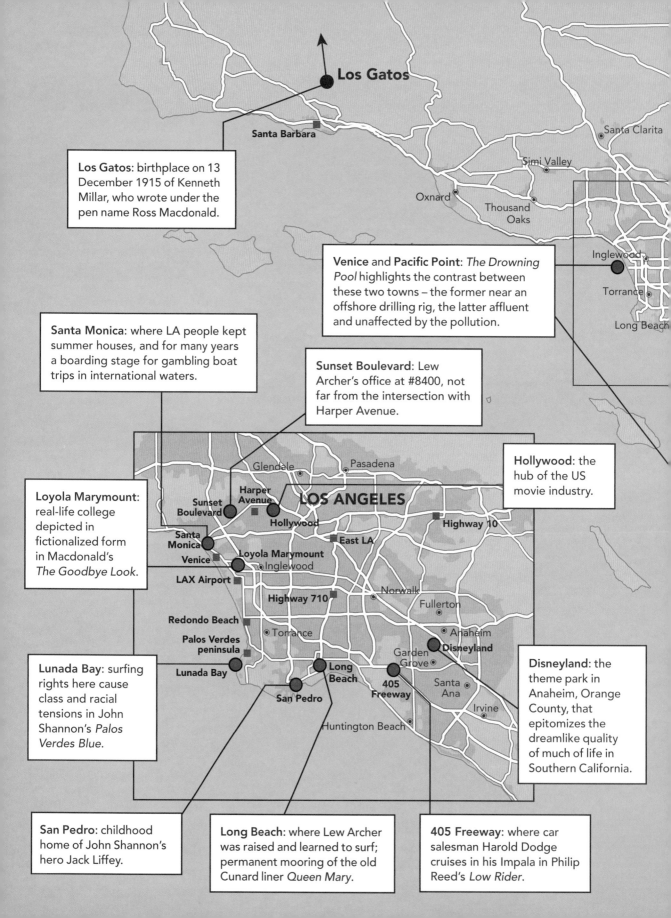

Los Gatos

Los Gatos: birthplace on 13 December 1915 of Kenneth Millar, who wrote under the pen name Ross Macdonald.

Venice and **Pacific Point**: *The Drowning Pool* highlights the contrast between these two towns – the former near an offshore drilling rig, the latter affluent and unaffected by the pollution.

Santa Monica: where LA people kept summer houses, and for many years a boarding stage for gambling boat trips in international waters.

Sunset Boulevard: Lew Archer's office at #8400, not far from the intersection with Harper Avenue.

Loyola Marymount: real-life college depicted in fictionalized form in Macdonald's *The Goodbye Look*.

Hollywood: the hub of the US movie industry.

Lunada Bay: surfing rights here cause class and racial tensions in John Shannon's *Palos Verdes Blue*.

Disneyland: the theme park in Anaheim, Orange County, that epitomizes the dreamlike quality of much of life in Southern California.

San Pedro: childhood home of John Shannon's hero Jack Liffey.

Long Beach: where Lew Archer was raised and learned to surf; permanent mooring of the old Cunard liner *Queen Mary*.

405 Freeway: where car salesman Harold Dodge cruises in his Impala in Philip Reed's *Low Rider*.

Santa Barbara

Santa Clarita

Simi Valley

Oxnard

Thousand Oaks

Inglewood

Torrance

Long Beach

Glendale

Pasadena

Harper Avenue

LOS ANGELES

Sunset Boulevard

Hollywood

Highway 10

Santa Monica

East LA

Venice

Loyola Marymount

Inglewood

LAX Airport

Highway 710

Norwalk

Fullerton

Redondo Beach

Torrance

Anaheim

Disneyland

Palos Verdes peninsula

Garden Grove

Lunada Bay

Long Beach

405 Freeway

Santa Ana

San Pedro

Irvine

Huntington Beach

Palm Springs: the southernmost point of Lew Archer's investigations in *The Drowning Pool*.

Valley Center: in Parker's *LA Outlaws* the home town of Suzanne Jones, history teacher by day, outlaw by night.

Barrio Logan: San Diego home of Art Keller, Drugs Enforcement agent in Don Winslow's *The Power Of The Dog*.

LANDMARKS IN SOUTHERN CALIFORNIAN CRIME FICTION

David Stuart Davies

ARTHUR CONAN DOYLE & SHERLOCK HOLMES'S LONDON

Sherlock Holmes's city is, of course, London, presented to us by his creator Arthur Conan Doyle, who grew up in Edinburgh and thus saw the greatly changing and evolving British capital in Victorian times from an outsider's perspective.

Indeed, Doyle wrote the first Holmes story, *A Study in Scarlet* (1887), while living in Southsea, Hampshire, and relied on his memories of various visits to London for background detail.

The formidable team

Victorian London, the hub of the British Empire, was Sherlock Holmes's hunting ground, although of course he did venture into the nearby shires from time to time. This brilliant consulting detective was based in the heart of the city at 221B Baker Street, where he shared rooms on the upper floor with Doctor John H. Watson. The pair first met when Watson had just returned from Afghanistan, invalided out of the army on a meagre pension. At this period of his life, Watson described London as 'that great cesspool into which all idlers and loungers of the Empire are irresistibly drained'.

Watson was keen to share lodgings with someone in order to keep his expenses down. One lunchtime in the bar of the Criterion in Piccadilly Circus he encountered Stamford, an old army friend who said he could solve Watson's problem. The friend took him to St Bartholomew's (Bart's) Hospital to a meet an unusual young man who was also in search of a co-lodger – a fellow by the name of Sherlock Holmes. Holmes was carrying out research in the lab at the hospital, 'beating subjects in the dissecting room with a stick... to verify how far bruises may be produced after death'. Sherlock Holmes's first words to Watson – 'You have been in Afghanistan, I perceive' – established his remarkable deductive powers and the rest is history.

When the stories were written, they were, of course, contemporary and therefore Doyle did not include conscious period dressing; this emerges in a subtle way, embedded in the text through a host of incidental references to locations, forms of transport, manners, dress and so on. In this fashion London emerges naturally in rich and varied detail,

providing a colourful backdrop to the great detective's investigations.

Doyle cunningly exploited the fascinating contrasts of the sprawling city in the stories. Thus we have Holmes in 'The Man with the Twisted Lip' (first published in *The Strand Magazine*, December 1891) slumming it in the Bar of Gold – an opium den in the fictional Upper Swandam Lane, 'a vile alley lurking behind the high wharves which line the north side of the river to the east of London Bridge' – and then visiting his brother Mycroft in the hallowed rooms of The Diogenes Club in Pall Mall in Whitehall. In the first Holmes novel, *A Study in Scarlet* (1887), the major crime is committed in a deserted house in down-at-heel Brixton, while in 'The Adventure of the Second Stain' (1904) Holmes solves the case in the grand town house of the eminent Trelawney Hope, 'the European Secretary' – a kingpin of the British government.

The developing capital

It is popular to view Holmes's world as one of fog-bound cobbled streets, ghostly gas lamps that fail at 20 feet (6 m) and dark old buildings. However, the facts present a different picture. During the years Sherlock Holmes spent in London – from approximately 1878 to 1904 – he lived through one of the greatest periods of change the city had ever known. The Victorian age (1837–1901) began with gas lamps, the telegram and the musical box; it ended with electricity, the motor car and the gramophone. Nothing remained constant.

HEAVY CASE LOAD

Sherlock Holmes appears in 56 short stories and 4 novels – *A Study in Scarlet*, *The Sign of Four*, *The Hound of the Baskervilles* and *The Valley of Fear*. All but four are written as if by Dr Watson. The exceptions are 'The Blanched Soldier' and 'The Lion's Mane', which are narrated by Holmes, and 'The Musgrave Ritual' and 'The Gloria Scott', in which Holmes tells Watson and Watson narrates in the third person.

'HOLMES IS THE MOST CONSOLING OF LITERARY ICONS. HE CANNOT ALWAYS PREVENT CRIME OR PUNISH THE CRIMINAL, BUT HE NEVER FAILS TO EXPLAIN WHAT HAS HAPPENED, AND HOW, AND WHY'
– TIMES LITERARY SUPPLEMENT (2007)

The change had actually started in earnest just after the young Queen Victoria ascended the throne. Even many of the locations referred to in the Holmes stories were relatively new. For example, the Criterion Bar in Piccadilly, noted for its Byzantine ceiling, was only completed in 1874, a mere seven years before Watson's fateful meeting with Stamford. In the same year, Liverpool Street Station, serving the Great Eastern Railway, was opened. Holmes departed from this station on his way to Norfolk in the investigation Watson called 'The Adventure of the Dancing Men' (1903); and Watson set off on his wild goose chase from here in 'The Adventure of the Retired Colourman' (1926).

Some other fairly new buildings mentioned in the stories include the House of Commons (1847), King's Cross Station (1852), St James's Hall (1858) and St Pancras Hotel (1872). The point is, of course, that what we may now view through the golden fog of nostalgia as being quaint and historical was fresh and new to the young Holmes and Watson. Here was a city, like the aspiring detective himself, eager to make a special mark on the world.

Facing the future

Among the greatest changes Holmes observed during his residence in London was its altering façade. In the final 20 years of the 19th century London virtually renewed itself. Buildings were constantly springing up to present freshly minted vistas for the inhabitants of the metropolis. Included in this changing architectural canvas were Aldgate Station, the eastern terminus of the Metropolitan Railway (1884) – it was near here that Cadogan West's body was found in 'The Adventure of the Bruce-Partington Plans' (1912) – and Hammersmith Bridge with its striking designs by Sir Joseph Bazalgette (1819–91), which is mentioned in 'The Adventure of the Six Napoleons' (1904).

Also during this period, numerous hotels were built to accommodate the increasing volume of visitors to London. These included the big curve-fronted Grand Hotel by Trafalgar Square, which opened in 1880. This is a candidate for the

THE STRAND
MAGAZINE

SOUTHAMPTON
STREET

359

EDITED
By
Geo:
Newnes
....
OFFICES

AN·ILLUSTRATED·MONTHLY

'THE MORE FEATURELESS AND COMMONPLACE A CRIME IS, THE MORE DIFFICULT IT IS TO BRING IT HOME' – SHERLOCK HOLMES, 'THE BOSCOMBE VALLEY MYSTERY' (1891)

Northumberland Hotel where Sir Henry Baskerville stayed and lost his boots in *The Hound of the Baskervilles* (originally serialized in *The Strand Magazine* between August 1901 and April 1902; first published as a novel in 1902). Farther along Northumberland Avenue was the Hotel Metropole (1885), probably disguised as the Hotel Cosmopolitan in 'The Adventure of the Blue Carbuncle' (1892), in which the Countess of Morcar had her precious stone stolen.

Indeed, the city must have looked like one giant building site. In *The Sign of Four* (1890), Holmes was able to conclude that Watson had been to the Wigmore Street Post Office by making some deductions about road works:

Observation tells me that you have a reddish mould adhering to your instep. Just opposite they have taken up the pavement and thrown up some earth, which lies in such a way that it is difficult to avoid treading in it in entering. The earth is of a peculiar reddish tint which is found, as far as I know, nowhere else in the neighbourhood.

Moving house

One of the most important buildings to be erected during Holmes's Baker Street days was the headquarters for the Metropolitan Police. It was built on reclaimed land on the Victoria Embankment. The architect,

Norman Shaw (1831–1912), designed what the contemporary writer A.P. Herbert (1890–1971) described as 'a very constabulary kind of building'. It was faced with granite, appropriately quarried by convicts on Dartmoor. The police moved there in 1890 and the building was named New Scotland Yard.

No sooner had this prestigious building opened than Holmes went to France on 'a matter of supreme importance to the French government' ('The Final Problem', 1893); then, shortly after, he had an encounter with a certain nefarious Professor Moriarty at the Reichenbach Falls. Presumed dead, Holmes disappeared for three years, a period known to Sherlockians as 'The Great Hiatus'. Perhaps he thought that with the new, modernized police headquarters, inspectors Lestrade, Gregson, Hopkins and company could manage without him. This turned out not to be the case. On returning to London in 1894, Holmes found that they were still struggling with their investigations – on this occasion with the murder of the Honourable Ronald Adair, who was shot with an airgun by a sniper – Colonel Sebastian Moran – while in his apartment in Park Lane. The events were recorded in 'The Adventure of the Empty House' (1903).

It is interesting to note that a near neighbour of Sherlock Holmes was Madame Tussaud's Waxwork Museum, which was located at 54–56 Baker Street until 1884 when it moved round the corner to its present site on Marylebone

HOLMES ON SCREEN

The following actors are among the most lauded of the hundreds of famous film and television portrayals of Doyle's deerstalkered sleuth.

IN FILM

John Barrymore *Sherlock Holmes* (1922)

Michael Caine *Without a Clue* (1988)

John Cleese *The Strange Case of the End of Civilization as We Know It* (1977)

Peter Cook *The Hound of the Baskervilles* (1978)

Peter Cushing *The Hound of the Baskervilles* (1959)

Robert Downey, Jr. *Sherlock Holmes* (2009)

Christopher Lee *Sherlock Holmes and the Deadly Necklace* (1962)

Vasily Livanov in five films (1979–86)

Raymond Massey *The Speckled Band* (1931)

Basil Rathbone in 14 films (1939–46)

ON TELEVISION

Tom Baker *The Hound of the Baskervilles* (1982)

Jeremy Brett *The Adventures of Sherlock Holmes* (1984-1994)

Benedict Cumberbatch *Sherlock* (2010)

Peter Cushing *Sherlock Holmes* (1965-68) *The Masks of Death* (1984)

Rupert Everett *Sherlock Holmes and the Case of the Silk Stocking* (2004)

Stewart Granger *The Hound of the Baskervilles* (1972)

Charlton Heston *The Crucifer of Blood* (1991)

Frank Langella *Sherlock Holmes* (1981)

Roger Moore *Sherlock Holmes in New York* (1976)

MODERN LONDON SLEUTHS

If the London of Sherlock Holmes is iconic, modern London and contemporary crime writing still prove frequent bedfellows. Important detectives operating now and in the more recent past include:

Mark Billingham's Tom Thorne, a North London copper whose cases have a capacity to disturb as he mines the psychological depths of evil in his investigations. Read *Bloodline* (2009).

Mark Timlin's Nick Sharman, a cheeky south London PI who treads uncomfortably on the wild side and was, briefly, portrayed in a British television series by Clive Owen. Read *Guns of Brixton* (2010).

Derek Raymond's nameless cop who operates from the Factory, a police station in Soho's Poland Street, and offers compassion and bleak, cold-hearted revenge fo the dispossessed. Read *I Was Dora Suarez* (1990).

John Milne's one-legged London policeman Jimmy Jenner, now working as a private investigator. Read *Daddy's Girl* (1982).

Dan Kavanagh's Duffy, another policeman in disgrace, operating between the lines of legality and crime. A pioneering character created by mainstream author Julian Barnes under a pseudonym. Read *Fiddle City* (1981).

Liza Cody's Anna Lee, arguably British crime writing's first resolutely modern female investigator. Lee appeared in six novels and was portrayed in a television series by Imogen Stubbs. Read *Head Case* (1985).

Road, taking with it 400 figures. One can imagine the detective visiting the exhibition so close to 221B as a divertissement when business was slow. Perhaps it was on one of these visits that he conceived the possibility of using a wax figure to aid him in some investigative subterfuge, as in the aforementioned 'The Empty House' and 'The Adventure of the Mazarin Stone' (1921).

During Holmes's detective career, new thoroughfares were grafted onto the old network of streets that patterned the city. The first really important new road was Victoria Street, connecting Victoria Station with Westminster Abbey. Holmes used Victoria Station on many occasions; in particular when, disguised as a venerable Italian priest, he was escaping the clutches of Moriarty in 'The Final Problem'.

The fact that new roads were appearing regularly meant that Holmes's knowledge of the city would need to be constantly updated and amended. However, he was equal to the challenge, as he demonstrated during the cab ride in *The Sign of Four* that leads him and his sidekick from the West End to Wandsworth Road, described as 'the howling desert of South London'. Watson observes:

At first I had some idea as to the direction in which we were driving, but soon, what with our pace, the fog and my own limited knowledge of London, I lost my bearings and knew nothing, save that we seemed to be going a long way. Sherlock Holmes was never at fault, however, and he muttered the names as the cab rattled through squares and in and out by tortuous by-streets.

While Watson's 'limited knowledge' suggests how difficult it was for an average fellow to keep up with the evolving geography of the city, Holmes's certainty of direction and location highlights his remarkable ability to keep abreast of the changing environment.

Touring the city

Most of the major institutions in London at the time are referred to in the stories. Holmes's investigations in 'The Blue Carbuncle' prompt him to visit Covent Garden Market; Holmes and Watson took relaxing walks in Hyde Park, notably in 'The Adventure of the Yellow Face' (1893); both the Foreign Office ('The Second Stain') and the Admiralty ('The Bruce-Partington Plans') feature; and, for dining out, the detective duo favoured 'taking something nutritious' at Simpson's Dining Rooms, situated on the Strand. While there is no record of Holmes visiting the Café Royal in Regent Street, it was outside this establishment that he was attacked by a hired thug in 'The Adventure of the Dying Detective' (1913).

Music played a large part in Holmes's life – he owned a Stradivarius and was an accomplished violinist. In several of the stories there are references to his visiting musical venues. For example, both Holmes and Watson attended a Wagner recital at the Covent Garden Theatre in 'The Adventure of the Red Circle' (1911); Holmes attended a concert by the celebrated Spanish violinist Pablo de Sarasate (1844–1908) at St James's Hall in 'The Adventure of the Red-Headed League' (1891); and at the end of *The Hound of the Baskervilles* the Baker Street duo got to see the opera *Les Huguenots* by Giacomo Meyerbeer (1791–1864) – the venue isn't mentioned but it is most likely to have been the Royal Opera House in Covent Garden, which had been rebuilt after a disastrous fire in 1856.

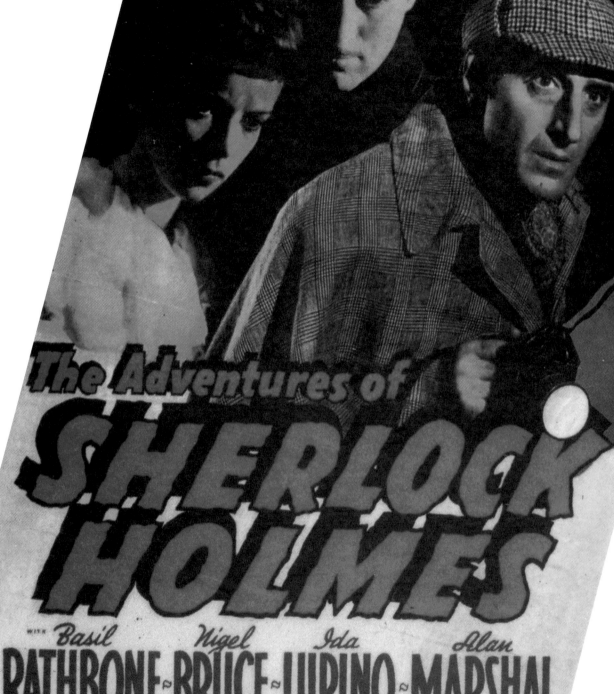

The Adventures of

SHERLOCK HOLMES

with Basil
RATHBONE ~ Nigel BRUCE ~ Ida LUPINO ~ Alan MARSHAL

and Terry
KILBURN ~ George ZUCCO ~ Henry STEPHENSON ~ E.E. CLIVE

A 20th CENTURY·FOX PICTURE ~ Darryl F. Zanuck
IN CHARGE OF PRODUCTION

DIRECTED BY ALFRED WERKER · ASSOCIATE PRODUCER Gene Markey

SCREEN PLAY BY EDWIN BLUM AND WILLIAM DRAKE
BASED ON THE PLAY "SHERLOCK HOLMES"

'HOW OFTEN HAVE I SAID TO YOU THAT WHEN YOU HAVE ELIMINATED THE IMPOSSIBLE, WHATEVER REMAINS, HOWEVER IMPROBABLE, MUST BE THE TRUTH?' – SHERLOCK HOLMES, *THE SIGN OF FOUR* (1890)

A change of pace

By the time Sherlock Holmes retired in the early days of the 20th century, London, his base and operating headquarters for 23 years, had become a different place from the one he had known when, after coming down from university, he had settled in lodgings in Montague Street, 'just around the corner from the British Museum', where he first set up as a consulting detective. At the end of his career, he had to a large extent becom a fixed point in a changing age. As a young man he had revelled in the whirligig of change, but as late middle age beckoned he felt like a fish out of water. He describes his retirement in 'The Adventure of the Lion's Mane' (1926) as 'a withdrawal' to the Sussex Downs from 'the gloom of London'. How different from Watson's view of the younger Holmes in 'The Adventure of the Cardboard Box' (1892):

He loved to lie in the very centre of five million people, with his filaments stretching out and running through them responsive to every little humour or suspicion of unsolved crime.

What once inspired, later depressed Sherlock Holmes. He felt the very human sensation that we all experience as we grow older: the pace of change becomes too fast and robs us of that sure ground that we thought we held. London with motor cars, cinemas, full electric lighting, and smooth tarmacadamed roads was a world in which Sherlock Holmes no longer felt at ease. In rural retirement, the great detective took up beekeeping and later wrote an authoritative book on the subject.

USEFUL WEBSITES

Walking tour of Sherlock Holmes's London
www.londonhorrortours.co.uk

The Sherlock Holmes Museum in London's Baker Street
www.sherlock-holmes.co.uk/home.htm

The world's most famous waxwork museum, as popular today as it was in Holmes's time
www.madametussauds.com/London

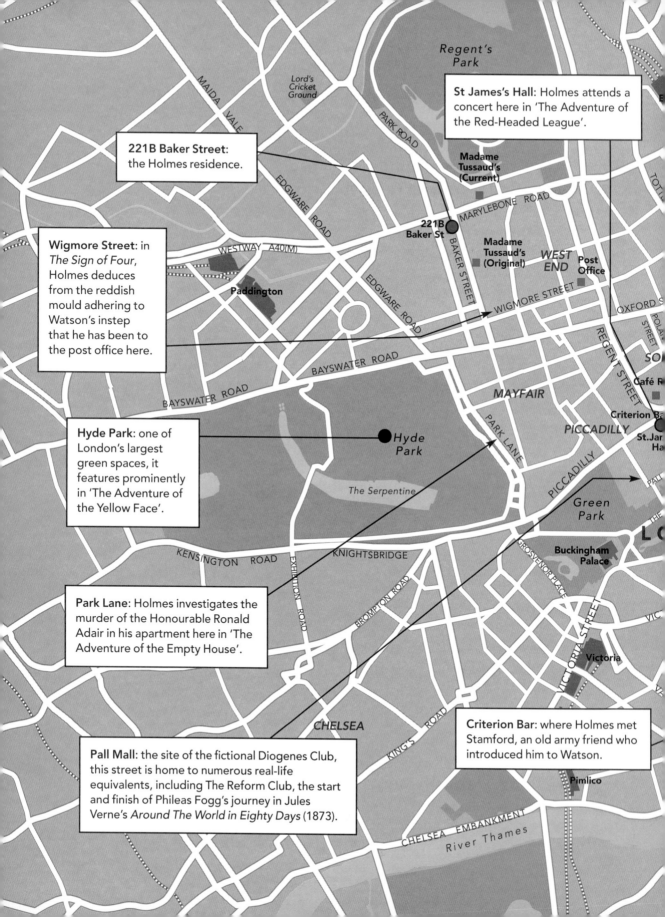

St James's Hall: Holmes attends a concert here in 'The Adventure of the Red-Headed League'.

221B Baker Street: the Holmes residence.

Wigmore Street: in *The Sign of Four*, Holmes deduces from the reddish mould adhering to Watson's instep that he has been to the post office here.

Hyde Park: one of London's largest green spaces, it features prominently in 'The Adventure of the Yellow Face'.

Park Lane: Holmes investigates the murder of the Honourable Ronald Adair in his apartment here in 'The Adventure of the Empty House'.

Criterion Bar: where Holmes met Stamford, an old army friend who introduced him to Watson.

Pall Mall: the site of the fictional Diogenes Club, this street is home to numerous real-life equivalents, including The Reform Club, the start and finish of Phileas Fogg's journey in Jules Verne's *Around The World in Eighty Days* (1873).

Regent's Park

Lord's Cricket Ground

MAIDA VALE

PARK ROAD

Madame Tussaud's (Current)

MARYLEBONE ROAD

221B Baker St

Madame Tussaud's (Original)

WEST END

Post Office

EDGWARE ROAD

WESTWAY A40(M)

Paddington

BAKER STREET

WIGMORE STREET

OXFORD

STREET

POLA

SO

EDGWARE ROAD

REGENT STREET

Café R

Criterion B

PICCADILLY

St Jan

Ha

BAYSWATER ROAD

BAYSWATER ROAD

MAYFAIR

Hyde Park

PARK LANE

Green Park

LO

The Serpentine

PICCADILLY

PAL

KENSINGTON ROAD

KNIGHTSBRIDGE

GROSVENOR PLACE

Buckingham Palace

EXHIBITION ROAD

BROMPTON ROAD

VICTORIA STREET

Victoria

VIC

CHELSEA

KING'S ROAD

Pimlico

CHELSEA EMBANKMENT

River Thames

Montague Street: Holmes took lodgings here after coming down from university (commentators are divided over whether he attended Oxford or Cambridge).

Liverpool Street Station: London terminus of the Great Eastern Railway that features in 'The Adventure of the Dancing Men' and 'The Adventure of the Retired Colourman'.

The scene of the crime in 'The Adventure of the Red Circle'.

St Bartholemew's Hospital: site of momentous first meeting between Holmes and Watson.

Grand Hotel, Northumberland Avenue: thought to be the inspiration for the Northumberland Hotel where Sir Henry Baskerville stayed and lost his boots in *The Hound of the Baskervilles*.

New Scotland Yard: designed by Norman Shaw, this was the London Metropolitan Police headquarters until 1967, when operations were transferred to Broadway, near Victoria Station.

Wandsworth Road: described in *The Sign of Four* as part of 'the howling desert of South London'.

DOYLE & HOLMES'S LONDON

Sarah Weinman

LAWRENCE BLOCK & MATT SCUDDER'S NEW YORK

There are eight million people living in New York City, and each one of them has a story. It's tempting to think that Lawrence Block has told most of them, considering how prolific he has been throughout his five-decade-plus career. In this case, the hyperbole is close to the truth.

Other writers have distilled New York's macabre essence in single masterful crime novels, but Block is to be commended for his ability to revisit his beloved city again and again, and find something new to impart to readers.

Block's early pulp fiction – published under his own name or various pseudonyms, and recently brought back into print at a trickle-a-year pace by the mass-market publisher Hard Case Crime – proffers a window into New York's darker corners, places that the working class might be aware of and wink slyly when asked about them by the more naïve middle class. *A Diet of Treacle* (2008),

originally published under the name 'Sheldon Lord' (the nom de plume Block used most often for soft-core fiction), is at first glance the story of one uptown girl's yearning for something deeper and more depraved below 14th Street, but on closer inspection the tale that unfolds is one of disaffected beatniks congregating in coffee houses like Cafe Wha? and Vivaldi. Even then, you could tell that Greenwich Village was Block's home, as it would be off and on until today.

Block isn't always so gritty about his home city: the Bernie Rhodenbarr novels, those delightful, erudite volumes of a witty burglar-cum-bookstore owner on the Upper East Side, attest to this. Bernie's world hovers somewhere above the real New York, never quite reflecting petty grumblings about subway delays, rats running amok or beer bottles litte ring the streets. Instead, we see the city as if it had been transformed into Sherlock Holmes's 221B Baker Street (*see pages 216–227*), or maybe a mix of P.G.

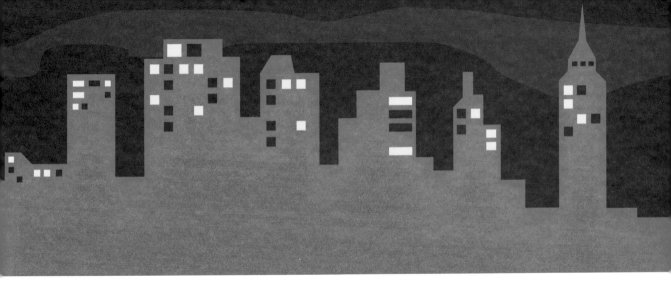

Wodehouse (1881–1975) and Rex Stout (1886–1975), if the two had co-written a Broadway musical libretto for Jerome Kern (1885–1945). Here is the New York of Leonard Bernstein's ballet *Fancy Free* (1944), except that there are priceless objects ready for stealing and inconvenient murders for poor Bernie to get mixed up in.

I suppose if you want to get a sense of New York City's full panorama, pick up a copy of *Small Town*, Block's 2003 magnum opus. It's a cracked kaleidoscope that runs high and low, east and west, from the Hudson to FDR Drive, up to the Bronx and down to the Battery, in open spaces and in secret corners, with astonishing sexual insatiability and a serial murderer hell-bent on avenging the 9/11 attacks in his own violent, anguished way. What ties this sometimes messy, often breath-defying novel together is no single human being, but the single character that is Manhattan. It opens its arms wide to newcomers and long-time denizens alike, to the comfortably upper class or the struggling man behind the bodega counter, to the woman who wants to get her freak on at all costs or

the tattooed collegiate hell-bent on escaping the Midwest to find other others who are just like him. Against the backdrop of violence and death, sex and communion, Block fashions his love song from the elements that continue to stoke his own literary fires.

Scudder and his demons

The purest distillation of Block's New York, however, comes from Matthew Scudder. The word 'distillation' is no

PASSPORT

United States of America

MEETING LAWRENCE BLOCK

Born in 1938 in Buffalo, New York.

Educated at Antioch College in Yellow Springs, Ohio.

Wrote soft porn for several years before surfacing with 'You Can't Lose', the first work he published under his own name.

Main pastime: Globetrotting – he and his wife, Lynne, have visited almost 9/10ths of all the world's countries.

accident: Scudder, the antihero who stars in 20 novels written over three decades, is preoccupied an inordinate amount of the time with drink. He's downing double shots of bourbon or whiskey in the early books, or attending AA meetings in the later novels. Matthew Scudder is the man who, in the closing page of *Eight Million Ways to Die* (1982), stands up at a basement meeting, 12 days sober, and announces to the crowd, 'My name is Matt. I'm an alcoholic'. Then he starts to cry.

But let's back up a bit. When *The Sins of the Fathers* was first published in 1976, readers and critics knew it was a harbinger of something important, but couldn't quite pinpoint what that something was. Did it emulate the masters of private-eye fiction – Dashiell Hammett, Raymond Chandler and Ross Macdonald? Certainly. Was Scudder, like Sam Spade, Philip Marlowe and Lew Archer, fond of drink? Absolutely. Did Scudder have personal demons that chased after him, whether he was on a job investigating (unlicensed, of course) or passed out in his West 57th Street hotel? Without a doubt. However, there was something darker, sharper, bleaker in that book, a tone that developed its despair further through six more books until Block called it quits on Scudder for a

few years, unsure how to bring the man back without the glassy haze of alcohol to help and hinder him.

Scudder came back in 1986 with a prequel, the even more masterful *When the Sacred Ginmill Closes* (which grew out of the excellent short story 'By The Dawn's Early Light', published the year before in *Playboy*). And here we really sense the rollercoaster nature of Scudder's relationship with the bottle, as he careens from bar to bar, night after night, but, like a pigeon with a better-than-GPS homing device, always comes back to his favourite haunt: Armstrong's. 'Christ, I lived there', Scudder says. 'I had my room to sleep in and I had other bars and restaurants to go to, but for a few years there, Jimmy Armstrong's was home to me.'

The changing scene

Armstrong's, a real-life bar, shut its doors in 2002 after the owner, Jimmy, died of a heart attack at age 60. Its last day came a little more than a year after I first arrived in New York City, loving the town as only an outsider expatriate Canadian could, shrugging off parental concerns about where to venture after dark alone and fiercely proud of riding the subway the day after 9/11. But Scudder's neighbourhood I took to, in part by

'WHEN I STARTED OUT, I KNEW I WAS GOING TO WRITE THREE BOOKS, AND HAD THE SENSE I'D BE WRITING ABOUT SCUDDER FOR A WHILE – BUT NOT FOR 25 YEARS AND 15 BOOKS!' – LAWRENCE BLOCK (2001)

BLOCK ON SCREEN

The best-known films made from books by Lawrence Block are *Burglar* (1987), starring Whoopi Goldberg as Bernie Rhodenbarr and John Goodman as Det. Nyswander, and *8 Million Ways to Die* (1986), directed by Hal Ashby with a screenplay by Oliver Stone and starring Jeff Bridges as Matt Scudder. Other works for screen, either written or based on novels or short stories by Lawrence Block include:

 ## IN FILM

The Antioch Adventure (1967)
Nightmare Honeymoon (1973)
8 Million Ways to Die (1986)
Burglar (1987),
Cleveland in My Dreams (2005)
My Blueberry Nights (2007), directed by Kar Wai Wong with Jude Law and Norah Jones
Gentlemen's Agreement (2009)
Abnormal Abduction (2010)

ON TELEVISION

Nothin' Short of Highway Robbery (1985), an episode of 'Tales of the Unexpected'
When This Man Dies (1987), an episode of 'Alfred Hitchcock Presents…'
Bradford in My Dreams (2003), an episode of the 'Spine Chillers' series; set in Yorkshire and featuring David Tennant
Rivered and *The Aftermath* (2005), two episodes of *Tilt*, a nine-part TV drama about poker players

necessity (I went to graduate school at John Jay College of Criminal Justice, just a few blocks away from Scudder's dingy hotel digs) and in part because, even now, its stubborn upper Hell's Kitchen soul hasn't quite abated.

The Armstrong's that closed was a block west of the fictional bar that Scudder drank heavily in and, even after years of sobriety, he returned to every now and then. The hotel digs were likely to have been in a Holiday Inn Express that gets the job done. There are good Thai restaurants and bad Thai restaurants; the college kids celebrate the end of semester by hoisting a few at the Coliseum, likely rubbing elbows with the people who still have jobs at CNN.

And, as the series went on, with Scudder aging, finding a wife (former hooker Elaine Mardell), settling down, solving his technological problems with the help of the streetwise TJ, growing comfortable in a station far above his worst days, Block was there to chronicle the city's deepening gentrification, obsession with money – lots of it – and the inevitable violent eruptions that Rudy Giuliani (Mayor of New York, 1994–2001) would have had you believe were swept away from Manhattan by the extra presence of cops on the streets.

Scudder made his final curtain call – for now, at least – in *All the Flowers Were Dying* (2005). He could use a long rest, in

The Chiara String Quartet at the Café Vivaldi in 2007.

'... SOMETHING THAT I REALLY ENJOY ABOUT WRITING ABOUT SCUDDER – I'M NEVER QUITE CERTAIN WHAT HE'S GOING TO DO NEXT. AND THAT APPEALS TO ME' – LAWRENCE BLOCK, INTERVIEW JANUARY MAGAZINE

light of the emotional and psychological damage inflicted upon him at the hands of a madman that is classic Block – hidden in plain sight, terrifying in his banality. I'm one of many who wonders what Scudder would make of the New York City of 2010, where the economy took its huge bite out of Wall Street, brought back the homeless to Central Park benches, drove up food prices (for a while, anyway) and brought out the violent, knife-wielding types on subways or street-peddlers with guns in Times Square. Maybe, to be frank, he is too old for all this, ready to cede the dirty work to the next generation, uninterested in taking part in social networks, happy to rest his aching bones and go gently into the good night.

It's not up to me. It's up to Lawrence Block. Nevertheless, I hope, as he continues to racewalk his way through Manhattan and elsewhere, he hasn't stopped mapping the city for those who, like me, never get tired of the small details made beautiful and spare.

USEFUL WEBSITES & ADDRESSES

New York Times guide to walking tours of literary Manhattan
http://travel2.nytimes.com/2006/05/14/travel/14going.html

Cafe Wha?
115 MacDougal Street
New York, NY 10012-1202
www.cafewha.com

Café Vivaldi
32 Jones Street
New York, NY 10014
www.caffevivaldi.com

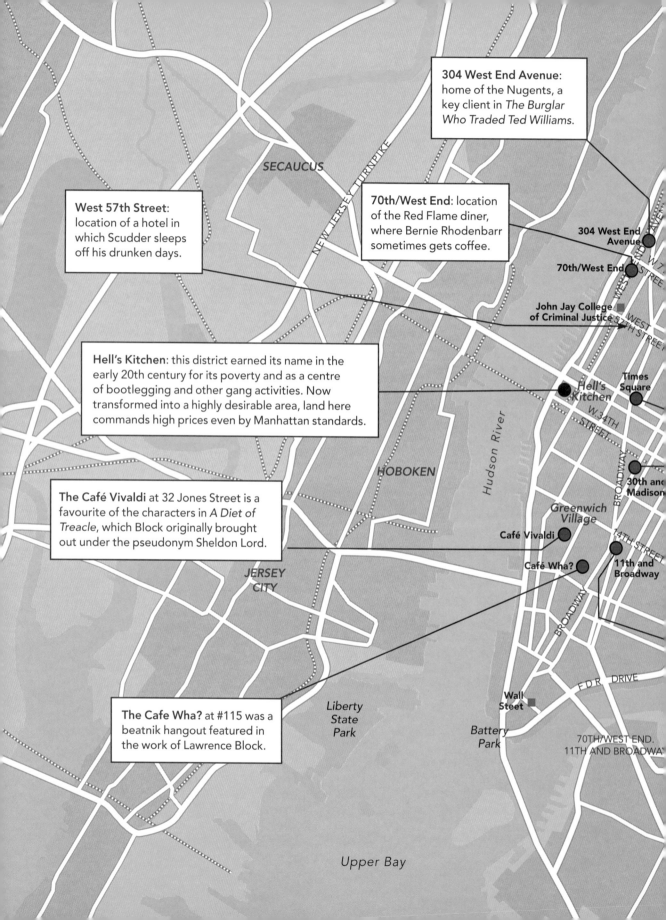

304 West End Avenue: home of the Nugents, a key client in *The Burglar Who Traded Ted Williams.*

West 57th Street: location of a hotel in which Scudder sleeps off his drunken days.

70th/West End: location of the Red Flame diner, where Bernie Rhodenbarr sometimes gets coffee.

Hell's Kitchen: this district earned its name in the early 20th century for its poverty and as a centre of bootlegging and other gang activities. Now transformed into a highly desirable area, land here commands high prices even by Manhattan standards.

The Café Vivaldi at 32 Jones Street is a favourite of the characters in *A Diet of Treacle,* which Block originally brought out under the pseudonym Sheldon Lord.

The Cafe Wha? at #115 was a beatnik hangout featured in the work of Lawrence Block.

SECAUCUS

NEW JERSEY TURNPIKE

304 West End Avenue

W. 7

70th/West End

WEST END AVENUE

John Jay College of Criminal Justice

WEST 57TH STREET

Hell's Kitchen

Times Square

Hudson River

W. 34TH STREET

HOBOKEN

BROADWAY

30th and Madison

Greenwich Village

Café Vivaldi

14TH STREET

Café Wha?

11th and Broadway

JERSEY CITY

BROADWAY

F D R DRIVE

Wall Steet

Liberty State Park

Battery Park

70TH/WEST END. 11TH AND BROADWAY

Upper Bay

Central Park: in Block's work this vast green space (bigger than Monaco) features as a place of recreation for the wealthy and overnight accommodation for the poor.

Upper East Side: site of the bookstore owned by burglar Bernie Rhodenbarr.

Times Square: the heart of the Theater District is a honeypot for many of the petty criminals encountered by Matt Scudder.

30th and Madison: Bernie Rhodenbarr meets a client here at the Martingale Club in Murray Hill.

The Bum Rap: Bernie and Carolyn sometimes meet at this bar.

ASTORIA

WOODSIDE

WILLIAMSBURG

Upper West Side

CENTRAL PARK

MANHATTAN

Elaine's

Upper East Side

NEW YORK

East River

BROADWAY

5TH AVENUE

MADISON AVENUE

F.D.R. DRIVE

GRAND CENTRAL PARKWAY

LONG ISLAND EXPRESSWAY

BLOCK & SCUDDER'S NEW YORK

OTHER NEW YORK DETECTIVES

At the crossroads of the world, and as a result, of criminal activity, New York City and its principal boroughs, Manhattan, Brooklyn, the Bronx, Queens and Staten Island, have been rightly celebrated in literally hundreds of books. In addition to Lawrence Block's novels, the city also comes under close and murderous scrutiny in the books of several other American writers of crime and mystery fiction.

Chester Himes placed his canny black detectives, Coffin Ed Johnson and Grave Digger Jones, in the heart of Harlem, to often explosive effect. Read *A Rage in Harlem* (1957).

Richard Price, also well known for his film scripts and his work on the TV series *The Wire*, is the poet laureate of the outer boroughs, where crime and poverty blend to harrowing effect. Read *Clockers* (1992).

Ed McBain is the legendary creator of the 87th Precinct cop procedural series, which extended into more than 50 volumes and, as Evan Hunter, the author of classic novels which also take New York as their background. Read *Cop Hater* (1956).

Dorothy Uhnak began life as a New York policewoman, and her novels catch the reality of Manhattan streets with a vengeance. Read *Law and Order* (1973).

William J. Caunitz was another New York policeman who trod the dark streets before incorporating his real life experiences in fiction. Read *One Police Plaza* (1984).

S.J. Rozan is one of the best chroniclers of contemporary New York in her outstanding series of novels featuring investigative duo Bill Smith and Lydia Chin. Read *China Trade* (1994).

Donald E. Westlake, under his real name (he also wrote the famed Parker series as Richard Stark) was the the creator of hapless but witty crook Dortmunder and his merry gang of failures whose tragicomic adventures criss-crossed the New York streets. Read *The Hot Rock* (1970).

Two film versions of books by Ed McBain (aka Evan Hunter).
Above: The Blackboard Jungle (1955). *Below:* Blood Relatives (1978).

INTERNATIONAL CRIME: AN OVERVIEW

If you think your reading list has run out of exotic settings for crime, then take a look at the following pages for an insight into other international crime and mystery fiction.

H.R.F. Keating
Inspector Ghote series, set in Bombay (Mumbai), India

The dogged Ganesh V. Ghote spends as much of his time fighting the unwieldy and often corrupt Indian justice system as he does apprehending the criminals in the first place. His wife, Protima, is dutiful and loving but infuriatingly argumentative. They have a son named Ved.

Read: *Inspector Ghote's First Case* (2008)

Shamini Flint
Inspector Singh series, set in Malaysia

A rotund Singaporean detective, Singh is drafted in to Kuala Lumpur, Bali and other parts of the East Indies to investigate serious crime. Unpopular with his fellow officers, Singh endears himself to readers with his warmth and eccentricity as well as his forensic skills.

Read: *A Most Peculiar Malaysian Murder* (2009)

Seicho Matsumoto
Inspector Imanishi series, set in Japan

Police procedurals in which the hero – a spiritual detective whose main interests are gardening and haiku poetry – solves crimes that bring him into sometimes abrasive contact with every stratum of Japanese society, from the most traditional to the most Westernized.

Read: *Inspector Imanishi Investigates* (1989)

Qiu Xiaolong
Inspector Chen series, set in Shanghai, China

Chen Cao runs the Special Case Squad responsible for political crimes but in his spare time he has a sideline translating English-language crime fiction into Chinese. The two sides of his life are reflected in his speech, which alternates between high-flown poeticism and banal Communist Party slogans.

Read: *A Loyal Character Dancer* (2002)

William Marshall: Yellowthread Street series, set in Hong Kong

The cops in this procedural series – DCI Harry Feiffer, a European born and raised in Hong Kong; Senior Inspector Christopher O'Yee, half Chinese, half American; and Inspectors Auden and Spencer, always at each other's throats – face bizarre crimes that often seem to have no rational explanation. The books are a masterly synthesis of violence, suspense and humour.

Read: *Thin Air* (1977)

Philip Kerr
Bernie Gunther series, set in Berlin

Gunther is a World War I veteran who became a private investigator under the Weimar Republic. He specializes in finding missing persons, the number of whom increases dramatically during the rise to power of Adolf Hitler. After World War II, he continues his work in Vienna.

Read: *A German Requiem* (1991)

Boris Akunin
Erast Fandorin and Sister Pelgia series, set in Russia

Erast Petrovich Fandorin is a fictional 19th-century detective who speaks Russian, English, German and Japanese fluently, can never lose a bet and possesses masterly investigative skills.

Read: *The Winter Queen* (2003)

Sister Pelagia is a crime-solving nun in Russia at the start of the 20th century.

Read: *Pelagia and the White Bulldog* (2006)

Marek Krajewski
Eberhard Mock series, set in Wroclaw, Poland

Mock has a messy private life that intrudes on his work as a police officer. His main personal problems are caused by his younger wife, Sophie, who spends more time at orgies than in the family home, and his scapegrace nephew, Erwin, who refuses to follow his father, Mock's brother, onto the railways because he wants to pursue what he believes is his vocation as a poet. Mock sometimes takes his subordinates off their normal duties to follow his erring relatives and report to him on their activities.

Read: *Death in Breslau* (2008)

Michael Walters
Nergui series, set in Ulan-Bator, Mongolia

The protagonist is a senior official at the Ministry of Security; his main assistant is Doripalam, head of the Mongolian Serious Crimes Team. Among the recurrent supporting cast is Drew McLeish, a CID officer seconded from the UK.

Read: *The Shadow Walker* (2006)

Diane Wei Liang
Mei Wang series, set in Beijing

The heroine, disgusted by the corrupt Chinese bureaucracy, packs in her safe civil service job and sets up as a PI. But her activities are illegal under communism, so she has to call herself an information consultant. Her sidekick is a young man who keeps her diary and duns reluctant payers.

Read: *The Eye of Jade* (2007)

Colin Cotterill
Dr Siri Paiboun series, set in Laos

The septuagenarian hero is the country's only coroner in the days immediately following the communist takeover in the 1970s. Siri is ably assisted in his investigations by Nurse Dtui and Geung, a mortuary attendant.

Read: *The Coroner's Lunch* (2004)

Leonardo Padura
Mario Conde series, set in Cuba.

Mario Conde is a Havana policeman who wishes he was a writer like his hero, Ernest Hemingway. He feels much greater sympathy with artists, madmen and drunks than with his fellow law enforcers.

Read: *Havana Red* (2005)

Paco IgnacioTaibo II
Hector Belascoaran Shayne series

The main character is an alcoholic, left-wing PI who hates the police and government corruption. His Spanish-born Mexican creator tried to kill him off, but like Sherlock Holmes the character was later brought back in response to popular demand and starred in a total of eight books.

Read: *An Easy Thing* (1990)

Manuel Vázquez Montalbán
Pepe Carvalho series, set in Barcelona

A northern Spaniard living in the fiercely nationalistic Catalan capital, a former communist and sometime CIA operative, Pepe Carvalho is a maverick PI whose thoughts and actions bring him into frequent conflict with the late-20th century Spanish state. The Sancho Panza to Carvalho's Don Quixote is the ever-dependable Biscuter.

Read: *Murder in the Central Committee* (1984)

Alexander McCall Smith
Mama Ramotswe series, set in Botswana

The cases handled by this female detective range from missing cows to runaway husbands. The background reflects the small details of African village life that the author – a Scot who spent part of his life in Zimbabwe – thinks tourists don't normally get to see.

Read: *The No.1 Ladies' Detective Agency* (1998)

Michael Stanley
Detective Kubu series, set in South Africa

The name of the hero – Setswana for 'hippopotamus' – gives an accurate picture of his physique and character – large and apparently docile but a formidable foe when the mood takes him.

Read: *A Carrion Death* (2008)

NOTES ON CONTRIBUTORS

EDITOR

Maxim Jakubowski

Following a career as an editor in publishing, Maxim opened the acclaimed Murder One bookshop in London in 1988. He has written extensively in the crime, erotic and SF and fantasy areas and has been a columnist for the *Guardian* and *Time Out*, among others. His books and collections include: *Paris Noir*, *London Noir* and *Best British Mysteries*. He was brought up in Paris and now lives in London.

NOTES ON CONTRIBUTORS

Dick Adler – Crime critic for the *Chicago Tribune*.

Declan Burke – Editor of *Crime Pays* and crime writer for the *Irish Times* and author of the crime novels *Eight-ball Boogie* (Citric, 2003) and *The Big O* (Hag's Head Press, 2007).

Michael Carlson – writer, broadcaster and reviewer for the *Financial Times* and the *Independent*. Author of several books on film, Film Editor for *Crime Time* and American sports presenter for Channel 5.

Oline Cogdill – Columnist for *Mystery Scene* and crime critic for the South Florida *Sun-Sentinel*.

David Stuart Davies – The UK's most eminent Sherlock Holmes specialist, with more than 10 books on the subject to his credit, and editor of Wordsworth's crime and horror list.

Martin Edwards – British crime writer and editor of the annual CWA anthologies.

Barry Forshaw – Reviews for *The Times* and the *Daily Mail*, and edits *Crime Time*.

John Harvey – Diamond Dagger award winning author and creator of the Charlie Resnick series. Also presented the BBC TV documentary on Wallander's Sweden.

J. Kingston Pierce – Editor of *The Rap Sheet* and author of a book on Dashiell Hammett's San Francisco.

Peter Rozovsky – Editor of *Detectives Beyond Borders* and reviewer for the *Philadelphia Inquirer*.

Sarah Weinman – US critic for the *Los Angeles Times*, the *New York Times* and the *Barnes & Noble Review*.

PERMISSIONS FOR MAPS, IMAGES & TEXT

Maps

Created by Encompass Graphics Ltd (www.encompass-graphics.co.uk)

Picture credits

A Journey around my skull: p.167; Ian Allen: p.128; Dominic Alves: p.144; AMK1211: p.229; Mark Anderson: p.176; Seth Anderson: p.49; John Armagh: p.173; Brandon Bankston: p.53; Mike Baird: p.208; Scott Bauer: p.17; Greg Beaver: p.232; Linda Iske Bergman: p.88; Molly Boiling: p.108; Peter Bond: p.212; Steve Cadman: p.115; Cathy257: p.196; Allie Caulfield: p.100; Leandro Neumann Ciuffo: p.40; Corbis: p.26 (Bettmann), p.148 (Philip Gould), p.180 top left (John Springer Collection), p.206 (Bettmann); David Coggins: p.19; Dennis in Amsterdam: p.228 bottom left; Laurence Edmondson: p.59; Ezicman: p.124; FEMA: p.149 bottom (Andrea Booher); Rodrigo Ferrgrezi: p.195; Salvatore Freni: p.121; Athena Gassoumis: p.228 bottom left; William Gathoye: p.122; Getty Images: p.66, p.116; Chip Griffin: p.104; Gryffindor: p.166; HarperCollins Publishers: p.194; Jason Hickey: p.132; Ruben I : p.68; David Iliff: p.140; Intangible Arts: p.134; Istockphoto: p.82 (James Harrop), p.101 (Laurin Johnson), p.109 (Juanmonio), p.130 (Cheng Chang); Loren Javier: p.189; Jazza5: p.110; Jblesage: p.48; Jorchr: p.90; Kiwinz: p.139; Florent Lansard: p.162; Library of Congress: p.32, p.98 bottom, p.182, p. 216, p.217; Loloieg: p.80, p.184; Thoralkur Ludviksson: p.58; Mark Kelland: p.20; Michael Maggs: p.219; Hynek Maravec: p.22; Annie Mole: p.218; JC Murphy: p.200; William Murphy: p.198; Michael Nyika: p.163; Orion Publishing Group: p.18; Leonardo Palotta: p.183; Press Association: p.98 top; Pruneau : p.79; © Ian Rankin: p.16; Rex Features: p.27 (ITV), p.29 (SNAP), p.36 (Action Press), p.46 (Susannah Ireland), p.47 (SNAP), p.70 (Charles Ommaney), p.78 (John Lawrence), p.138 (Andrew Hasson), p.160, p.170 (Julian Calder) , p.171 (ITV), p.181 (SNAP), p.186 (SNAP), p.209 (Everett Collection), p.224 (SNAP), p.237 top (Everett Collection), p.237 bottom (ITV); The Random House Group: p.57, p.114; Ronald Grant Archive: p.33; Ryanfb: p.85; Anneli Salo: p.56; Stock.xchng: p.37 (Sanja Gjenero), p.89 (Gayle Lindren), p.119 (Ramzi Hashisho), p.129 (Zvone Lavric), p.154 (Craig Toocheck), p.207 (Guilermo Ossa); Topfoto: p.180 bottom left (The Granger Collection); Travelling Fools of America: p.150; Philip Zaulig: p.203.

Contributors

Introduction
Raymond Chandler & Philip Marlowe's
    Los Angeles;
James Lee Burke & Dave Robicheaux's
New Orleans
© 2010 Maxim Jakubowski

Ian Rankin & Inspector Rebus's Edinburgh
Donna Leon & Commissario Brunetti's
    Venice;
Henning Mankell & Wallander's Sweden;
Peter James & Roy Grace's Brighton;
Georges Simenon & Maigret's Paris
© 2010 Barry Forshaw

Sara Paretsky & V.I. Warshawski's Chicago
© 2010 Dick Adler & Maxim Jakubowski

Arnaldur Indridason & Erlendur's Iceland;
Andrea Camilleri & Montalbano's Sicily
© 2010 Peter Rozovsky

John D. MacDonald & Travis McGee's
    Florida
© 2010 Oline Cogdill

Colin Dexter & Inspector Morse's Oxford;
Ellis Peters and Brother Cadfael's Shropshire
© 2010 Martin Edwards

George V. Higgins and Eddie Coyle's Boston;
Ross Macdonald & Lew Archer's Southern
    California
© 2010 Michael Carlson

John Harvey & Charlie Resnick's Nottingham
© 2010 John Harvey

George Pelecanos's Washington DC;
Lawrence Block & Matt Scudder's New York
© 2010 Sarah Weinman

Dashiell Hammett & Sam Spade's San
    Francisco
© 2010 J. Kingston Pierce

Declan Hughes & Ed Loy's Dublin
© 2010 Declan Burke

Arthur Conan Doyle & Sherlock
    Holmes's London
© 2010 David Stuart Davies

LOCATION AND BOOK TITLE INDEX

INDEX